'A Boy J Terry

Book Copyright © 2015 Terry Cavender

The moral right of the author has been asserted.

All rights reserved.

No part of this publication may be reproduced, stored in a retrieval system, or transmitted, in any form or by any means, without the prior permission in writing of the publisher, nor be otherwise circulated in any form of binding or cover other than that which it is published and without a similar condition including this condition being imposed on the subsequent purchaser.

Whilst every effort has been made to trace the owners of copyright material reproduced herein, I would like to apologise for any omissions and will be pleased to incorporate missing acknowledgements in any future editions.

Because of its nature, this book has stories with mature content and contains adult language.

Cover picture (behind front cover photo) by:
   Harry Turner (1908 – 2009)

DEDICATION

This book would not have been possible without the help and endless patience of my much loved wife Maggie and so is dedicated to both her and our treasured daughter Sara. Also humble thanks to fellow 'quill-dribbler' Brian (Harry) Clacy and his better half, Nicky for all of the help, advice, coffee and biscuits.

The words of this song say it all for me:

'A BOY FROM NOWHERE'

*The nights grow cold
My search for gold
Is leading nowhere
Whichever lonely road I take
It seems to go where
It's a fight to survive just until tomorrow
How can I display
What I know I'm worthy of
When they turn me away*

*The doors are closed to such as I
A boy from nowhere
But not to those who merely buy
The right to go where
They'll be met with respect
Not humiliation
A man's place on earth
I have come to realise
Is decided by birth*

*Another dawn, another boy
A boy from nowhere
My destiny will guarantee
I'll only go where
It's a fight to survive just until tomorrow
One more mouth to feed
And the way things are round here
That's the last thing they need*

Songwriters/Lyricists
MIKE LEANDER / EDDIE SEAGO

Published by
Lyrics © Warner/Chappell Music, Inc.

'HOW IT ALL BEGAN'

3 December 1947

Born prematurely at St John's Hospital, Keighley, in West Yorkshire, I weighed in at slightly less than 2lbs. I was one of the first new-born's to arrive via the soon to be instigated National Health Service (the NHS began on the 5th of July 1948). My parents had saved up the money to pay the Doctor for the 'mechanics' of my arrival, a requirement in those days, but didn't have to because of the kindness of our family Doctor who, fortunately, was a supporter of the National Health Service in principle and decided to forego the 'delivery' charge. I think that my beloved Mother was a tad disappointed when I arrived early on the morning of the 3rd of December, because she was in fact expecting a roll of lino to be delivered - but instead got yours truly.

January 1963

After having signed the attestation papers for joining the Army in 1962, on a very cold January day in 1963 I travelled by the 'Devonian' steam train down to Taunton, then on by road to the Junior Leaders Battalion, Royal Army Service Corps (RASC) based at Norton Manor Camp, Taunton, Somerset. There as a Junior Private, aged 15, I began training in order to become a professional soldier, a finely honed fighting machine (Clerical) and model citizen. It was to be a rather rude awakening!

October 1992

I eventually left the Armed Forces as a crusty old Major and returned to Civvy Street' much older and considerably wiser, hair gone, wind broken, but having discovered along the way some of the mysteries of life. Not the answers, just the mysteries.

'AND THEN'

There you are, that's saved you hours of unnecessary reading about Yorkshire people wearing clogs, string vests, flat caps etc and you'd have probably flipped through the first few chapters anyway (that's what I normally do). Personally I'm not normally interested in someone's Great Auntie Bertha, so I concentrate on what happened to me once I'd said TTFN to Her Majesty and left her to manage the Empire without the benefit of my assistance. I do, however, dip back into the past here and there – so be warned. There's a bit of a 'lead-in' to me handing in my spurs and my departure from the Khaki World. Please bear with me whilst I do a bit of flitting back and forth, it'll all make sense eventually.

So here's my first 'flit' - let's step back in time to long before my departure from H.M. Forces; bear with me for a while whilst I set the scene for you. I'm going to tell you just a bit about some of my family. My Mother, Maureen, (Mam) is sadly no longer with us. Maureen Cavender (nee Hugill) had three other sisters, Kathleen and Isobelle (Belle) and Glenis. Glenis was just a year older than me and we were more like brother and sister than aunt and nephew. Times were excruciatingly hard for them, they were poor but happy (no they weren't)! My Grandad, John Hugill – their Father, had done a runner, singularly avoiding his parental responsibilities and failing to provide any form of financial support by lurking in a tent somewhere up in North Yorkshire with the Territorial Army and denying all knowledge. He eventually saw the light and returned home to the 'bosom' of his family. Things must have gone relatively well as his fourth daughter Glenis eventually arrived on the scene.

Because Grandad hadn't provided any money for his family whilst he was away soldiering, my Nan had to do the best that she could to keep everything together in his absence. My Nan, Margaret Hugill (nee Carolan), was a small. fiery, red haired character – more of her later. At that time, there were three girls in the family but only one set of footwear – a pair of men's boots, so they had to share the boots – taking it in turns to go to school wearing them, St Anne's Catholic School on Skipton Road, Keighley. One day it was my Mother's turn to wear the lace-less boots. A Nun at St Anne's made a point of humiliating my Mother by pulling her to one side, sniggering and pointing at her boots then loudly taking the piss out of them. My Mother was made to go and stand in a corner of the school yard until playtime finished, being deemed unfit to mix with the other pupils. She was ashamed and mortified and the insult still rankled right up until her final years.

Justice, however, was lurking in the wings. When my Nan heard about it, the very next morning she went down to the schoolyard, arriving there at playtime, sought the Nun out and promptly felled her with a nicely timed blow to the chin. All hell broke loose, Priests and Nuns running around like demented penguins. My Nan didn't care, her daughter had been demeaned and she had therefore wreaked vengeance as best she knew how. The Sister had been well and truly 'leathered' and family honour was restored. My Mother told me that the Nuns at her school were, in the main, very cruel to the children, disciplining them harshly for the slightest transgression. Needless to say, my Mam was left alone from then onwards, the Nuns wishing to avoid being the recipients of a well aimed knuckle sandwich.

My Mam, Maureen, was extremely intelligent and was also a gifted artist, indeed she won a scholarship because of her artistic capabilities, but unfortunately couldn't afford to go to college. How could she when the family couldn't even afford footwear? Regrettably like many of her friends she was destined for a life in the mill. What a bloody, shocking waste of a golden opportunity. Who knows what she might have achieved. It makes me seethe just writing about it now.

Mam told me that my Nan had to work in a local mill on the night shift because if she'd worked during the day there would have been no-one at home to look after the girls and the authorities would have arranged for them to be taken away from her and put into local care! Go figure. They lived in a small council house at Woodhouse on the outskirts of Keighley. My Nan would make sure that her lasses were as comfortable as they could manage on their very limited resources, some good, plain food, a little fire burning in the grate etc, before she sneaked off to the mill on 't'night shift' to earn some brass.

For some inexplicable reason, my Nan had forked out a couple of bob from her meagre wages, and bought an old piano. It took pride of place in their front room, both as an instrument and a piece of furniture to be admired by the neighbours. She encouraged the girls to try and play it.

One dark winter's night Nan had gone off to work at the Mill and the girls were gathered around the fire trying to keep warm, when the piano started to play all by itself. The girls were frightened stiff as the keys magically tinkled away. Eventually, the eldest, my Auntie Kathleen, plucked up the courage to go and investigate the mysterious music. She told me that she could see the keys on the keyboard moving up and down as if being tapped by some invisible hand. Much to her relief when she lifted the piano lid and peered inside the piano she saw a mouse running in and around the hammers! The mouse had been busy munching on the felt that covered the hammers and in doing so it caused the haunting music..

As a young girl, my Nan had heard about a job working as a Lady's Maid for local luminary Lady Butterfield, (wife of Sir Henry Butterfield who made his fortune from owning Mills and other such things) at Cliffe Castle, described as being a modernised Tudor castle, situated on the outskirts of Keighley. The Buttefield's had homes in Paris, New York and Nice, so weren't short of a few quid. It would have been a good job for Nan to get, one with prospects. My Nan said that at the interview, where she'd done her very utmost to look her best, Lady Butterfield had looked her up and down then apparently said, haughtily, "Carolan (*maiden name*) – I don't like your face. It borders on insolence!" My Nan realising that the interview was going nowhere, gave her the 'evils' (it is quite conceivable that Lady Butterfield could well have been heading for some of what the Nun had copped, which was termed in the vernacular of the day – "a reyt good belting") – but order was maintained. Not to be outdone, Nan said to Lady Butterfield, "No – and I don't like your sulky, spoilt bloody face either!" before sweeping out of Cliffe Castle, leaving Lady Butterfield to sniff her smelling salts. Cliffe Castle is now a local heritage museum, the Butterfields having departed into history. Nan went off to work in t'mill.

Back to the subject of boots. In the mid to late 1950's, my Grandad, John Hugill, had returned home to Keighley from his military adventures and things settled down to such an extent that my Aunt Glenis had been sired, rounding the family up to a total of six, including the parents. My Grandad, who was nicknamed 'Buck' - not because of his propensity to sire girls but because he loved watching black and white cowboy films starring an actor called Buck Rogers. Buck (Hugill) retired from work in his very early fifties because he was badly bronchitic and had breathing problems, despite continuing to smoke 20 'Wild Woodbines' a day. In addition, he had a devout aversion to any form of work. Naturally money was still a contentious issue at home and there wasn't a lot of anything to be had. They muddled along.

One Saturday my Nan returned from Bradford 'thieves' market where she had purchased a fine pair of men's brown lace-up 'booits' for Buck, at what she considered to be a knock-down price. She made him try them on and insisted that he wear them at all times as they looked 'reyt grand.' He said he would try them out and take them for an airing. "You might try walking to the Labour Exchange in 'em!" was one fruity comment. After a few days, he complained bitterly that the boots, although made of high quality leather, weren't at all comfortable, indeed he began to develop a very bad and obvious limp.

To cut a long story short, it transpired that the 'booits' had originally been crafted for someone who had been suffering from Ricketts and who had had a deformed, shortened leg. One of the 'booits' had a disguised inner wedge to compensate for the original owner's shortness of leg and that's why they were so cheap. The original owner had passed over the great divide, thus freeing the 'booits' for someone else to use. So Buck had been hobbling around in boots that had been produced for some unfortunate disabled person. The boots were returned to the market stall in Bradford the following Saturday by my Nan and exchanged for something more appropriate. Notwithstanding, Grandad never made it to the Labour Exchange, with or without boots. He earned a few quid on the side by playing the drums with the popular 'Albion Trio' an accordion band that played in local clubs and at weddings, things like that. A much loved character, a very pleasant man, greatly missed. Buck, (Grandad), departed this life early one fine summer's morning when he suffered a fatal heart attack getting out of bed! Say no more. He was a big lad, I helped carry the coffin at his funeral and sported a serious bruise on my shoulder for many weeks afterwards.

We lost our little Nan in a tragic car accident many years later. Unfortunately the car she was travelling swerved and hit the kerb. The rear door sprang open and she was thrown out of the vehicle and died of her resultant head injuries, (pre-seat belt days). It was a very sad and undeserved ending for a very much loved lady. If you can think of someone and smile, then they couldn't have been that bad, could they?

My cousin Paul Milligan and my Nan, Margaret Hugill

I should just mention that my very first 'published' work was back in the late 1950's when I had a small verse reproduced in either of these non-technical journals - the 'Dandy' 'Hotspur' or the 'Beano' - it was so long ago that I can't remember which one. The verse was something along the lines of:

To market, to market with my brother Jim,
Somebody threw a tomato at him.
Tomatoes are nice when they're inside a skin,
But this one they threw, was inside a tin!

Not my own work and 'lifted' from my Dad I'm afraid. Notwithstanding – it won for me what was then the princely sum of 10 shillings (about £10 in today's money). A postal order duly arrived for that amount which was handed over to my Dad "for safe keeping" and which was undoubtedly exchanged for several 'Timothy Taylor' ale tokens at the British Legion Club, before the sun set over the yard arm. I may have received a bag of sweets for my efforts, can't remember. Nevertheless, a brief moment of local fame and the glimmer of realisation that the printed word could, with a little effort and imagination, bring in a couple of bob, (which it certainly hasn't done so since then).

During my formative years, times were relatively happy for me in Keighley, a smog filled Northern mill-town (can you hear the brass band playing gently in the background, the birds coughing in time with the music as we ate our Wonderloaf sandwiches made with Stork Margarine and jam if we were lucky). I used to lie in bed, wrapped in a greatcoat (I made that bit up) listening to the mill-workers trudging off to work very early in the morning, their clogs making a hellish racket as they walked along the pavement and off to t'mills. They were hard times for the majority, but at least there was work to be had. We had originally lived in a hovel in Hill Street, Keighley which had no electricity, no running hot water with the 'tin bath once a week' routine and the house was lit by gas mantles. The lavatories were communal and sited at the end of the houses. They were emptied weekly by council workers. Ah sweet mystery of life.

Our only entertainment, apart from neighbours arguing when the pubs emptied was from a radio supplied by 'Radio Rental' which was piped into the houses. I recall listening, with much joy, to things the 'Goon Show' 'Three Way Family Favourites' and stuff like that. Eventually, in the mid-1950's my parents managed to obtain a council house for us all which, joy of joys, had electricity, an indoor lavatory and a proper bath with hot water provided by a back boiler hidden behind the open coal fire. Living the dream. We even got a refrigerator which was powered by gas – I could never work out how the heat of a gas flame could freeze things, but it did.

We 'flitted' (moved) from the hovel in Hill Street with a few items of goods and chattel on the back of an old truck, whilst Mother and we children, I had a brother, John, by then, walked 'up' to our brand spanking newly built palatial council residence at 55 Whin Knoll Avenue, Keighley. I recall that we had an old three piece suite, a small table on which the newly obtained electric radio sat in isolated splendour and the front room floor was covered with oil-cloth (linoleum). We had to wait a while for carpets to appear. There was a nice fire-place and the coal could be lit by an archaic implement called a gas poker which I'm sure that these days would be banned for health and safety reasons. We all loved Whin Knoll, particularly the children. The houses in the area were surrounded by green fields and not too far away were the delights of 'Bluebell Woods' and 'Tinker Bridge' and the local 'Tarn' which wasn't too deep and ideal for paddling and splashing about. There we could while away the days 'laking out' (playing). It was bliss.

Just after we'd moved in, I recall that my Dad organised a housewarming party which included a noisy four piece band. Things went swimmingly well until about four o'clock in the morning, when our next door neighbour, a delightful man, Mr Jack Mitchell, quite rightly came around and asked for the festivities to be toned down a bit as no-one could get to sleep. By that stage, vast quantities of Timothy Taylor's Ales had been consumed by the party-goers and sensible, diplomatic discussions were not the order of the day. Voices were raised and fisticuffs duly commenced. Struggling male bodies and shrieking females were thrashing around in the front garden knocking seven bells out of each other, until the local constabulary eventually arrived to restore order. Much handshaking and apologies were made the following day and normality was resumed. I started at a new school, Guardhouse, and thus my education continued. Incidentally, my Dad had taught me to read when I was three years old and I was reading comics before I started at the National Infants School, commonly referred to as 'Nashpots.' Clever move by Dad really as the comics maintained my interest.

'LITTLE COINCIDENCES'

Life is a series of strange little coincidences and you never know what's around the corner. For example, one freezing cold December night I was travelling back to my home town Keighley, West Yorkshire from Taunton, on leave. I was a boy soldier at the time and could have been more than Fifteen and bit. As the weather was appalling, the trains were struggling to get through but I managed to get as far as Shipley and then had to wait for a couple of hours for the connecting train to Keighley. In those days British Rail had decent waiting rooms with blazing open coal fires. I was alone in the waiting room, so making myself as comfortable as I could I settled down near the fire with my feet on my suitcase and drifted off.

After about an hour's worth of dozing I was woken up by a noise. Sat opposite me was an old, trampily dressed bald headed man, tattooed and sporting a large gold ear-ring. There was definitely a touch of the 'Gypsy Rover' about him (think Sergeant Obadiah Hawkswill in Bernard Cornwell's 'Sharpe' series). Outside the wind was howling and the snow continued to fall. As there was no-one else around, I started to get a bit twitchy. He looked at me and said, "Travelling far, son?" "Er, yes," I replied, "I'm going to Keighley on leave." I should add that members of the military were allowed to travel on public transport wearing uniform in those days. He moved closer to the fire. "Ah, I used to live in Keighley," he said "And I used to be in the Army, during the war. I was a Redcap (*Military Policeman*)." "Ah," I replied, wishing that the train would hurry up. Strangely, he looked vaguely familiar.

"What's your name, lad?" he asked. I replied, "Terry Cavender," He looked startled, "What, Jim Cavender's lad?" "S'right," said I. "Blimey son,

I'm your Uncle George. George Waterhouse. What are you doing here at this time of night?" "I'm on leave. I'm off home to Keighley." "Oh right, well say hello to your Dad for me," said Uncle George. I nodded, "Will do. Are you travelling on to Keighley?" I asked him. "No," he replied, "I'll just warm my bones here for a bit longer then I'll be off." We sat there quietly.

Much to my relief the train finally arrived and I legged it, delighted to get away from my 'Uncle' George, who made me distinctly nervous. On the final part of the journey to Keighley I remembered my Dad once telling me that Uncle George wasn't a particularly nice man and that during the war he'd been employed as a hangman with the Army in Egypt. Bloody charming. Much to my relief our paths never crossed after that. I did briefly, though, bump into his son Gerry, who was 'on the trot' from the Coldstream Guards Band, in which he'd played the flute. He told me that he'd never really learnt to play the instrument properly but just used to disguise his lack of expertise by whistling away merrily through his lips whilst carrying out public duties like the 'Changing of the Guard' at Buckingham Palace etc. Gerry eventually returned to his unit and served a bit of time behind bars before being hoofed out of the Services. Following that he did a spot more time at Her Majesty's pleasure for, would you believe it, robbing a small sweet shop – scaring the poor shop keeper half to death, with a shotgun! He eventually fell off the radar and, like his Father, we never saw him again. I would have like to have got to know Gerry a bit better though, just to see what made him tick.

My Dad's brother, Uncle Jack, Jack Cavender, had a lovely singing voice and could also play the acoustic guitar beautifully. He was, as a younger man, in a trio that played regularly on Radio Luxembourg and was starting to make a name for himself. He was appearing in a show on the Isle of

Man with Max Bygraves who was a big name even back then.

The entertainer Max Bygraves

Uncle Jack was accompanied by his wife, a most marvellous and colourful character, my Auntie Gladys. To say that Uncle Jack and Auntie Gladys liked a tipple would be something of an understatement, they lived life at full pelt. They were young, vibrant and talented. All was going swimmingly well until late one afternoon at the Isle of Man Airport when the cast of the now concluded show were assembling to fly home. Max Bygraves was at the bar having a quiet drink when Auntie Gladys hove into view, slightly the worse for wear from an afternoon boozing session. Uncle Jack was nowhere to be seen. She sat next to Max Bygraves and started chatting to him, assuming that he would recognise her as being the wife of a fellow performer who had shared the billing in his show. After all, they'd been there for the full season.

Not recognising her, he said something along the lines of "Look, I'm happy to give you an autograph, then would you please leave me alone!" Auntie Gladys, a lady not to be tampered with, took great offence at his acute ambivalence and said something along the lines of, "I'll have you know that I'm Jack Cavender's wife!" "And?" replied Maxie, "He's in your show!" she said. Max replied, "So What?" then turned away, ignoring her. Bad move Maxie.

She took great offence at the dismissive way he had spoken to her and so, swinging her handbag, (probably containing a bottle of spirits) she thwacked Maxie on the head, who then promptly slumped to the floor, dazed. "You arrogant bastard! My Jack's got more talent in his little finger than you've got in your entire body," shouted Auntie Gladioli. At that moment, enter Uncle Jack who viewed the carnage and was mortified. He knew, looking at a dazed and bleeding Max Bygraves, that his career in show-business was over from that moment on – and it proved to be true. His name was mud, his bookings tailed off and he had to go back to 'normal' work.

My Uncle Jack was a rather heavy drinker and it was only very many years later that I discovered that during the war as a young man he'd served in the Royal Navy on Destroyers before becoming a Submariner. He spent a lot of time on the Murmansk run and that's when the drinking started. He, like others, had been through some exceedingly hard times whilst a Submariner and his mental welfare hadn't been a consideration. Nevertheless, he survived and went on to lead a very colourful life, eventually finishing up being in charge of a power station in Zambia for a couple of years before being invited to leave the country after getting horribly pissed at a Cocktail Party and saying something extremely rude and dismissive to their President, Kenneth Kaunda. Uncle Jack was given a couple of weeks to sort out his personal affairs and then would have to leave Zambia. Unfortunately whilst awaiting repatriation, his wife my Auntie Gladys, died in her sleep cradled in his arms which did nothing for his rapidly deteriorating mental state and made his drinking even worse. Auntie Gladys was eventually laid to rest in Zambia. I don't think that she'd be particularly happy about that, being a Yorkshire lass.

Uncle Jack eventually returned to England, where in due course he married my Auntie Clara – (which made her my Auntie Clara twice as she'd been partnered with Uncle Bert Woolley - Sheep Rustler). Uncle Jack sadly, died of cancer. Without the demon drink in his life, Uncle Jack could have been a glittering success at whatever he chose to do, but it wasn't to be. Both him and my Auntie Gladys were very dear and colourful characters and I still miss them both. It was always such fun being in their company.

Jack & Gladys Cavender- in Zambia

Strangely, whilst I was serving with 8 Regiment RCT in Munster, West Germany, I was sat with the Memsahib in our married quarter one evening having drinks and small eats with a couple of friends. We didn't have English TV in those days so made our own entertainment. One particular evening we were playing around with a Ouija Board and asking it all sorts of questions. One of the questions I asked of the board was – "Is Auntie Gladys still playing Uncle Jack up?" The message we got from the board was – "Not anymore!" A few days later, I kid you not, I got a letter from my Mother telling me that Auntie Gladys had died in Zambia. I haven't touched a Ouija board since.

My Father despised Winston Churchill with a vengeance and the very mention of the Churchill name was banned in our house when we were growing up. To even allude to his name invited a lug-holing. Dad considered Churchill to have been an arrogant, self publicising adventurer. As I approached adulthood I found out why. My Father very rarely mentioned the war and his activities in it. We knew that he'd done his bit for 'King and

Country' but that was about all we knew. He just never discussed it with us. He had several medals which he proudly wore when on the Annual Armistice Day parades.

After a try-out with the Duke of Wellington's TA from 29th June 1936 until the 10th of February 1938, he'd joined up as a Royal Engineer on the 11th of February 1938 as a Blacksmith's Striker/Engine Hand when he was 18 years old. He stayed on in the Army until being discharged as being medically unfit for further service on the 10th of April 1946 after having served with the colours for 8 years and 149 days, – so saw things through to the bitter end. I know that he was extremely disappointed by being discharged as he wanted to stay in the Army and continue as a regular soldier. He was tossed on the scrap-heap along with many other young lads.

Rather shockingly his medals, which he kept in a little metal tin, were stolen and the medals sold on. He knew who'd stolen them but alas they were never recovered. In one of those strange coincidences, I was to bump into the young man who'd stolen the medals when I was at Taunton where he was also undergoing training as a Junior Leader. Naturally he denied taking the medals when I asked him about it and that was that. The tea-leaf didn't survive the army training and thankfully disappeared into the ether never to be heard of again.

Without going into mountains of details and statistics, (information that is freely available elsewhere), apparently Winston Churchill had decided in the early 1940's that there should be a more active phase to the Norwegian Campaign, after all, Norway was strategically important and whoever held Norway had the advantage of its ports. At the start of the operation, British Expeditionary Forces (BEF) numbered some 38,000 of which, at its conclusion, some 600 were evacuated – with 1,869 killed, wounded or listed as missing. I've read in my Dad's discharge documents that he was 'in theatre' during the period 21st April 1940 to the 8th of June 1940, so that's when he experienced his particular horrors.

*My Dad - Sapper James (Jim) Cavender RE
(November 1943)*

As a young 18 year old Royal Engineer he had been very badly wounded, some of the tips of his fingers had been shot off, he'd received a severe leg wound that gave him a slight limp and also had a nasty shrapnel wound in his stomach that left a rather large hole there. He was granted a paltry war pension by a 'grateful' nation. I only ever saw his wounds once, he always kept them hidden away because he was ashamed of his mutilated body. He'd been a member of the ill-fated military expedition to Norway where things had gone very badly, resulting in the Brits having to withdraw and try and get back across the channel to the safety of home. Dad and the others had been told that anyone who was wounded was to be left behind. He'd also been informed that the enemy forces were not taking any prisoners and that they, the Germans, were executing the wounded. The normal 'niceties' of war were being totally ignored. My Dad and his mates knew full well that Adolf Hitler had issued an edict called a 'Fuhrerbefehl' which stated something along the lines of:

'From now on all opponents captured by German troops in so-called commando operations in Europe or in Africa, even when it is outwardly a matter of soldiers in uniform or demolition parties with or

without weapons, are to be exterminated to the last man in battle or while in flight. In these cases it is immaterial whether they are landed for their operation by ship or aircraft or descend by parachute. Even should these individuals, on their being discovered, make as if to surrender, all quarter is to be denied them on principle.'

How about that – '*on principle*!' As usual, these rules were dictated by the heroic Hierarchy usually from the safety of a cushy bunker somewhere far from the field of battle.

Along with some of his buddies, my Dad was making his way back to the Norwegian port, probably Trondheim, through the freezing fog and snow, for which, quite naturally being British, they were ill-equipped. It's strange that no matter what, historically our Servicemen and Women always seem to be 'ill-equipped' for the tasks that they are given – but always manage to survive despite the efforts of 'the staff.' Anyway, Dad was heading towards the port, hoping for repatriation, when a British Army staff car drew up containing a Colonel, well wrapped up to protect himself from the bitter cold, wearing a British 'Winter Warm' Overcoat, scarf, gloves etc.

He wound the staff car window down and asked the lads what they were doing, which was presumably patently obvious – they replied that they were making a strategic withdrawal, as was he. After they'd explained, the officer then said something along the lines of "Well, carry on chaps, do your best!" and also reminded them that the wounded were to be left behind. With that he wound the car window up and drove off leaving them stood there. He could easily have offered some of these freezing and frightened young men a lift to the docks, but apparently chose not to do so. Presumably it was a class thing, couldn't have the 'lower decks' travelling with a senior officer, what.

As the soldiers headed for the docks, the small party that my Dad was travelling with came under very heavy enemy fire and unremitting dive-bombing from the Luftwaffe. As he was climbing out of a hurriedly scraped snow trench, that's when he received his wounds, as a result of which he was too badly wounded to be able to continue under his own steam. His mates made him as comfortable as possible as they could but they had no option but to leave him behind, as ordered. Dad said that he remembered being laid there, alone, in the snow, slowly bleeding to death in the freezing cold when suddenly a number of ski troops appeared in the distance. He could see that they weren't British. My Dad knew full well that Adolf Hitler had issued the 'Fuhrerbefehl' edict and that he could expect no mercy when they found him. No prisoners to be taken alive!

The ski troops arrived and stopped to look at Dad. He was convinced that they were going to execute him and, quite understandably, through loss of blood and shock, he lost consciousness. Fortunately for him the ski troops weren't Germans, but brave Norwegians. They collected Dad and took him to a local village Doctor who 'repaired' him as best he could. He was then hidden underneath the village school with several other wounded soldiers whilst arrangements were made to repatriate them all back home to England. Had he been discovered by the Germans both he and his helpers would undoubtedly have been executed.

Some days later, one dark night on the 8th of June 1940, he and the remainder of his wounded comrades were transported by boat out to a British destroyer that had been sent to rescue the wounded and take them home. When they eventually reached Port Glasgow on the 9th, my Dad was stretchered off the destroyer. He said that the civilians in the port were booing and spitting at them because for some reason they thought they were German Prisoners of War.

Another little coincidence – my Dad didn't realise it but his brother, my Uncle Jack was a crew member on the very same Destroyer that rescued him, but in the confusion of war they didn't meet up. As part of his staged recovery Dad was employed at Glasgow Central Railway Station as a lance corporal with RE Transport and Movements and apparently had a little side-line earning quite a few quid selling railway warrants to the troops. I never did find out the full story but apparently he did rather well out of it.

Eventually, after a relatively lengthy recovery period, my Dad was invalided out of the Army because of his wounds and 'awarded' a meagre medical pension. In his military discharge book it states: *'Has proved himself a most efficient and conscientious worker. Of sober and steady habits and thoroughly trustworthy.'* He was issued with the standard demob suit, given a few quid, (boosted by the illicit railway warrant profits) then was left to get on with his life. He considered that Winston Churchill had been the cause of his misfortunes and never forgave him.

Dad, like many others who had been through similar experiences, became a heavy drinker, although that never stopped him from working extremely hard, which he did for the remainder of his life. There was no 'Help for Hero's' or 'Combat Stress' to turn to in those days. He worked hard all of his life, a decent and salt of the earth man, until eventually succumbing, cruelly, to lung cancer. His life was a colourful and interesting one. What I do know is that he was extremely intelligent, talented and funny. Given the right opportunities who knows what he also might have achieved. If.

And that is why one couldn't mention Winston Churchill in my Dad's presence. When you could, very rarely, get him to speak about the war (usually when he was well bladdered), he always said that he felt that the Norwegian campaign was a badly planned and ruinous adventure and that as usual the cannon-fodder suffered immensely because of that. Whilst those at the top had simply spiffing times in London, the 'lads' were out in places like Norway, badly equipped and poorly officered, but trying to do their best. Lions led by Donkeys. Not much has changed.

The Right Honourable Sir Winston Spencer Churchill KG OM CH TD DL FRS RA Churchill died and was accorded a state funeral attended by the great and good on the 30th of January 1965. I was at that time a Junior Leader under training in Taunton. On the day of the funeral our Platoon had to sit reverentially in the Television Room, properly dressed, and in respectful silence watch the entire state funeral as televised and eulogised on the BBC.

Conversely, when my Dad died, on the 16th of May 1975, Lance Corporal James Daniel Cavender, late Royal Engineers, his family and friends attended a simple service at a Funeral Home in Keighley, followed by his cremation. There were no television cameras, Kings or Presidents at that one. Dad would have been proud to note that bringing up the rear of his funeral cortege of grieving family and friends was a Timothy Taylor's Brewery Waggon. Thus it ever was and ever will be.

Like my Uncle Jack, Dad also had a beautiful singing voice and I'm sure that he could have made a good living from it, but chose not to do so. Life takes us all in different directions. I often remember Dad telling me that times were very hard when he was young and that until he'd left school and got a job he and his brothers and sisters had to stand at the dining table for their meals. They only got the privilege of sitting on a dining chair once they started bringing some money into the house. He'd only just started working and getting a few quid together when the war loomed and everything changed.

Dad was a highly intelligent man and having thought about it over the years, it is now evident to me that his wartime experiences had damaged him both physically and mentally and like many of his colleagues he was hung out to dry by an uncaring government after the war. He lived and played hard. All our family loved reading and we were always surrounded by books and comics in our house, even when television, from a conversely named 'Radio Rentals' made an appearance in the late 1950's. We were then able to watch exciting adventurous programmes like 'Waggon Train' 'Robin Hood' 'William Tell' 'Juke Box Jury' '6-5 Special' and things like that. The last two were 'pop' music programmes which my Dad would switch off at every opportunity, to howls of complaint from all of us.

Most of my generation were home schooled in many ways. Some examples:

My Mother taught me to *APPRECIATE A JOB WELL DONE:*
"If you and your brother are going to kill each other, do it outside."

My Mother taught me about *RELIGION:*
"You'd better pray that'll come off the lino, lad."

My Father taught me about *TIME TRAVEL:*
"If you don't shut it, I'm going to knock you into the middle of next week!"

My Father taught me *LOGIC:*
"Because I bloody well said so, that's why."

(*Usually followed by a clip to the ear from his iron hard hands*).

My Mother taught me *MORE LOGIC:*
"If you fall off that swing and break your neck, you'll get your arse cracked."

My Nan taught me FORESIGHT:
"Make sure you wear clean underpants, in case you get knocked down by a tram."

My Father taught me IRONY:
"Keep crying, and I'll bloody well give you summat to cry about."

My Mother taught me about the science of OSMOSIS:
"Shut your mouth and eat your dinner."

Whilst thinking about the contents of this book, I recalled 'out of the blue' one particular Christmas, it would be round about 1957 or 1958. Things weren't going too well on the employment front and a lot of people were desperately competing for what few jobs there were to be had. The several large mills, Cloughs, Heaton's etc that operated in and around Keighley were churning out materials, which up until then had kept local people like my Mother in work, but 'foreign' workers were arriving and taking what was perceived to be 'our jobs' working for lesser money. I remember that this caused a lot of ill feeling in the community and stretched Yorkshire tolerance to the limit, particularly as it put people like my Mother out of work. It made things difficult for a lot of people. This wasn't really the fault of immigrant workers, who themselves were working to survive, but I recall that it did cause a great deal of bitterness at the time.

My Mother lost her job which meant that both she and Dad, unfortunately, were in between jobs. My Dad was at one time the Verger of Keighley Parish Church, but lost that post when the Vicar found out that he'd been earning a little extra on the side by hiring out the bell tower to courting couples. My Dad had been warned that the Vicar had been sniffing around, but took little notice – the bells made him deaf. We were so poor that Mam used to sew rubber pockets in our trousers so that we could steal soup.

Apparently our larder was bare so my Dad, aided and abetted by my fabulous Uncle Bert (a handsome, talented and dashing man who at the weekends was the lead trumpeter in the 'Bert Woolley Trio' a musical trio who were big in the area, particularly at the local British Legion Club, performing there every Saturday night), decided to do something to resolve the lack of food situation. Uncle Bert was the proud owner of a much cherished ancient motorbike, (pre-owned by the military), now with a cleverly self-constructed side-car attached. The side-car was made entirely out of spare bits of acquired wood and resembled a coffin with a supporting wheel. It had the luxury of being fitted with two seats obtained from an old ambulance and a hinged sheet of Perspex, shielding the person riding shotgun from the elements.

Attached to this coffin-like appendage was a converted vacuum cleaner tube emanating from the side-car, connected to Uncle Bert, the chief pilot. His long suffering beloved not quite wife, my Auntie Clara, (they lived 'ower t'brush' for many years), would blow down the tube if she wished to converse with Uncle Bert whilst the contraption was in motion. She would holler into the tube and issue instructions to the pilot. Quite how Uncle Bert heard anything above the roar of the motorbike engine I can't imagine – particularly as he always wore a leather helmet and goggles, looking for all the world like a demented Kamikaze pilot. Incidentally, Uncle Bert also used his motorbike at the weekends to do some competitive hill-climbing, with his beloved, my generously proportioned Auntie Clara, firmly clamped in the side-car as ballast, shrieking encouragement, "Go on lad! Give it some bloody clog!" whilst he thrashed up and down some very muddy Yorkshire hills. Notwithstanding, the motorbike and side-car served its purpose admirably for many years before heading off to the local scrap-yard. I recall that it was replaced by an old Co-op van with sliding doors which gave many years of loyal service, often taking us all off on trips to t'sea-side, usually Morecambe.

One Christmas, when money was in short supply, Dad and Uncle Bert made a policy decision that starvation was not to be tolerated in their respective residences and that by hook or by crook they would 'acquire' some food for their families. Quite what their thought processes were I don't know (I would imagine that drink was involved), but eventually they decided to head for Ilkley Moor and rustle a sheep. They set off in the dark of night and headed for the hills. Apparently much of the night was spent hurtling across the moors chasing sheep, falling into ditches, treading in sheep poo, that sort of thing. Eventually they succeeded in wrestling a poor animal to the ground, it was then stunned with a lump hammer and unceremoniously heaved into the side-car before being transported back to Cavender Towers in Keighley. The sheep was gagged and removed from the side-car (in the middle of a council estate in what was now the early morning). There was much thrashing around and muted "Baa Baa-ing" going on until eventually the unfortunate animal was corralled in our coal-house where it met an unfortunate and mercifully swift demise. Imagine the uproar if they'd have managed to get a cow in the side-car!

There was deep joy as the freshly butchered meat was distributed amongst the fortunate few, ensuring that many a hearty meal was enjoyed by all that merry Christmas. I recall that virtually every bit of the sheep was eaten, conveniently ensuring that there was no evidence of the crime remaining. Not a hundred years earlier, if the rustlers had been caught they would probably have been branded and transported to Australia. My apologies at this late stage go to the unfortunate Farmer who had the sheep illicitly removed from his flock, but at least it was put to good use and many deserving and empty bellies were filled on the strength of it. Needs must when the devil rides (back to Uncle Bert again)!

Our council house was constantly cold as we couldn't afford to purchase a 'sack o'coil' from t'coalman' to light a fire. Most mornings when it was freezing we, Dad, Mam, me, my younger brother and sister would assemble in the kitchen and the gas oven would be lit for a short time whilst we had our breakfast. We had a gas meter that gobbled up what little money there was, so we had to be careful. I remember that the gas meter took shillings and when a shilling wasn't available my Dad would file down a halfpenny to the appropriate size. Even the water in the toilet froze, so we often had to wait until we got to school to use their 'facilities.' Some mornings we reached school in record time, red faced and not daring to break wind. Strange term that 'Break Wind.' I'd love to know how that came about. Reminds me of an old Army saying, "You can beat and egg, you can beat a drum, but you can't beat a good fart." Back in the kitchen we'd gather around the open oven door to warm our hands and whatever else could decently be exposed. Mam would make a pan of porridge for our breakfast, which wasn't particularly appetizing as we didn't have any milk, she had to use water. Even now, all these years later I can't face a bowl of claggy porridge.

Baaaaack to the sheep for a moment, (see what I did there). One day we asked our beloved Mother what we were having for tea (which loosely translated 'oop North meant Dinner), because of the delightful smell emanating from a huge cooking pot on the kitchen stove, replied "sheep's head broth. It'll put hairs on your chest!" She went over to the gas cooker with a ladle and gave the pan a stir then scooped something out of the innards of the pan – it was a sheep's skull, grinning evilly. The broth had the usual turnips, potatoes, lentils etc slung into the mix to pad it out. The skull was returned to the bubbling liquid. "A bit more Bisto I think," said the Master Chef. Questions you wish you'd never asked. I should say that after 'Dinner' not a drop of the broth remained, just the poor sheep's grinning skull rattling around a now empty pan, undoubtedly happy in the knowledge that it had fed a clemmed (starving) family. I am now a Vegetarian and would rather remove my appendix with a rusty scalpel than eat sheep's head broth. I am 'dry gipping' (retching) just thinking about it.

As parts of the council estate where we lived were still being constructed (Whin Knoll Avenue/Black Hill), there was a mountainous pile of industrial strength coke (the stuff you burn on a fire – not drink or sniff) deposited at the rear of the Watchman's hut on the huge building site. A Council Watchman was supposed to keep an eye on all of the valuable building materials throughout the night. This particular evening he had obviously fallen down on the job because Dad returned to the house with a wheelbarrow full of coke, which was immediately deposited in the coal-house, the charnel house that had been the scene of the sheep slaughter (now renamed the coke/coal-house). The barrow used in the crime, also on temporary loan for the occasion, was quietly returned to the building site and no-one was ever any the wiser.

So, now we had something to heat the house - and in addition could also heat the boiler at the rear of the fire-place to produce lashings of hot water (we could never afford to switch the electric cistern on). One unfortunate by-product of the coke that we didn't know about was that it being industrial standard, once ignited it gave off copious amounts of toxic fumes, and could have been fatal. We would all sit there, warm as toast, gently drifting into the arms of Morpheus. The coke was actually meant to be burnt outside in the open air, in a brazier in order to keep the Watchman warm throughout the evil winter's nights. I'm sure that he wouldn't have minded sharing a bit of it with us though.

Having feasted on rustled sheep, we all gently drifted off in front of a blazing fire, sucking in the noxious fumes from the industrial coke, whilst listening to 'Journey into Space' on our little valve radio. Living the dream. We were content – warm and well fed. We didn't have a car or a telephone, nor did we have many material things. No-one did. A lot of our clothing was obtained second hand (pre-worn) from the local Army & Navy Stores. For two years I went to Guardhouse Junior School dressed as a Japanese Admiral (you can have that). Happy days.

Just recalled that Dad found a supplier of hens eggs, a local Farmer from the nearby village of Laycock, from whom he purchased the eggs at a knock-down price - then had the bright idea of manufacturing a rubber stamp with the 'Little Lion' logo, impressing it upon the egg shell with red ink, which immediately upped the perceived quality (and therefore the asking price) of the eggs when they were sold on. They went down a storm. Dad had a family to support in between jobs and used his initiative to do so. His 'rustling' colleague, my Uncle Bert, provider of the infamous motorbike and side-car, used the said machine to help transport these delicate and precious objects to clamouring recipients. Jim and Bert, the Keighley version of 'Bonnie and Clyde.'

I should add that my Dad worked extremely hard throughout out his life and ensured that we never really went without and were at least fed and watered when times were difficult, which was frequently. In addition to bringing up a relatively large family, my Mother never stopped working when jobs were available, often having to look after us lot, cooking, washing and cleaning throughout the day then toddling off onto the night shift at some local mill or other, surrounded by suffocating smog, to be paid a pittance. Don't know how she managed it all. Both of my parents were complex characters who were much-loved and are sorely missed.

One of life's little coincidences occurred the other night. I'd repaired to my bedchamber early, (bit of a sacroiliac problem - someone near and dear had mentioned gardening), so I went for a rest. Picking up a book that my beloved had purchased on one of her jaunts, entitled '1001 Answers to Correspondents.' I thought that a gentle meander through its pages would help me get off to sleep. Bear with me.

When I was at Highfield Secondary School in Keighley, back in the early 1960's, I had to undergo the indignity of council purchased school dinners, as did many of my contemporaries whose parents were in the unfortunate position of being out of work or just hadn't got enough money coming in for them to pay for school dinners. Each school day at 'dinner-time' we would be herded into a converted classroom to be fed whatever the school cooks had prepared for our delectation. Those children whose parents could afford to pay for school dinners sat at one table, whilst the great unwashed, like me, whose meals were paid for by the council, were segregated and had to sit at a different table. The Teachers used to burn a cross on our foreheads so that we could be distinguished from the 'normals.' (They didn't, but that's how you were made to feel). The school dinner ladies always seemed to be rotund, red-faced and very fierce, often perspiring profusely, their sweat dripping into the rice pudding or sago. We cared not a jot – we were always clemmed (hungry).

We always knew when lunchtime/dinnertime was approaching because the smell of boiled cabbage used to waft around the school like stale fart. One particularly memorable day I was enthusiastically consuming what can only be described as 'Yorkshire Haute Cuisine' (Sausage and Mash surrounded by glutinous gravy). I'm sat there at the 'unfortunate's' table and, not knowing any better, speared the waiting banger from off the plate with my fork, lifted it up to my mouth and bit a piece from the end of it.

Suddenly I was knocked spinning from the table after receiving a very fierce slap to the back of my head from the Teacher who was supervising the lunch meal. Silence descended in the 'dining room' as I sprawled on the floor with my head ringing. This was followed by the shouted guidance – "Cut a piece off the sausage, boy! Then eat that piece and continue in the same fashion until you have finished masticating!" (I had to look that up afterwards). Slap number two was administered swiftly, to ensure that his direction had been received and understood. I returned to my seat at the table, bright red with embarrassment and shame. Everyone else having lunch/dinner there sat sniggering, eating their sausages properly and secretly pleased/relieved that it hadn't been their turn to be singled out.

Puce with embarrassment, I finished eating my 'main course' and moved on to the sweet. I was on safe ground there, it was rice pudding and I managed to finish that off without any further dramas. Normally we would mix the dollop of jam in the centre of the rice/sago until the whole thing turned a gruesome reddish colour – but not on this occasion. The only reddish colour was my lugholes. I just wanted to finish eating and get out of there.

To this day, whenever I eat a sausage (Quorn, before you ask) I am reminded of that occasion and that sausages must be cut into munch-sized pieces pre-mastication. State education is such a wonderful thing. If I ever got invited to lunch at Buckingham Palace – I'd have no qualms if sausages were on the menu.

Anyway, back to where I'm laid in bed reading the book, '1001 Answers to Correspondents,' where I came across a small paragraph explaining why we use the phrase 'As Daft as a Brush.' The writer gave the following explanation –

'As I'm now in my 70's and clearly remember my grandmother and her twin sister using a similar expression, it must cast doubt on the idea that it originated in the last war. The full version used by those ladies was: 'As daft as a brush baht bristles.' Baht means without, as in Ilkley Moor Baht 'at, and it meant as useless as a brush without bristles.'

As I finished reading the paragraph I noted that the information had been provided by a Mr Bill Hensman of Keighley, West Yorkshire, the very

Teacher who had given me the in-depth lesson re the correct way of eating sausages (I can still feel my outrage at the injustice of it). Incidentally, when I got home from school on 'Sausage Day' I informed my parents what had happened. That was a given because if news of disciplinary action filtered back home via other channels and you hadn't 'coughed' then another lug-holing would definitely be in the offing.

When I explained to my Dad what had happened, he was highly indignant and stated that he was going to go down to the school the very next morning to 'sort that bloody Teacher out.' I was mortified at the prospect and wished that I hadn't mentioned it. Oh my God – no, the shame! My Dad was going to 'leather' a Teacher.

Dad: No one, ah sed, no-one clatters you lad, except me and your Mam! I'm going down to that bloody Highfield School in the morning and I'll lug-hole him! I'll decide how you eat sausages, not some bloody snooty Teacher! What's his name this Teacher, eh?

Me: Mr Hensman, Dad.

Dad: What, Billy Hensman?

Me: Yes Dad.

Dad: Bugger me I was at school with Billy, he lived next door to us when we lived up Ingrow. When the war started I went into the Army and he went into the RAF as a fighter pilot. He always had his arse hanging out of his trousers when we were lads. Brave little bugger though.

I received a stinging clout from my Dad (I was doing rather well on the old 'Cloutometer' that day). My Dad had hands like Workhouse shovels and one soon learned the art of ducking a blow and heading for the hills:

Dad: Sither lad - next time, eat your bloody sausages properly! And don't show me up again, you uncouth lout!

Me: My apologies, Father. Could you pass the Port please? (*I made that bit up*).

Nevertheless, much to my horror, Dad went down to Highfield School the following morning and spoke to Mr Hensman about the sausage incident. I don't know what was said between the two, but no more clouts were received by me from Mr Hensman. I was quietly removed from the school dinner lists, which meant a long walk home each lunchtime if I wanted any lunch. Sausages had caused me much grief. Maybe that's why I eventually became a Vegetarian?

When thinking back across the years, I was most fortunate with the Teachers I had, (including Mr Hensman). My admiration for them knows no bounds. They taught us all the vital importance of the three 'R's.' At the very least those leaving school in those days could read and write. I wasn't particularly up on logarithms and vulgar fractions myself, but then I can't recall one occasion when they've been required.

There was a Mr Howarth, a Form Master who used to 'mangle' his sentences superbly so that you never really knew what he was asking. He would say things like, "Did I not say this morning that apostrophe's were to be used in sentences? Is it not so? Was it not true?" When we submitted our written work for his perusal he would cast an eagle eye over it and say, in stentorian tones, – "Hmmmm

– you can't educate pork. You can only try and cure it. Is that not so? Do it again boy!"

Mr Hensman's particular forté was maintaining discipline in his classroom with a twelve inch steel ruler. He was old school, 'Spare the rod, and spoil the child.' Miscreants, male or female, would be summoned to the front of his classroom, made to touch their toes and then he would expertly flick his wrist; the metal ruler would flex and land on the cheeks of the victim's braced arse, stinging like a branding iron. Transgressors would then hurtle around the classroom, bellowing like a bull moose on heat until the fire on their sizzling rumps eased off. It was a very effective punishment and Mr Hensman maintained an orderly, well run classroom. It sounds much worse than it actually was, in fact it was a punishment very rarely used – but the threat of it was constant. Because of the sausage incident, I was spared that particular indignity.

Mr Hensman had his hands full with some of the pupils who were, shall we say, a little lacking in social skills. On one memorable occasion there was a bout of fisticuffs between Mr Hensman and a pupil called 'Twit' Whittaker. We all sat in horror as we watched the altercation roll out of the classroom and into the corridor. I recall that we all sat in shocked silence as the sound of battling Teacher and Pupil disappeared into the distance. I can't recall what the upshot of it all was but I remember that Mr Hensman returned to the classroom and 'Twit' didn't. Our big fear though was to be sent to the Headmaster, ex-Army Major, Mr Frank Walton, to be disciplined and no-one wanted that to happen. It was the ultimate disgrace and would inevitably end in tears. Ours not his!

I have a sneaking suspicion that if such methods of punishment were used today, the prisons would have a surfeit of members of the hallowed teaching profession lurking within their hallowed portals. We had a woodwork teacher, a 'Silas Marner' lookalike who shall remain nameless. He would take great delight taking you into a little corner of the woodwork classroom, out of sight of everyone else, then thrash you mercilessly with various lengths of dowelling rod for very minor transgressions. They were fear-filled lessons. We would all have our heads down working on our benches as we heard the howls of the victim being thrashed.

I was at the same school and time as my 'Aunty' Glenis (Hugill), who although being my Aunty was only a year older than me. As there wasn't much money around in either of our families, we two used to have to share a simple white apron, her for cookery classes, me for woodwork. She'd be doing cookery one day, with my wood shavings falling all over the domestic science classroom and I'd be in the woodwork class, usually the following day, with clouds of her flour and bits of dough falling all over my woodwork bench. Pupils shared woodwork benches, one on each side.

For one particular woodwork lesson we were making footstools. My opposite number and I got our respective stool 'legs' mixed up and the stools wouldn't fit together. We were taken into the Teacher's little office and 'got the stick' for that outrage. The smell of wood glue or the mention of a mortise and tenon joint gives me butterflies, even to this day.

The Headmaster of Highfield School, retired Army Major, the very dapper Mr Frank Walton, would arrive each day at the school just before the nine o'clock bell rang summoning us out of the playground and into the school gymnasium for assembly. Mr Walton drove a magnificent and impressive two-tone Armstrong Siddley car. He always wore a nice suit, hanky in breast pocket, a mustard coloured waistcoat and sported his regimental tie (Royal Engineers). Mr Walton always looked well scrubbed and smelled of quality aftershave. We, the underlings, only ever really saw him at morning assembly or when sent to his office for a spot of remedial discipline.

I only ever received 'the stick' from him once though, which was quite enough thank you. If you merited his attention for a particularly serious transgression, you would be sent to stand outside his office, crapping conkers every time the door handle moved. You weren't allowed to knock on his door, you had to wait for it to be opened and for his beady eye to settle on you (bit like the apprehension whilst you were queuing to see the School Dentist or Nit Nurse). The School Secretary, quite deliberately in my opinion, kept popping in and out of the office deliberately leaving the door opened as wide as possible so that the Headmaster would eventually see us stood there, trembling. We would then be summoned into his lair for wheedling explanations.

The apprehension of waiting for that door to open was intense and a punishment in itself. I once got three strokes on each hand for dropping a lit penny banger (firework – not sausage) into someone's blazer pocket, blowing a hole in it, during one particularly joyous playtime. I was sent to see the Headmaster. I entered the Headmasters 'killing ground' where Mr Walton was expecting me. He kept several other canes behind his desk, each of different thicknesses, which he used to swish through the air whilst choosing the appropriate one to use. On this occasion he was flexing a mean looking piece of cane. It was if he was dueling with some unseen opponent, wildly waving an épée (dueling sword) about his person.

He actually said to me, looking very sad, "This is going to hurt me more than it'll hurt you,

Cavender!" Bloody liar! It stung for days, although I was hero worshipped by my class mates when they saw the bright red weal's on the palms of my hands. Badges of honour. That lesson was, however, well and truly learned. It was obvious to me that 'Bangers' of any sort and I just didn't get on. Needless to say, I never mentioned that I'd had 'the stick' to my parents. That would have attracted a further 'leathering.'

There were occasions, albeit rarely, at the school's morning assembly when those who had committed some really serious transgression, like stealing sweets from the sweet shop across the road from the school, were frog marched onto the stage at the front of the assembly hall, with the entire school watching, aghast, and were then publicly berated before being caned by the Headmaster. You could have heard a pin drop, the only sounds being those of a swishing cane and arses being thwacked, echoing around the hall. The punishment was always preceded by the Headmaster saying "Touch your toes boy!" and then the old flexing of cane ploy whilst the victim waited, bent over in an undignified position, for the 'Cane of Damocles' to descend on his posterior. This was usually followed by the victims being frog marched back into the body of the hall, usually weeping and rubbing their throbbing arses, whilst a beaming Headmaster would then piously lead the singing of the hymn of the day, such as – 'As now thy lonely children kneel,' or 'Amidst the wrath, remember love.' All hits in their own right.

I was at that time (1962) in the school's 'A' stream, which was for those pupils who although academically sound, were unsuited for the Grammar School or Technical College, and who were fully expected to gain GCE's etc and maybe, just maybe, have the opportunity to get to University to achieve something 'decent' in life, like being a Chemist or a Teacher, (with the power to thrash miscreants). Something along those lines. Once I told my Form Teacher that my Dad had taken me to the Bradford Recruiting Office where I had been signed up for the Army I was, with indecent haste, moved into the 'B' stream, which was cunningly designed to educate at a different level and was aimed at those pupils destined to work in Peter Black's Shoe factory, spending their lives making felt slippers etc. That's how it was in those days. One's educational ruination began with 11+ failures. Mr Walton, a retired Army Major himself, had strangely tried to dissuade me from joining the Army, believing that I could do well at school and forge a better career for myself. That decision, though, had already been taken for me. There was to be no turning back, a life of khaki beckoned. There was to be no turning back. I had to lurk in the 'B' stream at school until such time as I left to join the Army.

'GONE IN A FLASH'

What I'd like to do next is give you just a bit of a flavour of what happened to me once I'd joined the Army which, I suppose, moulded and morphed me into what I am today.

It all really began for me in late 1962 when my Father, an ex-Royal Engineer who did more than his bit in World War 2, meandered up to our house one Sunday afternoon with an Army Recruiting Sergeant friend of his in tow, both hoping to cop a Sunday dinner. Drink had been taken at their favourite watering hole, 'The Reservoir Tavern' and it had been decided there and then that it would be a good career move were I to sign on the dotted line and take the 'Queen's Shilling.' My Dad very rarely spoke about his time in the Army, mainly wartime. In retrospect I suppose that it was all too painful for him. When I used to ask him about it, he'd always brush it off with a daft story like – "I was a hand grenade instructor during the war. I used to change the pin on your nappies then throw you over the back of the couch!"

Back to the Recruiting Sergeant. On the Sunday in question, Taylors Ales had been consumed in copious amounts. Dad said to me something along the lines of, "Reyt lad, I've made an appointment for thi at Bradford Army Recruiting Office for next week. I'll come with thi. Tha's joining up. I'm not having you going into t'mill or that daft shoe factory like all the other silly young buggers." "Right Dad," was my respectful reply as I turned back to the television to continue watching 'Corky the Circus Boy.' One didn't question one's parent's decisions in those bygone days, you just did as you were told - blind obedience was the order of the day. My upbringing hadn't been overly strict, but we always did as we were told (when I was a child my Father never raised a hand to me - he used to kneel on my neck).

The dastardly recruitment day came around and off we travelled to Bradford on t'bus. I completed all the tests, academic and physical, had my private parts caressed by a Doctor with extremely cold hands, but nice eyes, to see if everything was present and correct, followed by the duty coughing bit etc. On receiving the results of the tests I was informed that because I'd achieved such good overall results I was destined for a slot in the Army Catering Corps. "No he's bloody not. No son of mine's going to be a water scorcher!" Dad said. The Recruiting Sergeant took one look at his face and said "I'll just go and speak to the Major, Mr Cavender." When he returned his face was beaming – "What about your lad joining the Royal Army Service Corps as a Driver/Clerk, dual tradesman Mr Cavender?" "That's more like it - just the job," was Dad's reply. I sat there absolutely clueless. "Sign here please, young Cavender." Dad saved me from becoming a 'Slop Jockey' for which I am forever grateful.

I duly signed the proffered piece of paper and was thence committed to a 22 year engagement in the Armed Forces with options to leave at the 9, 12, 15 and 18 year points. I had not a clue. If my Dad was happy, then so was I. The Recruiting Sergeant informed me that I would eventually be reporting to the Junior Leader's Battalion RASC at Norton Manor Camp, Taunton, Somerset early in January 1963. It all sounded quite exciting. Even more exciting was the fact that both my Dad and me were given expenses by the Recruiter – i.e. our bus fares, some cash to buy lunch (Pie and Peas in Bradford Market) and I also got a day's pay. The days pay was handed to my Dad for safe-keeping, never to be seen again – (the money, not Dad) and I was permitted to keep the bus fare. I was awash with cash.

On our way back home I was informed by my Dad, "Incidentally lad, if anybody asks, you're now a Methodist." He'd had my Army attestation papers adjusted accordingly. Up until that point I'd been Church of England. "It'll save you all sorts of grief on Sunday's" he said. I didn't understand what he meant at the time, but I did much later – and was thankful on many a following Sunday morning when I was able to remain festering in my bed at Norton Manor Camp, whilst the 'C of E' element were marched off to Church, in uniform, accompanied by the Regimental Band. There they were harangued by the Padre (Chief God Botherer) for a couple of hours about such things as the perils of masturbation "Mark my words – you will all go blind!" (he should have known as he wore thick, pebbled lensed spectacles) and over imbibation of the local brew, natural cider!" etc.

Those Army 'high church' church services were very class conscious i.e. the officers and their family's got the front pews with kneeling cushions whilst the reminder of the lower decks sat according to their rank and status, finishing up with the Junior Leaders towards the rear of the Church, sat on the planks, gently drifting off or slyly reading a smuggled in Sunday paper (usually the News of the World), obtained from the Cookhouse that morning at breakfast. Often there was fierce competition, apparently, to see who could produce the loudest fart or belch at a key moment of the Vicar's diatribe. The Permanent Staff certainly had their hands full at these gatherings. I, fortunately, being a lapsed Methodist, remained oblivious as I lay in my pit, impatiently waiting for the cookhouse to open for Sunday Dinner. We were all obliged to attend the unit cinema every Sunday afternoon to watch a specially selected film.

Then it was back to the billets to spend the rest of Sunday preparing our uniforms for the next morning's working parade. Blancoing belt and gaiters, bulling boots, pressing the crappy uniform with a ridiculous little non-steam iron etc. There was only one iron for each billet. Join the queue mate! Sometimes you couldn't get to the iron until after 'lights out' which meant doing your ironing in the semi-darkness. How ridiculous was that. A lot of us bought our own irons, Londoners usually having those that emitted steam!

Prior to departing for Taunton, I was actually doing rather well at school (Highfield), academically speaking. I was in the 'A' stream (GCE level); a House Captain (Nelson), a Lance Corporal in the Boy's Brigade Band and was expected to do quite well for myself eventually. As I explained previously, once I announced to my Form Teacher that I was joining the Army, within minutes I was accorded leprosy status, hoofed out of the 'A' stream classroom and placed into the 'B' stream along with those others deemed to be plodders. I fartled about wasting time at school for a couple more months until the Army paperwork eventually arrived confirming my acceptance as a Junior Leader. In due course I was instructed to proceed in an orderly fashion to Taunton in Somerset along with all of the details of how I was to achieve that. I had no real inkling of what was waiting for me, but it all sounded incredibly exciting and glamorous.

Being a Junior Leader, apparently, meant plenty of well cooked food, tons of sport, lots of leave, I would be knee-deep in qualifications, great mates for life and to top it all – paid a more than generous wage. Food and accommodation was free! Also, if you were really alert, you could see a pig flying past the billet windows. My Dad eventually sent me on my way with this intellectual gem – "Allus remember lad, never trust a thin Cook or a fat Medic!" I didn't know what he meant at the time, but in essence it proved to be sage and valuable advice.

This is an excerpt from the 'official' spiel that was churned out by the Junior Leader's Battalion RASC at that time to those about to join the Battalion:

'The young soldier in the Army of the 60's can get to the top of his profession if he has the ambition and the will to get there. In a Battalion such as the Junior Leaders Battalion RASC, all the same training facilities exist as those to be found in a first-class public school, the main differences being that our young soldiers are fed much better than their counterparts and are paid a liberal amount of pocket money by the Exchequer instead of by the parent!

A survey carried out of boys who have attended Junior Leaders Battalions and Regiments (or their equivalent in earlier years) shows in the Royal Army Service Corps that of the 1,032 now serving in the Regular Army, seven per cent are holding commissioned ranks, five per cent Warrant rank, thirteen per cent are Staff Sergeants and Sergeants and twenty per cent Corporals. It shows also that forty per cent of all Junior Leaders leaving the Battalion achieve NCO rank within the first year of adult service, twelve per cent achieve the rank of Sergeant before their sixth year of service and fifteen per cent are promoted to the rank of WO2 before their thirteenth year of service, which is at the age of approximately 30. Fourteen of the nineteen one-time ex-Apprentice Tradesmen and ex-Regimental boys still serving in the non-commissioned ranks with 21 years service, are Warrant Officers Class I.'

So, all to play for!

I'd started to prepare for my departure. My Dad came home from the British Legion Club one evening where he'd won a small suitcase, more of a briefcase really, that was full of small bottles of

O.B.J. ('*Oh Be Joyful*') beer. This, he insisted, would be just the job for me to take my 'stuff' to Taunton in, once the beer bottles were removed, naturally. I didn't realise at the time, but the initials O.B.J. stencilled onto the side of the case would cause more than a little confusion as my initials were T.J.C. My little Nan, who couldn't afford much, bought me a job lot of soap from a door-to-door salesman, which actually was quite niffy and must have been made from recently boiled horse. I remember that it lasted for months before I managed to switch to Imperial Leather. I was also presented with my Dad's shaving kit in a little leather case containing a hairbrush, comb, toothbrush and a safety razor, which I still have. Finally, my Dad loaned me his 'British Winter Warm' overcoat, which I was instructed to send back home at the earliest opportunity after my arrival at Taunton so I only got to wear it the once. Although I was fairly tall at the time, I wasn't as tall as my Dad and when I wore the coat I must have looked like 'Jim Crint' of the Goon Show as the bottom of the overcoat was just above my ankles. Still, it kept me warm and I was grateful for the loan of it.

Back in January 1963, for those who may not have been around at the time, there was a spot of very bad weather; a group called 'The Beatles' started out (what ever happened to them?) and I was unfortunately unable to report for duty on the appointed date because not only was there severe flooding throughout the Nation, but the majority of our main roads were blocked with snow. Everything had ground to a halt - and nothing, including trains, was moving, I decided to do the same. Eventually though, what few bits I owned got crammed into the 'O.B.J.' suitcase and I made my familial farewells. There was much snottering and floods of tears (but I managed to stop eventually). Off I went to a soot stained Keighley Railway Station, clutching a second class railway warrant and some sandwiches for the journey, (wrapped in a grease-proof 'Wonderloaf' bread wrapper – the sandwiches, not the warrant). The mountain of potted meat sandwiches had been lovingly prepared for me by my Mother, who was convinced that she'd never see me alive again. I sniffled and simpered all the way to Leeds and then decided to accept the great adventure that awaited me.

Interestingly, whilst I was waiting for my connecting train to Bristol I saw the late Jimmy Savile stood on the station platform, apparently, waiting for the arrival of the singer Sandie Shaw or it could have been Dusty Springfield. He was surrounded by a coterie of young admirers even then and was name dropping furiously. It all seemed very exciting. A new career beckoned and here was I in the presence of pop stars. My train, the exotically named 'The Devonian' eventually steamed into the station, I climbed on board and off we went. It was all rather heady stuff, I travelled all the way to Doncaster, Bristol and thence to Taunton. That might not seem very thrilling to you dear reader, but to me who had not been much further than Bradford Recruiting Office, it was akin to travelling along the Amalfi coast. I was just 15 years and a few weeks old and it was an exciting leap into the unknown.

I eventually arrived at Taunton Railway Station where I saw an Army Corporal pacing up and down on the platform as I alighted from the carriage. It was by this time pitch black (can you still say that?) about ten o'clock at night, snowing and absolutely bloody freezing. I meandered across to the Corporal, clutching my O.B.J. briefcase. He was quite obviously nithered and wearing a hairy greatcoat with large, very shiny buttons. I thought I'd better make my presence known to him. He was busy sucking on a Woodbine (cigarette). Just as an aside - Squaddies refer to cigarettes as "Doofers," as in "Two's up on your doof, mate," i.e. people with not a lot of money sharing the luxury of their ciggie. Apparently the word "Doof" comes from the phrase used by soldiers in World War One. "That'll doof-fer me!" Anyway, moving swiftly on and back to the Platform, I addressed the Corporal politely:

Me: Excuse me.

(I was wearing Dad's very smart British Winter Warm overcoat, (with epaulettes and brown leather buttons), which undoubtedly impressed him, because he replied):

Corporal: *(Politeness personified)* Yes sir?

Me: Are you taking recruits to Norton Manor Camp?

Corporal: Yes I am, and your name is?

Me: Terry.

Corporal: Not your first name, you gormless twat, *(he had by this time made the assimilation that I was an underling),* your surname!

Me: Er, Cavender, sir. That's like Lavender, but with a 'C.'

He ticked my name of a list on his mill-board.

Corporal: Right, that's good 'cos you're the last one to arrive. See that truck over there - get yer arse on it - now!

I joined several other young shivering potentials in the back of the truck, a Bedford RL, fitted with a protective canopy - which was not fastened up at the back, so we were exposed to the elements. This was either sheer idleness on the driver's part, or a deliberate ploy to commence the toughening up process. In the gloom we nervously introduced ourselves. The lads were from diverse places such as Scotland, London, Birmingham, and Leicester etc. We sat there shivering and wondering what would come next.

The Corporal sauntered across to the truck, more than a little pissed off because he'd been stood around a cold Taunton railway station for hours on end waiting for recruits to arrive. By then we were all chattering happily (well our teeth were) whilst he leapt into the cozy cab of the truck. Before the driver cranked it up, the Corporal glared at us malevolently and shouted something erudite along the lines of:

Corporal: You lot - shut yur fuckin' gobs!! Save your energy – you'll be needing it where you're going! I'll have the next bastard what speaks!

(What did he mean, "Have us?" - a deathly silence descended in the back of the vehicle. This did not augur well).

The threat of military disciplinary action had reared its ugly head for the very first time. It was rare that I'd encountered that sort of sort of ripe prose and regarded it as being the absolute height of vulgarity. Our Boys Brigade officers would have been mortified. We definitely wouldn't have used that sort of salty language in the 1st Keighley Company of the Boys Brigade – the Captain, (the late Tom Mitchell) and his eloquent, erudite Lieutenant (Brian Thurling) would have made us hand our belts in – the ultimate disgrace. I recall clearly sitting there in the rear of the truck, shivering, wondering just what I'd gotten myself into, particularly when, to my horror, one of the Londoners flashed the Corporal a reverse Churchill and said, 'sotto voce' 'Ah fuck 'im, the tit!" and lit a roll-up. We gathered around the glowing end of his cigarette to warm our hands (no we didn't, I made that up to get the sympathy vote). He had to light up his cig covertly as the law stated quite clearly that you couldn't smoke until you were 16 years old. Within a few short weeks, however, we would be smoking and swearing like seasoned members of a hoary Portsmouth Royal Naval Press Gang (although I gave the smoking a miss).

We eventually arrived at Norton Manor Camp and although it was by then eleven o'clock-ish at night, pitch black and still freezing, the civilian contract Barber was waiting for us and we were shorn by his red hot shears, reducing us to look-alikes. The brain-washing and equalizing of the masses had begun. Then it was off to the QM's (Quartermaster') Stores to be issued with a baffling mountain of kit and equipment before being semi-marched over to the wooden spiders (billets) where we had been allocated the bed-spaces that were to become the centre of our universe for the next three months.

The billets were freezing cold because apparently the heating was turned off at 10 o'clock each evening to save money (they had heating targets even back then – some tight-arsed Quartermaster (QM) angling for an MBE probably). Our kit was chucked unceremoniously into a metal locker, then we were invited, individually to see the Padre in the Platoon office. There we were thrust to our knees for a quick blessing and handed a small copy of the English Bible before being hoofed out of the office back to our bed-spaces where we were ordered to change into our military jim-jams (the design of which were, I'm sure, based on what was once issued to POW's – a very fetching blue with white stripes).

We climbed into our pits and the all powerful Room NCO switched the lights off, plunging us into pitch darkness. It was so cold in those rooms that we had been instructed to put our newly issued Greatcoats on top of the two blankets. I recall being in bed, freezing cold, more than a bit scared and surrounded by strangers. Someone called out for permission to go to the lavatory and was told to shut up and get to sleep. As I laid there in the dark I listened to the sound of heartrending sobbing, fearful of what horrors the next day would bring and wondered just what I'd let myself in for. Surely things couldn't get much worse, could they? I wondered if this was what life was like in an orphanage? Of course it wasn't – it was worse. I was just 15 and a couple of weeks old. This was the start of my new life.

The Winter in 1963 was one of the worst on record. Everything froze. Once we became a little more 'savvy' we used to iron our sheets with a hot iron before getting into bed. One had to wait one's turn in the queue for the one hot iron that was available – there was a pecking order being established even in the early days, usually with the gobby, street-wise Londoners always at the front of the ironing queue.

The next morning, Day 1, in the pitch black, at something like 5 o'clock (oft referred to in military vernacular as 'Sparrows Fart'), the shaping process began. Upon hearing reveille blown on a Trumpet by the Regimental Bugler, we all leapt out of our pits (beds) wondering where Mummy was with the full English, then were berated constantly by our Room NCO's. We washed and shaved using cold water (it was that early that the boilers hadn't kicked in – bloody QM again), no plugs in the sinks – just issue lavatory paper (the shiny stuff – San Izal) stuffed in the sink plug-holes – and my first shave with my Dad's what was laughingly described as a safety razor. So wearing an ill-fitting, itchy uniform, huge leather boots that felt like diving boots and with strips of bleeding flesh hanging off my face courtesy of the mis-named Wilkinson's Safety Blade, it was outside into the freezing cold where me and my fellow inmates were formed up as a Platoon, in the dark, and 'marched' to the Cookhouse for an early breakfast.

Fortunately for us, the Cookhouse wasn't too far away from the living accommodation. The road along which we marched was 'bottle' ice and when we were halted, because our boots had studs and metal on the heels, a goodly portion of us went arse over tit and in doing so smashed our newly issued ceramic one pint mugs, and hurtled our KFS (Knife Fork and Spoon - Diggers) into the snow – many not to be seen again until the snow melted. There was a nice little trade going on in replacement Mugs and Diggers. It became normality to hear "Squaaaaaad – Halt!" Smash!

Getting food in the Cookhouse was something like a scene from 'Oliver.' You stood in a huge queue for ages, whilst a porky, sweating, swivel eyed member of the Army Catering Corps (ACC) slapped some greasy, questionable food, onto a cold plate. You were issued with a slice of bread and a square of frozen margarine, which wouldn't spread and usually with the Cook's thumbprint on it. Breakfast had to be scoffed in record time as the dreaded cry of "Get outside you nob-heads!" would echo around the Cookhouse after what seemed like only a couple of minutes. Tough cack if you hadn't finished eating, you had to wolf it down like the clappers.

A nice little psychological touch was that the Orderly Sergeant or Officer would be stood in the pan-wash area where you handed your plates in on your way out of the Cookhouse. If there was any food left on your plate you had to finish it off there and then. No waste allowed. It was a chargeable offence not to go to breakfast so you couldn't avoid those early morning torturous and mindless procedures.

In addition to the various complexities of learning a new way of living, we also had to learn a new language based on military mnemonics, very quickly, otherwise you wouldn't have got through the day. Things like:

NAAFI - (**N**avy **A**rmy and **A**ir **F**orce **I**nstitution) (or as renamed by the troops - **N**o **A**mbition **A**nd **F**uck all **I**nterest).

CO - Commanding Officer.

OC - Officer Commanding.

QM - Quartermaster.

RSM - Regimental Sergeant Major.

CSM - Company Sergeant Major.

WRVS - Women's Voluntary Service (later the Women's Royal Voluntary Service –'Weevers' as the troops called it).

Full Screw - Full Corporal.

Lance Jack - Lance Corporal.

Gob Doc - Dentist.

M.O. - Medical Officer

etc, and so my military education had begun.

One of the first things that we sprogs were taught was how to salute commissioned officers properly. It was stressed that saluting was very important. Saluting is a strange habit that continues in the Armed Forces to this day, waving one's right arm around in the air, finishing with the right hand forefinger just touching one's right eyebrow, in the approved fashion, i.e. "Longest way up, shortest way down. Lad!" Failing to salute got you into deep cack and was a chargeable offence. The only exception to saluting was/is, I believe, when in a combat situation/area where an officer by being saluted could be singled out and spotted by the nasties. I am still convinced that saluting is one of the many means devised by the ruling classes to maintain subservience in what they consider to be lesser beings.

Learning and absorbing the military rank structure was complex and confusing. At first, the 'grown ups' were all 'Sirs' to the likes of me. A commissioned officer stopped a young recruit who failed to salute him when passing:

Officer: You boy! Haven't you been taught how to salute?

Recruit: (*Trembling and cheeks of the arse cracking walnuts*): Yizzah! I've been taught how to salute - but not who to salute.

For the next two and a half years we were beaten, (*metaphorically*), into shape and constantly had it drummed into us that not only were we eventually to become professional soldiers but that we were the future Warrant Officers and Officers of the Corps. Our first taste of the 'Carrot and Stick' method. For a lot of us that prediction turned out to be true as many of us unexpectedly and against all odds achieved their predictions. Many others bit the dust and returned to civilian life to let their hair grow back and try some other occupation. Military life, understandably, wasn't to everyone's taste.

One particular piece of good news in those dark and distant days was that as we had all been three weeks late in reporting for duty because of the inclement weather, we were entitled to three weeks' pay – which was duly handed over. It should have been sent to our homes prior to our departure, but the Pony Express couldn't get through the snow. Deep joy and straight off to the NAAFI for Beans on Toast, extra tins of 'Duraglit' and 'Blanco.' All of our uniforms, from the posh Battle Dress Uniform down to what were referred to as 'Drawers Dracula' (a perverse form of green underwear which one fastened using strange rubber buttons – no elastic), was provided free of charge by Her Majesty. Civilian clothing was not authorized to be worn for your first three month 'term.' Uniform and shorn heads was a great leveller. Accommodation, food provided 'free of charge,' education, tons of sport, two films a week and on top of that you got paid – and – something like ten weeks paid holiday a year (Boy Service perk). What more could a young lad ask for, eh? Who needed Peter Black's Shoe factory when we were living the Junior Leader dream at Taunton.

In truth, once settled and familiarised with everything, I had a marvellous time at the Junior Leaders Battalion RASC (which eventually morphed into a Regiment of the Royal Corps of Transport (RCT) one day in August 1965), the RASC having been consigned to the history books to be replaced by the RCT. Many years later the RASC was to resurface cunningly disguised as the Royal Logistics Corps (RLC) – (despite all of the current denials to the contrary). Meanwhile, in May 1963 I had joined the Regimental Band in what was known as Clayton Platoon and had a great time. Once trained up to the required performance standard and a fully fledged member of the band, it meant that we got to get out of barracks and travel all over the place, including the Royal Albert Hall, the Military Tattoo at Earls Court, Bristol City Football Ground, local Carnivals, Village Gala's things like that. Hey, I was a member of a boy band! One particularly memorable engagement at the Royal Albert Hall was when we shared the bill with the Dagenham Girl's Pipers and top pop singer, the delicious Susan Maughan singing her top ten hit - 'I want to be Bobby's girl':

60's Pop Singer - Susan Maughan

backed by the magnificent Ted Heath Band. Miss Maughan, who was toppermost of the poppermost at that time, was very patient with a multitude of spotty, panting, smelly Junior Leader's, posing for photo's and signing autographs for all of us. That was on the evening of the 24th of October 1964. We were full of it and living the dream. Happy Days!

Our dressing room in the Albert Hall was located immediately adjacent to the Dagenham Girl Pipers dressing room. There was a small hole in the wall and one of our lads spotting it told everyone about it. One squaddie, missing the point, said, "If they want to look at us, let 'em look!"

The Dagenham Girl Pipers

On that particular occasion, during the interval, one of our lads was approached by a rather posh 'Knight of the Realm' who had been watching the show from one of the plush boxes in the Albert Hall. He had slyly slipped some money into the lads trouser pocket, ruffled the lads hair and asked him to pop into his box (metaphorically speaking) after the show, for a glass of something and perhaps a little chatette. It didn't take the brains of an Archbishop to work out that there was some form of intended debauchery in the pipeline. Our adult

Trumpet Major, who never missed a trick, heard about what was going on when he saw the young man delightedly flashing a couple of five pound notes. He was promptly relieved of his ill-gotten gains, which was then changed for coin and distributed equally to each member of the band. 'All for one and one for all!' We all legged it, clutching our newly acquired wealth, back to Regents Park Barracks straight after the performance, leaving behind a disappointed and frustrated Knight sat in his plush box all by his little self, no doubt quivering with outrage and disappointment. Dodgy place, London.

I started off in the boys band as a Trumpeter (the 'E' Flat Cavalry Trumpet, (for those with a musical bent) until one day when out firing on the ranges, a round jammed in a Light Machine Gun (LMG) and exploded in the barrel right next to my lug-hole, perforating an ear-drum. I was what was known as the Number 2 (right next to the barrel), the firer being Number 1. Once my head had stopped ringing I reported the incident to my Platoon Sergeant, hoping for tea and sympathy. He just said, "Oh dear, how sad, never mind, you're now a Tenor Drummer," which was rather pleasing to me as I got to wear a leopard skin as part of the uniform. It didn't register that perforating an ear drum would have repercussions throughout my life. Many moons later my eardrum still plays me up. I often hear it squeaking when I sneeze. If I go swimming without ear plugs, my head fills with water and I sink (made that bit up). I eventually became the Drum Major, leading the band and just loving the theatre of it all. It couldn't last but it was fun whilst it did.

Scrubbed up nicely as - Junior Drum Major Cavender

When the Corps changed over, I was informed that I wouldn't be selected for transfer to the Royal Army Ordnance Corps (RAOC) but would remain with the newly formed Royal Corps of Transport (RCT), because, presumably, I wasn't numerate enough to count blankets. I didn't know whether to be pleased or disappointed. I remember on the afternoon of the 15th of July 1965 at 1400 hours, (sorry I can't be more specific than that) being on parade on the drill square at Norton Manor Camp when a portly and highly mottled full Colonel presented me with my new RCT cap-badge and collar dogs – which was great because they were 'Stay-bright' and didn't have to be furiously polished every night using a yellow NAAFI duster and a tin of smelly 'Duraglit' (metal polish). We had a Company/Squadron Sergeant Major (CSM/SSM Fred Sears) who used to call us 'Duraglit' when we were getting bollocked. "Do you know why I call you Duraglit?" he'd say sarcastically, "It's because you're a bright boy!" You had to be there. The rebadging from one Corps to another had momentous significance which didn't sink in at the time. I was more concerned about getting to the NAAFI for a crusty roll before the shutters went down.

Parades were OK but it was a right royal pain continually having to blanco gaiters and waist-belts, as if interminably bulling Boots Ammunition Pairs 1 wasn't enough. For those of you denied the joys of Blancoing, a bit of information. Blanco was a compound used primarily by soldiers throughout the Commonwealth from 1880 onwards to clean and colour their equipment. It was first used by the British Army to whiten Slade Wallace buckskin leather equipment, and later adapted to coloured versions for use on the cotton Web Infantry Equipment, Pattern 1908 webbing. Blanco became widely used throughout both world wars (presumably it was good for deflecting bullets)? I know that you feel better for knowing that little gemette. You want more? Look it up on the Internet, you'll have many happy hours filling yourselves in. Oh, all right, I'll save you a bit of time then. Have a butchers:

Blanco initially came in either powder manufactured by the Mills Equipment Company (who designed and were a primary manufacturer of the webbing it was used on), or round cake form, much like soap, manufactured by Pickerings and which used the trade-name "Blanco" and was used as a cleaning and colouring compound. (The compound was manufactured in Canada as "Capo".) Capo is an abbreviation for "Canadian Colouring Compound". Blanco was applied with a brush and water, and rubbed into the woven cotton material of load bearing equipment, to provide a consistent colour to equipment worn by soldiers in the same unit, and as a method of cleaning the gear. Post-war experimental rectangular waxy blocks became available with greater waterproofing abilities but after 1954 Joseph Pickering & Sons Ltd introduced a tinned paste product that didn't need the addition of water and could be applied directly from the tin. Other manufacturers made competing tinned paste products until the 1980s.

The most common form of Blanco, for us anyway, was the original No. 7 (British No. 61 Buff), a "khaki" colour which in practice was a tan shade, or one of two shades of green, either No. 9 or British

No. 3 Khaki Green. Other colours included black (used by Royal Armoured Corps and rifle regiments per regimental custom), white (for ceremonial duties or military policemen on traffic control duty) or blue (by air force units), the latter being a shade known as "RAF Blue" for use on the RAF blue-grey web equipment.

The majority of our meagre wages got spent on items of cleaning equipment such as Boot Polish, Brasso/Duraglit Metal Polish (also used for cleaning barrack windows), yellow dusters and the aforementioned dreaded Blanco. I've just recalled that we were each issued with a pair of 'pumps' to be worn for physical training purposes, which were a strange shade of orangey brown when new. The rubber toe sections had to be carefully melted smooth with a hot spoon, (heated over a candle flame), and then the pumps had to be highly shined with black Cherry Blossom boot polish. When the pumps got wet, which they often did, some of the black polish would soak through to one's feet. Why couldn't the QM just get back plimsolls? We would have still had to melt the toe sections, but would have saved a fortune in shoe polish.

Whichever sadist thought the 'polishing pumps' one up is, I fondly hope, burning in blanco hell alongside the man who invented bulling boots and 'boxing blankets' - which for those who have served before the mast will well know is absolutely nothing to do with sport but is a tortuous and time consuming method of folding bedding.

There were constant foot inspections, usually prior to enjoying some form of physical training when 'pumps' 'daps' were worn. These checks were made by the permanent staff to ensure that Junior Leaders were complying with the strict hygiene rules. Those found to have manky feet had their toes stamped on, despite protestations of innocence and that it was actually boot polish stains. Inspections were usually carried out in the Gymnasium by the professional sadists of the Army Physical Training Corps (APTC) – (Muscle Benders). One particular punishment for those found to have manky feet was that they had to remove their navy blue issue PT shorts (no underwear as that was deemed to be unhygienic whilst wearing PT kit), miscreants had to place the shorts over their heads and then had to complete several circuits of the gymnasium whilst simultaneously being walloped viciously on their bare arses and hocks by other trainees, using their rubber soled pumps.

If the APTC Instructor deemed that the punishment was insufficient i.e. not enough solid blows had landed, then further circuits of the gymnasium were required. I can hear the shrieks of anguish in my head as I write this. This punishment was probably something that morphed from public schools. Aye, but we were happy and it made men of us. Go figure!

As I was not going to go to the RAOC as a Staff Clerk, my short-hand training ceased with immediate effect. How handy that would have been in my life had I been able to write in short-hand, particularly as I've never had a particularly retentive memory. I started to do my driver training – in an Austin Champ (with a Rolls Royce engine). At the same time I underwent Clerical Training, being taught by two delightful old retired officers from the Indian Army no less. They did an excellent job teaching me and my fellow potential quill-dribblers to type etc. The instructors had one of those old wind- up gramophones and we typed along to some old scratched musical records in order to ensure that our little pinkies maintained the correct typing speed. Sounds dotty, but it worked. Whenever I hear the tune "Wheels" it reminds me of that classroom. Life was beginning to get interesting.

One thing I do recall though, is travelling back to Taunton at the conclusion of a much enjoyed leave at home where my every whim had been catered for. No queuing for breakfast there. I was still a spotty, pre-pubescent boy soldier, aged somewhere between 16 and 17, returning by train to my unit at Taunton. In those days 'we' had to travel wearing uniform. That was all stopped eventually when the IRA nastiness kicked off, but at that time it was considered safe and OK to be seen out and about in your uniform. It was also a matter of personal pride.

As the train 'clickety-clacked' along the track I decided to be a bit daring, (I was under 18), and go and buy myself a can of beer (Newcastle Brown was the tipple of the day). I made my way to the buffet restaurant, deepened my vocal delivery and ordered a can of Nukey B. At the bar stood a tall, distinguished, elderly, white haired gentleman who had also ordered himself a drink. He said hello and smiled at me. I though that he looked a bit important, so I'd better behave with decorum. "Morning Sir!" He asked me where I was going. I think I may have said something gormless like "Back to my compartment sir." "No, I meant where are you travelling to?" "I'm returning from leave to Taunton, Sir," I replied. He asked me my name and all about my unit, what I was doing there etc then said that as he was a little unsteady on his pins, why not come and have a chat with him and his wife in his carriage. I thought it wiser not to refuse – he was obviously important and super posh and this would be my first opportunity to travel 1st Class. He was probably just an old Officer wanting to have a chat and reminisce with one of the 'lads.'

We walked back to his 1st Class carriage, where there was a sticker on the window stating, rather grandly, reserved for 'Lord Avon and Party.' We went in and sat down. He introduced me to his wife and I recall that bit quite clearly. She was sat, rather daringly I thought, perched with her feet on the seats - reading a copy of 'The Times.' Milord said, "Darling, this is Junior Private Cavender. He's returning to Taunton from leave." His wife, Lady Avon (Clarissa Spencer-Churchill), peeped over the top of her newspaper, gave me a disdainful glance as if she'd discovered something untoward on her shoe and said something like – "Eeeeough, really!" then disappeared back behind her newspaper. Lord Avon smiled and then we chatted about all sort of things until finally the train pulled into Bristol Railway Station.

He was a very cultured and pleasant man, easy to chat with. Milord told me that that was where they were leaving the train at Bristol, so taking that as my cue to leg it, I grabbed my (by now) empty can of 'Nukey B', shook his hand, nodded respectfully at Lady Avon (ignored) and returned to my 'normal' seat in steerage. I realised afterwards that Milord had been sipping his drink out of a glass whilst yours truly had been necking the 'Nukey B' straight out of the can! Where the train stopped, parked right next to the platform was a large, immaculately polished, black limousine and smartly dressed chauffeur, waiting to collect Lord and Lady Avon. Before getting into his car, Lord Avon turned and looked across at the carriages, saw me gazing out of the window, smiled wistfully and waved before being helped into his limo and being driven off. I remember thinking something along the lines of "What a nice old geezer."

The Right Honourable the Earl of Avon KG MC PC

As Junior Leaders we were made to write home at least once a week, so shortly after my return to Taunton I wrote home and told my parents that I'd been sat chatting with Lord Avon on the train. My Dad eventually replied, something along the lines of "Did you know, lad, that you were sat with Sir Anthony Eden, who was Foreign Secretary three times and Prime Minister! Also that during the course of his career, Sir Anthony had met people like Winston Churchill, Joseph Stalin, Franklin D Roosevelt, Adolf Hitler, Benito Mussolini, General de Gaulle, Stanley Baldwin, Ramsey Macdonald, General Dwight D Eisenhower etc and now Junior Private Cavender!" The names that my Dad mentioned were vaguely familiar to me but didn't really register until I was a bit older. I just thought at the time that Lord Avon was a very nice posh bloke and that his wife was a bit snooty. In essence as he looked as if he was worth a few quid I'd hoped that he'd buy me another can of Newcastle Brown (which he didn't). So, I've shaken the hand that shook the hand of Stalin, Roosevelt and Eisenhower etc – how historical is that! I've never washed it since.

Now that I'm retired and have time to sit and watch various documentaries on Sky TV's History Channel etc, I'm amazed to think that I'd spent some time with a man who'd been right in the thick of making history - World War 1, World War 2, the Suez Crisis etc and a man that had been involved with so many historic and influential figures. Lord Avon was clearly an erudite and educated person; apparently he spoke fluently in French, German, Persian, Russian and Arabic. Quite how he made sense of a young Yorkshire lad's nervous mumblings eludes me, but he did. So that's one of my claims to fame. When I talk to people about it now, which I do very occasionally, unless they are of a certain age they haven't got a clue just who I'm talking about, which is a great shame.

Train journeys, for me, had their moments. I remember being stuck in Bradford Railway Station waiting to get my Taunton connection. Because the weather was so bad there was a lengthy delay in the train arriving, snow on the track probably. For some reason known only to British Rail, the waiting rooms were locked and we had to sit on a windswept, freezing platform. It became unbearably cold so I decided to go and sit in the men's lavatories. They, at least, were indoors and had some form of heating. I put my penny (!) in the lock, entered, lowered the lid on the lavatory and settled down on the pan for a couple of hours.

I'd just started to drift off when I was woken by a strange grating noise. I glanced to my left at the old-fashioned glazed brown brickwork and saw that one of the bricks in the middle of the wall was sliding back into the next stall. I was dumbstruck. A pair of ferrety eyes appeared where the brick had been and a Kenneth Williams type voice said – "Heeeeelloooo!" then winked. God help me, I couldn't even keep warm in safety. I hurriedly made my excuses and returned to the platform. I may have been relatively innocent at that stage of my life, but not that innocent that I didn't know what he was after. I should have poked him in the eye!

Travelling back to Bristol by rail one winter, there was – naturally – nothing to eat or drink on the train and the carriage heating was non-existent, which was virtually standard operating procedure on British Rail in those days. As the train pulled into I think it was Burton-on-Trent it decelerated and I thought that it would be stopping to let passengers on and off. As there was usually a wait of a couple of minutes I decided that it was an ideal opportunity for me to nip off and buy a cuppa and a sandwich from the station buffet. As the train slowed I opened the carriage door, nipped off and looked for the buffet. To my horror the train kept going and it was obvious that it wasn't going to stop, so I had to thrash along the platform, sprinting like Sir Roger Bannister, and dive back onto the train, which by now was picking up speed. I returned to my seat, screaming for breath, well and truly lathered.

The Guard had seen all this going on and sought me out. He gave me a severe bollocking for my stupidity then took me into the Guards Van where he handed me a mug of tea and we had a good chat. Luckily for me he was an ex-soldier, so we had something in common to chat about. The Guards Van had a little stove and was lovely and warm. Being an ex-Serviceman he told me all about his World War 2 experiences and, joy of joys, made us both a bacon sandwich on his little stove. Living the dream. Leaving the train at Bristol I boarded another train for Taunton, which was also freezing cold. What was it with British Rail?

To cut a long story short, (I can sense that you're drifting), I eventually left the Junior Leaders Regiment RCT, by then qualified as a dual-tradesman – Group B Class 3 Driver & Group B Class 3 Clerk (some cunning bastard at the MOD had invented the first 'Twofers') and I was posted to Headquarters the RCT Training Centre at Buller Barracks, Aldershot, where I was employed as the lowest form of clerical life, tea boy, delivering Part One Orders etc. Again, luckily, I'd landed on my feet and it turned out that I had a superb time there. In our office was a brilliant, gifted young Corporal called Adrian (Andy) Ball who was theatre mad and had just written a marvellous musical comedy play called 'Hercules.' His enthusiasm for all things theatrical was infectious and I was persuaded to join a little theatrical group that he'd organised and take part in 'Hercules' the show he was producing at the

Garrison Theatre, adjacent to 'God's Half Acre' cricket ground at Buller Barracks.

I loved it and had quite a good part in the play, managing to stop the show each evening because of the huge amounts of laughter at my performance! I'm not boasting, it just happened that way and was really down to the tremendous quality of Andy Ball's writing. I was a success darlings. Thinking about it later, the laughter was probably generated because of the sight of my legs hanging out of an indecently short Toga, (some wag commented that the last time they'd seen a pair of legs like mine, they'd been hanging out of a birds nest)!

It was great fun working in the Headquarters, there was always something going on. I made a lot of new friends, civilian and military by being in the play and each day something interesting seemed to be going on. I remember being put in charge of tidying up the filing system, which might seem terribly boring but it wasn't. I kept finding interesting things like the file that had been prepared for the funeral procedures and transport requirements for the funeral of The Queen Mother who was still alive and kicking at the time.

Sir Billy Butlin MBE, the man behind the Butlins Holiday Camp Empire, had been in the first World War as a soldier himself so had an affinity with the military. Sir Billy had been invited to be the inspecting officer for a recruit passing out parade at Buller Barracks in Aldershot. It was round about 1966. We were all stood in the front offices of the Headquarters RCT Training Centre, watching the parade. Sir Billy had been driven onto the main parade square, seated in the rear of a large white American open topped car. He was wearing a white suit, topped by a Stetson hat and waving to everyone, clearly enjoying the moment. Not your normal "Hello Chaps!" Inspecting Officer.

Some pompous staff officer, (clearly jealous), said "Look at that vulgar little man!" I remember thinking that Sir Billy hadn't done too badly for himself – a Knighthood, an MBE, loads of holiday camps around the country and creaming the money in. Last but not least he had a stunning blond maiden sat next to him in his limousine. If that's what being vulgar was, bring it on!

Incorporated into our Headquarters building was the RASC/RCT Corps Museum. One of my duties was to ensure that the Headquarters Building was secure at night once everyone had finished work. In its way it was a fairly important task. All of the doors and windows had to be secured and there were two or three safes that had to be checked to ensure that they were locked. The best part about it for me, though, was ensuring that the Corps Museum was safe and sound. Alone, I spent hours in the archives there, having a look through all of the old uniforms, medals, documentation, publications etc which was very interesting.

There were mountains of old uniforms, medals, hat boxes, swords, cavalry boots with spurs still attached. These were all, presumably, loaned to the Museum and were there to be catalogued for exhibiting in due course. I don't know why, but one evening I decided to put one of the uniforms on for a laugh, so I got togged up in full Service Dress which had belonged to a General. I wore a Service Dress jacket covered with medal ribbons, badges of rank and red tabs, a pair of Jodhpurs, some brown cavalry boots with spurs, a leather swagger stick – and to finish the rig off – a pith helmet. I know – silly – but I was just a young lad having a laugh and in a world of my own.

I swaggered around the Headquarters, slapping my thigh with the swagger stick, carrying out my security checks. I was shouting and bawling out instructions as I pretended that I was now a very senior officer inspecting the troops on parade etc. I thought I was safe because everyone had gone home. When I clumped upstairs, spurs jangling, I ponced into the Brigadier's Office, swishing the swagger stick and bawling something like "This is filthy, look at the bally dust" etc. I must have looked and sounded like Major Dennis Bloodnok of the Goon Show, an officer who suffered from terrible flatulence who every time he appeared broke thunderous wind, then said his famous catchphrase – "No more curried eggs for me, Jim!" Those of a certain age will know just who I'm talking about.

T C – a.k.a. Major Denis Bloodnok of 'Goon Show' fame

To my abject horror I discovered that the Commandant, Brigadier Lindsay J Aspland, was sat at his desk, still working. He glanced up from his paperwork and looked straight at me, saying "Yes, what is it?" I saluted, bashing my fingers on the pith helmet, and said "Er, good evening sir, just locking up." He shook his head, smiled and said, "Carry on, Cavender!" as if seeing someone dressed like a reject from the Indian Empire was the absolute norm. I reversed out of his office as fast as the old cavalry boots would let me, spurs jingling and returned the illicit accoutrements back to the Museum, running like a man possessed. Expecting to be summoned by my boss, the Superintending Clerk, the following morning for a dressing down about dressing up (see what I did there) I was pleasantly surprised to hear nothing further about it.

The Brigadier often smiled and nodded at me in an understanding and avuncular fashion whenever we crossed paths. After that I went low profile and continued in my subservient role as collector of the sticky buns from the WRVS Mobile Van.

The Brigadier's office was situated in the upstairs segment of the building, which was reached by walking up an impressive curving staircase. One particular evening, properly dressed this time, I was running up the stairs in order to get my security duties completed fairly rapidly, when around the top part of the stairs came Brigadier Aspland. We tried to pass each other on the stairs, performing some sort of mincing tango, but collided. The Brigadier lost his footing then wildly 'luged' down the stairs, roaring profanities and clutching his briefcase. I ran after him, helped him up, dusted him down and apologised profusely. He "harrumphed" and said, "Cavender, you're a bloody nuisance!" then hobbled on his way, limping badly. He didn't turn in for work for the next few days as apparently his back was playing up. He must have been startlingly patient because there was no comeback on that incident either. Those were the days when your feet wouldn't touch the ground as you headed to the Guardroom to be slung in a cell for some very minor transgression. I kept well away from the Brigadier from then on. He was probably more relieved about that than I was.

There was time in those days to have a bit of fun. A group of us from the Headquarters – the "Theatre set" - would often jump into a convenient car and head off for the West End of London to see a show. I remembered going to see 'Hello Dolly' starring the late Dora Bryan with a group of fellow thespians. It wasn't a particularly long drive from Aldershot to the West End in London and anyway the drive was part of the fun. In those days there wasn't too much difficulty finding a parking space in theatre-land either. On the way to the theatre we drew up at a set of traffic lights. I recall that several of us were crammed into a small Fiat, clutching and swigging from bottles of cheap Italian wine along the way, considering ourselves to be very 'continental' and with it.

A highly polished and large Jag drew up alongside us. There was just one occupant in the vehicle, a smallish, well dressed man who stared straight ahead, ignoring us. Someone said, "Hey, that's Peter Sellers," and it was. Being a long time Goons fan, I was thrilled. Naturally we shouted a few kind comments to him like, "Yoo Hoo - Mr Sellers!" "Alright mate?" "Hello Min!" that sort of thing. We all admired him and were fans. He turned and glared at us, I recall that he was very sour faced – but then he'd probably been filming all day and was heading for home for a well earned rest and to count his millions. Anyway, he looked as if he was sucking a lemon. By then we were mischievously shouting "Hello Jim?" and "No more curried eggs for me!" He totally blanked us. The traffic lights changed, he put his foot down and headed off into history. Ah well, a little smile and a wave wouldn't have hurt him – after all we'd paid for his Jag in a roundabout way. Unabashed, we continued slurping our wine and headed for a memorable night at the theatre. After the show we went into London to an Italian Restaurant for a meal before legging it back to Aldershot. About two years ago I was in London and saw that the restaurant was still there. I went inside for a meal and the only things that had changed were the staff and the prices. It was like stepping back in time. A lovely experience.

Back at work, one day I was summoned into my immediate boss's Office, the grandly titled 'DAA & QMG,' (Deputy Assistant Adjutant and Quarter Master General), the late Major D J (Derek) Murphy RCT, who was to die tragically from a heart attack at a very early age, and was told, "Cavender, my boy, you've had enough fun. It's time you did a bit of proper soldiering. You've spent enough time at the WRVS van! I'm going to ring our Manning and Records Office and sort out a decent posting for you. Where do you want to go to, the Far East, Middle East or Near East?"

I didn't have a clue what he was talking about. My main responsibility and raison d'être at that particular time was to make sure that I got the crusty roll orders right for the Headquarters when the WRVS van came around each morning. Major Murphy said, "Listen chum, I've just returned from Singapore missen. I was with the Air Despatch. Fancy a bash at that?" "Yes sir," I replied, having no clue whatsoever about what the Air Despatch was or indeed where Singapore was (other than the fact that there's been a balls up in World War 2 and that 'our lads' had suffered badly as a result). Anyway, I nodded dutifully and that was it. Major Murphy made the call and confirmed with me that I was about to join the very specialized world of RCT Air Despatch. I was to be posted to 15 Air Despatch Regiment RCT, based at RAF Seletar in Singapore.

Purely by coincidence I'd been to the local cinema in Aldershot, with a couple of my Army mates, to see the then newly released film 'King Rat.' We were sat chatting about it in the office the next day saying what a brilliant film it was, when we were summoned (by a very loud, bellowing voice) into the office of the late Major (Retired) L H J (Larry) Sadler, who was employed in the Headquarters in a Retired Officer (RO) capacity. We stood in front of his desk like naughty little schoolboys, whilst he proceeded to soundly berated us for saying that we'd enjoyed the film about '"those bloody Japs!" for whom he had a very special dislike. He then sat us down and told us a few 'home truths' about Singapore and in particular Changi prison where he'd had the gross misfortune to have been a Prisoner-of-War and had suffered terribly at the hands of the Japanese as a result. We clueless young squaddies left his office duly chastened and a little bit wiser and with the knowledge that not everything that came from Hollywood was just an exciting adventure, grossly exaggerated to make it entertaining.

Little did I know that before too long I would be given a guided tour of Changi Prison, which included, with a touch of gruesome theatricality, the death cell. For us young, easily impressed squaddies, 'King Rat' was just a film, for Major Sadler it was a diminution of the real-life horrors that he had experienced and was all still fresh in his mind, World War 2 having not been all that long ago at that time.

On reaching Singapore, as a new arrival, after settling in, I was taken on a guided tour of the island, which included a fleeting glance at Changi prison as part of our in-theatre education. We used to have educational tours to various places around Singapore, one of which was inside Changi Prison. I recall during the tour being shown an old notebook that was held in the prison chapel, listing those many British (and other nationalities) and how they had died i.e. Beaten to Death, Starved, and other such unspeakable and unforgiveable horrors. Those pencilled notes in that book brought the starkness of war and 'man's inhumanity to man' well and truly home to us all.

We just couldn't understand how the Japanese, a supposedly cultured nation, could do such cruel things. I remember also that our guide for the tour of the prison purported to be the last British Prison Officer on the staff at Changi Prison. He was a sallow faced Peter Cushing lookalike. At the end of our tour he invited us into the Prison Officer's Club for a beer and I recall quite clearly, with a shiver, him saying something along the lines of "You know the best part of my job, lads? We shook our heads dutifully. He leered, "I've got the keys for the

Women's prison and can go in there whenever I feel like it, day or night!" then laughed – "Mwwwha ha ha…." It was one of those rare occasions when you could feel the hairs on the back of your neck rising.

During our prison walk-about he'd taken a perverse delight in pointing out various prisoners and reeling off their offences, such as "See that jolly little chappie over there?" we looked at the little Chinese guy who was working in the bakery, "Well he set fire to his Mother. He won't be getting out of here in a hurry!" he looked at the man and shouted "Oy You! Get on with your work! You'd better not burn that bread! " then gave us another graveside laugh. As we got towards the end of the tour he said, "Don't forget lads, you can pop in here at anytime for a nice cool beer! Just ask for me – and if I'm in a good mood I might lend you my cell keys!" Not bloody likely.

During our visit we were also shown around the condemned cell, which was all a bit spooky. It was painted a manky shade of green and had an ominous looking metal hook embedded in the ceiling just above a trap-door in the floor. There was a great sense of collective relief when the tour finished and the prison gate finally clanged shut behind us and we headed off to Singapore City for a refreshing beer or three.

Watching a documentary on Sky TV very recently I saw that Changi Prison was about to be demolished and replaced by a more up-to-date rebuild elsewhere. A group of old ex-Prisoners of War (British and Australian, male and female) were being allowed to have a final look around the prison. It was a very touching programme as they tearfully relived their obviously extremely unpleasant memories. Their bravery, spirit and dignity shone through. Funnily enough, I remembered clearly the main gates of the prison from my visits in the 1960's but little else of the inside. It did, though, remind me of that menacing Prison Officer.

I was fortunate enough to go on several guided tours of the Tiger Breweries in Singapore. Someone in authority had decided that it would be most educational for the troops to see the beer being brewed, (particularly as most of our wages were spent on it). The tours always culminated in us drinking copious amounts of the produce, which was provided free of charge, in the delightful little bar in the brewery before staggering out into the heat, boarding the transport and heading off for Singapore City, awash with free alcohol. I eventually stopped going on the 'Tiger Tours' as some of the brewery staff started to recognize several of us 'frequent flyers.'

I've digressed. Bear with. Back to Aldershot, where I'd received a posting order sending me to Headquarters 15 Air Despatch Regiment RCT at RAF Seletar in Singapore. I was by that time 18 years old. On my final working day at the RCT Training Centre, the last thing I did was to nail the Post Lady's favourite slippers to the wooden floor in her mail room. She hadn't been particularly pleasant to me during my time there, so I decided to take retaliatory measures. I would be out of the country when she stepped into them. It was a bit mean I suppose, particularly as she had feet like curly Cornish pasties and on a daily basis hobbled painfully around the headquarters, delivering the office mail wearing the manky slippers that in truth should have been condemned as being unfit for human purpose. "Cor, the old plates are playing me up today!" etc. I never heard the outcome of the nailed slippers ploy, for which I now formally apologize. I sincerely hope that she didn't slide her deformed feet into the slippers then go arse over tit when she 'stepped off' to do her postal rounds. Had she been nicer to me I would only have nailed one slipper to the floor.

My 'Far East' kit was packed, items like the new 'Gortex' uniforms, Stockings Footless (eh?), Boots Jungle Pairs 1, Hats Jungle 1, stuff like that, final farewells made, injections galore whacked into the old rump then off to RAF Brize Norton to fly out to Singapore. As we were flying out fairly early in the morning, we had to report to Brize the night before. I think the place I overnighted in was called 'The Gateway' but I can't really remember. I do remember going for a rather swish pre-flight breakfast the following morning. One had to be properly dressed i.e. suited and booted for flying in those days and I had scrubbed up particularly well. As I sat there eating a full English I remember thinking to myself, "How very civilized the RAF is," Breakfast was served to us by respectful white jacketed Stewards and it was all done with great panache, decorum and a flourish that you don't get now, even in some of the best hotels.

It was only when I was leaving the dining room after breakfast that I read, to my abject horror, inscribed on the door - 'Officers' Mess.' Cheeks of the arse cracking conkers I thrashed off out of the building, but not before signing the required breakfast chit! That's one chit that never did get cleared. The Officers that I had breakfasted with must have wondered who the young Army vulgarian was in their midst, but probably wrote me off as just another a dense crap-hat.

I worried that the 'Snowdrops' (RAF Police) might be waiting for me, waving an unpaid breakfast chit, as I headed for the aircraft departure lounge. Several of us were not allowed to board the aircraft, an RAF Comet, because we hadn't had the required Yellow Fever jab. This was remedied when we were swiftly taken to the Medical Centre, where a tutting RAF medic made several stinging comments about Army administration and then begrudgingly gave us our jabs. We then returned to the aircraft, arms throbbing but ready to meet Yellow Fever head on. 'Tally-ho' – and off we went, heading for Singapore via some very exotic locations, starting with Cyprus, Bombay (now Mumbai), Sharjah and last, but not least, a final re-fuelling stop at a beautiful gem of an island, RAF Gan. I felt very 'Mr International Traveller.' I remember the palm trees, the white sandy beaches and very clear blue water as we flew into RAF Gan. It was like something out of a movie.

Apparently we'd experienced a bit of a heavy landing at RAF Akrotiri in Cyprus where we'd bounced along the runway, damaging the landing gear and as a consequence had to overnight there whilst the aircraft was put back together again. I was totally oblivious of the landing as it was my first ever flight. The RAF, organised as ever, laid on a film for us that night, some decent scoff and some welcome cold drinks. Their welfare system was beyond criticism, all very civilized. As a crap-hat I was used to be shouted at and told precisely what to do. The RAF people were very grown up about things and allowed you use your initiative. Whilst there I adopted a low profile just in case they'd been notified that I had an outstanding mess bill hanging over me from breakfast. I was only a lad and these sort of things loomed large.

We eventually flew in to RAF Changi, Singapore, late in the evening, where I was greeted by two familiar faces, ex-Junior Leader friends of mine, Geoff Lukins and Mick Hosie. The stench of rotting vegetation was quite appalling, but that wasn't Geoff's fault – he didn't handle the curry very well. With them was a well-known Corps name, Tom Broadfoot, another ex-Junior Leader. It was reassuring to see such familiar faces when one was so far away from home at the other side of the world. After a bit of back-slapping, they took me up to RAF Seletar in a Land Rover, where I was allocated accommodation, got changed into something bordering on lightweight, (Aldershot - Marks and Spencer) and off we went to savour the delights of Singapore City.

I remember that my military accommodation, 'H' Block RAF Seletar, didn't have a mattress on the metal bed and I had to kip on the bed-springs until the stores opened the following day when I could sign out a mattress and some bedding. The RAF would never have allowed that to happen. The next morning I looked as if I'd been flogged, the bed springs having left a pattern across my back. How terribly vulgar, but I couldn't have cared less – jet lag combined with gallons of the newly discovered delights of both Tiger Beer and Anchor Beer made me oblivious to bed-springs or anything else that night.

The next few years flew by and I had a truly brilliant time. It was all Charwallahs, Punkawallahs, Dhobiwallahs and Singapore Dollars. I didn't clean a pair of boots/shoes, wash a shirt or make a bed for the next three years. Those who served out there will know the unabashed luxury of which I speak. So began my adult military life with the Air Despatch. I soon got into a routine and was enjoying life. It wasn't all tea and biscuits, though.

Ah, I was going to tell you about the time I was the 'Diarist' in a Riot Squad at RAF Seletar. It was time to grow up. I hadn't been there for more than a couple of months when the locals, who had taken great offence with the Brits because Harold Wilson had tinkered with the value of the pound, devaluing it and knackering their investments/savings. Up until then the pound had been as safe a bet as the American dollar. Anyway, a very large, furious crowd of Singaporeans had assembled in the nearby local village of Jalan Kayu and were heading for the main gates of RAF Seletar. The Snowdrops (RAF

Police) had beaten a hasty strategic retreat behind the main gates and the Army Air Despatchers were summoned to help restore order. Knowing that something like this was bubbling under, we had been practicing riot drill for a few days on the main square outside Headquarters 15 Air Despatch Regiment RCT.

It was all rather exciting being in a Riot Squad, fully 'tooled up' and raring to go. We quickly 'debussed' forming a square just outside the camp gates and must have looked quite fearsome. Along with the usual, bricks and bottles that came our way, some of the locals were wielding a particularly nasty type of 'weapon.' They were wielding long bamboo poles with razor blades embedded in their ends, swishing them at troops. Tempers were getting very short, particularly as we were extremely uncomfortable physically, sweaty uniforms clinging to our bodies, faces awash with perspiration inside our respirators (gas masks) in the mafting heat of the afternoon sun. I could hardly see anything as my spectacles kept steaming up inside my 'gas mask.' Wonder if Harold Wilson was having the same sort of discomfort in Downing Street?

I was right in the centre of the riot squad as the 'Diarist' – which was a legal requirement, scribbling in a sweat stained register key events such as the time, what incidents had taken place, what orders were given by the officer commanding the Riot Squad and what action was taken. I was very twitchy because I only had a pistol, whilst the other members of the squad had 'proper' weapons. The odd shots were fired and a few skulls were cracked (theirs) before things eventually calmed down and returned to normal. I'll leave the full story of what happened that day until another time, suffice to say that the Singaporeans never really forgave us for devaluing the pound – or for sending out the Riot Squads with their new secret weapon. Me.

As a relatively young soldier of some 18 summers, I did a variety of jobs in Headquarters 15 Air Despatch Regiment RCT at RAF Seletar. At one stage I was the Regimental Sergeant Major's (RSM) clerk. This was quite a cushy number because no-one dared interfere with you (metaphorically speaking) as you were working for a key man. You were the RSM's 'bitch.' Things all went swimmingly until the then incumbent of the RSM's post was granted a commission and a new RSM arrived to take his place. The 'new' RSM's fearsome reputation preceded him. I won't name the individual concerned, for obvious reasons i.e. he might come back and knock seven bells out of me. He was a little turd who wasn't adverse to taking those miscreants that had transgressed around the back of some quiet building and offering them the choice of either a thrashing or formal disciplinary action. He would then coldly beat them up before they had the chance to consider their options. I think the phrase at the time was 'receiving a severe twatting.' Those that had volunteered for a hammering inevitably regretted it because not only did they get a severe seeing to, but formal disciplinary action inevitably followed anyway. A 'double whammy.' The RSM was a tough, mean little swine and everyone, regardless of rank, tip-toed very carefully around him. That's just the way it was back then. RSM's held positions of seemingly unassailable power.

I remember being in the office one day, typing up a couple of letters or something, when an outraged Air Despatch Corporal marched in to see the RSM, complaining bitterly that someone had been writing extremely rude verses about his wife on the Other Ranks (OR's) lavatory walls. The Corporal said something along the lines of, "I don't mind what they're writing sir, but they keep spelling her name wrong!" I thought it hilarious and sniggered. The RSM summoned me over to his desk – "Cavender, do you think that's funny then?" Brainlessly I replied, "Well, yes sir." "Right them," said he, "Double over to the Quartermaster's Stores, sign out some steel wool, a tin of Vim and a fire bucket. Fill the bucket with water then get your arse over to the shit-house and remove all of the graffiti off the OR's bog walls!" Fortunately for me there wasn't any rude writing on the walls of the Officers facilities – and even if there had been, spelling wouldn't have been a problem.

The OR's lavatories were sited downwind of the Headquarters in an elongated shed with a tin roof and about twelve stalls. Each of the distempered stall walls, to my dismay, had copious amounts of crude obscenities and witty ditties, written all over them. I realized that I daren't go back to the RSM to discuss which particular stall required having the walls scrubbed and it was with sinking heart that I knew that they'd all have to be restored to a pristine condition by yours truly.

So I sat there perspiring profusely in the mafting Singapore heat, swatting mosquitoes and scrubbing the Cludgie walls with wire wool until they were spotless. The fact that I was in there scrubbing walls didn't stop several hairy-arsed and mean minded Air Despatchers coming into the place in order to 'open their bomb doors.' I'm sure that the mean spirited RSM ordered everyone in the Regiment to go in there and defecate to their heart's content throughout the renovation process as part of the 'teaching me a lesson' process. It took me two very long days to complete the task.

Naturally in a very hot and sweaty country where ferocious curries were the norm, it made for very unpleasant and unsanitary working conditions in the Cludgie. Having said that, as a consequence I learnt some very funny limericks/verses which came in handy later on when I was writing pantomimes. Want to read a couple? OK then:

> *The boy stood on the burning deck,*
> *The flames near drove him crackers,*
> *A spark shot up his trouser leg,*
> *And set fire to his knackers.*
>
> *The boy stood on the burning deck*
> *As all around him did wilt,*
> *But it bothered not this Scottish lad,*
> *He was wearing his asbestos kilt.*
>
> *They went to Spain, but never again,*
> *The Señor's there drove her crackers,*
> *They stood beneath her window at night,*
> *Shacking their Maracas.*
>
> *He once had a box of soldiers,*
> *He knocked off the General's head,*
> *He broke all the Sergeants and Corporals*
> *Now he plays with his Privates instead.*

I eventually returned to my duties as RSM's Clerk, lesson learnt, chastened and with red raw hands, keeping a very low profile. From then on the office was a snigger free zone and the RSM was placed well and truly in the twat category.

I recall quite clearly the event that brought about his removal. One day the entire Regiment was stood in the blazing heat on the main parade square outside the Headquarters of 15 Air Despatch Regiment RCT at RAF Seletar, where we were rehearsing a parade for a forthcoming visit. For aficionado's – we were wearing 'White's' which I think was termed 'Number 3 Dress' but I may have that wrong with the passage of time. It was during the monsoon season, the heavens had suddenly opened and we were all stood there absolutely pissed wet through as the rain lashed cruelly down. We didn't mind too much as it cooled us down. A corporal from the Headquarters (Corporal Dave Powell – another ex-Junior Leader) marched onto the square and halted smartly in front of the RSM. Because of the rain beating down, a shouted conversation, something along the following lines, took place:

Corporal: Colonel's compliments, sir, could you please stand the Regiment down, immediately.

RSM: What's that?!

Corporal: Colonel's compliments, sir, could you please stand the Regiment down immediately, sir.

RSM: I'll stand the Regiment down when I'm good and ready – now fuck off - Corporal!

Corporal: Yizzah!

Corporal Powell executed a sharp turn to the right and exited smartly, undoubtedly secretly thoroughly delighted that he could pass on the RSM's comments verbatim to the Adjutant (thereby doing his little bit to drop the RSM into the deepest of deep shit). He passed the RSM's message up the chain of Command to the Adjutant and the Adjutant informed the CO, in the time honoured fashion. The Commanding Officer (an officer of the 'old school' and a future General) was not to be tampered with. The upshot was that the RSM was relieved of his duties in very short order, and told to pack his kit as he was to be flown back to the UK the following morning in deep do-do. One does not cross a Commanding Officer, whatever the circumstances. There was deep and abiding joy throughout the Regiment at the departure of this odious little creature, and his going was not a moment too soon as far as we all were concerned. He was a very special sort of person, one who lit up a room when he left it.

His replacement was a man who had been my Sergeant Major in Boy Service at Taunton, RSM Fred Sears. Mr Sears was a delightful chap, very popular with us Junior Leaders, a sort of a surrogate father figure and a very colourful character who worked hard to ensure that an air of normalcy returned to Regimental activities within days. Happy times continued. I am unable, to this very day, to read graffiti on lavatory walls without the memory of scrubbing those 'bog' walls in Singapore with steel wool for hours on end returning to haunt me.

Someone at the 'War Office' decided that a full Regiment of Air Despatcher's was not required in FARELF (Far East Land Forces). 15 Air Despatch Regiment RCT at RAF Seletar was to be disbanded and the Air Despatch element reduced from a Regiment to a Squadron. After all, the 'Confrontation' had finished and things had quietened down. Eventually I and several others were moved to 55 Air Despatch Squadron RCT a few miles down the road at RAF Changi. We moved lock, stock and barrel into the RAF living accommodation at RAF Changi which was undoubtedly an improvement on the billets we had in 'H' Block at RAF Seletar.

RAF Changi, Singapore, the date – sometime in 1967. Broadcasting at the time was RAF Radio Changi, a Tannoy speaker in every room, linked in with the British Forces Broadcasting Services (BFBS). Blasting out over the Tannoy System was the latest hit from the hottest selling artiste of the moment, a young Tom Jones, warbling 'The Green Green Grass of Home,' a song guaranteed to increase levels of home-sickness amongst the troops. Great things were to happen to both me and to Tom. One of the BFBS broadcasters was the lovely Miss Sara Kennedy who eventually went on to better things with the BBC and also Stephen Withers, a name that many who served in BAOR will remember. I was selected for promotion to Lance Corporal and Tom Jones eventually got a knighthood and a few million quid in the bank. Didn't we do well.

I had my very first interview on RAF Changi Radio with Warrant Officer Bill Cater – talking about Pantomimes. I had started writing pantomime scripts and he'd heard about it. He was very gentle with me when I was sat trembling in the studio, it must have been patently obvious that I was a bit nervous, particularly as my top lip kept sticking to my teeth. I must have looked and sounded like Humphrey Bogart. Anyway, I got through the interview and enjoyed it. That was my introduction to the magic of radio. I particularly love radio as if done properly it is thoroughly entertaining and lets you paint pictures in your mind. Who hasn't said, when seeing a photo of a much admired disc jockey or announcer for the first time – "Wow he/she doesn't look anything like I imagined." I once met a DJ whose voice on radio was rich, mellifluous and butch but in the flesh he was a screaming queen with a totally different 'Off Air' voice and effete demeanour. Still, he's a nice, talented bloke and now broadcasts very successfully for the BBC. No names, no pack-drill!

We, the common foot soldiers, were allowed to inhabit the ground floor of an RAF accommodation block at RAF Changi, recently vacated by the 'Brylcreem Boys.' Once we'd settled into our accommodation i.e. got rid of the RAF's red silk curtains, the smell of 'Brut' after-shave, seductive lighting and wall to wall carpeting etc, we started to enjoy life. Purely for historical purposes, I am about to move off at a tangerine (as an old Sergeant once said, trying to impress us with his command of English). Another one said "Gentlemen, let us syncromesh our watches." After only a few months it was decided that we would be moved out of RAF Changi and into old fashioned wooden 'spider' accommodation situated a few miles away from the main base in a delightful little place called Telok Paku. At Telok Paku we were sited right at the bottom end of what was then the RAF Changi runway (now Changi International Airport), but more importantly our billets were just across the road from the beach. It was rumoured that we were moved from the accommodation at RAF Changi because not only were the crap-hats' a divisive influence on the Brylcreem Boys, in their opinion we lowered the tone of the place.

At Telok Paku we were co-located with the Far East Air Force (FEAF) Band, also probably a divisive influence – "Musicians don't you know"…. which led to many merry nights. A great bunch of blokes. We would all get horrendously slaughtered on either Tiger or Anchor Beer, whilst the lads from the band played all of the latest hits, late into the night. Occasionally there was the odd whiff of Ganja as we partied oft into the late hours. We often decamped to across the road to the beach and thrashed around pissed as newts in the warm South China Sea. Happy days.

One evening I was sat in my room in the accommodation block, waiting for 'Pop's Canteen' to open, feeling a tad homesick, a bit sorry for myself and thirsting for an ice-cold Tiger Beer. In those days, once posted to Singapore it was more than likely that if you were a 'lower deck' you remained out in the Far East for a full three year tour. Occasionally the gentry, commissioned officers, would fly back to the UK for a holiday or to do a spot of shopping. That of course was, quite naturally, only right and proper as they were the ruling classes. My three year posting had been extended by a further three months as the Squadron was due to be closed down and everything military was about to be handed back to the Singaporeans. Can you believe it – I whinged! I wanted to go back to Blighty. I'd done my time and wanted to get back home. My whining was ignored in the time honoured fashion and I soldiered on. Oh, the innocence of youth.

Another three months of Local Overseas Allowance (LOA), the loyal services of a Punkah Wallah to do all of the mundane things like shoe cleaning, laundry, bed making and then there was the additional bonus of three months unlimited access to the watering holes of Singapore. Gradually all my mates left for the UK and we were reduced to a relatively skeleton crew. It was a bit sad really because we were like a large family. That's what happens in the Army. You move on, leaving old friends behind and make up for it by making new ones. It's the nature of the beast.

Back to the tale. In the billets, every now and again in the evenings a small, rotund Chinese lady, possibly in her mid to late sixties, wearing traditional black silk trousers and top, white straggly hair scraped tightly back into a bun, would come into our rooms carrying a small handbag and a little three-legged wooden stool. She didn't speak English and I only spoke Yorkshire, so we never really conversed. Smiles and nods were usually sufficient. I remember asking one of the lads who she was and what was she doing there. The reply was "Oh that's the 'Sew Sew' Lady. She repairs our torn clothing and sews buttons back on shirts, stuff like that. She's OK." 'Sew Sew' would sit on her little wooden stool and carry out various repair jobs before copping a handful of Singapore dollars from the troops and then departing into the night, highly delighted with her 'haul.' A brave and memorable little lady.

I noticed that 'Sew Sew' had several colourful medal ribbons pinned to her dress. It transpired that 'Sew Sew' (I never did find out her 'proper' name) lived in Singapore before, during and after the Japanese invasion in World War 2. The story was that she had saved a fair few Allied prisoners lives during the Japanese occupation by smuggling what little food she could get her hands on to those incarcerated in Changi prison. Unfortunately someone had 'blagged' on her and she was arrested by the Japanese military, jailed and brutally tortured. I'll leave it to your imagination to work out the indignities that this brave lady suffered – just one of which was that she'd had all of her teeth knocked out.

'Sew Sew' was a lovely person who would sit on her little stool, sewing whilst giggling at the soldier's antics as they got dressed into their best bib and tucker prior to hitting the delights of downtown Singapore, usually starting at the Union Jack Club and finishing off in Bugis Street. I can't recall which particular night 'Sew Sew' would come around the billets, but I do know that all but the most niggardly of us often deliberately ripped stitches on shirts, tore items of other clothing and cut off buttons so that they could be handed to 'Sew Sew' for repair. She was far too dignified to accept hand-outs from us nor would we have insulted her by offering them to her. The money she earned from her work was our way of helping her maintain her dignity and an opportunity for us to say thanks for what she'd done for us and how we fully appreciated how she'd suffered at the hands of the Japanese. It was the very least we could do. Rumour had it that 'Sew Sew' wasn't in receipt of any sort of pension so had to work just to survive. That was the way of the world back then.

I often wonder what happened to this truly heroic little lady. One day she just stopped coming into the billets and we never saw her again. I assume that she must have died. There were many more like our 'Sew Sew' Lady. Their bravery and loyalty should never be forgotten.

'MOVING ON'

As I stated previously, we the 'Lower Decks' couldn't really afford the exorbitant cost of the air fare back to the UK at that time, that was a privilege reserved for the upper echelons, or those with RAF contacts who could then scrounge flights for them. To be perfectly honest, who would want to come back to a wet and miserable UK when such fun and games could be had abroad? But it all has to come to an end sometime and I'd had a good run at it. It was time to go home. I was in relatively good nick physically on my return to the UK, rather bronzed, a full head of hair, all my own very white, flashing teeth, a few quid in the bank and ready to give it my best shot. I was entitled to something like ten weeks leave, some entitlement and some carefully accumulated, so I had that to look forward to before having to report back for military duty.

BBC's Radio 1 had just started in the UK. The DJ Tony Blackburn ruled the roost and Tom Jones was still at it. The 'Green Green Grass of Home' as you would expect, was totally different to the lush vegetation of the Malaysian jungle and horror of horrors – you couldn't get your hands on any Tiger Beer. Tetley's or 'Double Diamond' ("Works Wonders, so drink some today" – was their particular jingle) – so I did and it did. Timothy Taylor's wasn't a bad drop of stuff either, not quite as exotic as 'Tiger' though. I wasn't to see Tiger Beer for many years – but now of course it's freely available in all good supermarkets. Go on – try one – you'll love it!

As expected, I got bored after a couple of weeks ligging and decided to do a bit of work on the side. I got a job with my Uncle Dennis working with his little demolition crew. They were helping to pull down old houses in central Keighley and there I was with them one day helping to rip cabling out of the houses (lead) and tottering up on to the roof tops helping to recover some quality Yorkshire slate. Don't know how I managed that particular aspect of the job as I'm not too keen on heights, but I did it – man-handling huge slate tiles across to a ladder, where they were slid down onto the back of a mattress covered truck and whisked away for reclamation. Purely by coincidence I helped to demolish the little house that I'd grown up in, 12 Hill Street, Keighley. I couldn't believe how small and manky those houses were, but at least it had been a roof over our heads. I took great delight in wielding a ten pound hammer and heartily smashing the walls down. They were so damp that the it was like hitting wet card-board. They were a strange combination of horse-hair and plaster. Manky. It hadn't been too long before that people lived there, in fact in one of the houses beneath the 'landing' one of the occupants, and elderly man by the name of 'Joe Pump' (I kid you not) was holding things up by refusing to move. He been there for many years and certainly since I'd lived there in 1947. He had to go eventually. You can't beat the developers.

My first home - 'The Landing,' Hill Street, Keighley, (just prior to being demolished)

After a week or two, thankfully, the demolition work finished, so my Mother kindly arranged for a couple of more weeks work for me at Dalton Lane Mills, next to the Railway Station in Keighley. She was determined that I wasn't going to fester in bed all day. Anyway, quite rightly, she figured that going out to work would probably keep me out of the pubs and out of mischief.

Working in a mill was a first and an unusual experience for me. On day one I had to report to something called the 'steam room.' The Steam Room had a trapdoor in the ceiling and every now and then the finished wool products would tumble down a chute into baskets called 'Skips.' They were then packed by us in an orderly fashion into other skips after having been steamed in a boiler like contraption before being moved onto the next department for onwards transmission, presumably to clothing manufacturers etc. There were three of us working in there, two lifers, and yours truly. It was a miserable little hole and in one gloomy corner was a bloke called the 'Overlooker.' Let's called t'Overlooker Jim, because that was his name. Jim stood at a lectern tucked away in his little corner, making notes in a book relating to the amount of mill product that passed through our hands. He was a very old-fashioned sort of bloke without a single ounce of humour. He just kept his beady eye on us, licking his pencil and making suspicious annotations in his book throughout the day. He was part of the long established 'command team,' knew everything and was not to be tampered with.

A highlight of our mid-morning and mid-afternoon breaks was when the tea trolley arrived, pushed by two very cheerful ladies who looked just like those Rubinesque ladies often depicted in Beryl Cook paintings, dispensing huge buttered tea cakes containing thickly sliced ham, a selection of sandwiches, pies and other health foods. We were also able to buy pint mugs of hot, sweet invigorating tea. Their visits broke the crushing monotony. In principle, it was very similar to the much loved NAAFI breaks. The right stuff at the right time.

A key part of the job was when articulated lorries would arrive throughout the day containing mountains of rough, new wool crammed into elongated hessian sacks. These sacks were about nine feet high and roughly four foot round. They were off-loaded in the enclosed yard outside our steam room and then had to be man-handled and moved, by us, onto ancient sack barrows then trundled to the other side of t'mill where they were processed through the mill system - same principle as a sausage machine. Sausages figure big in my life. The sacks themselves had a life of their own and were mean spirited bastards, doing their utmost not to stop on the barrows and continually flopping onto the floor. They were the devils own job to get back onto the sack barrows and I spent many frustrating hours struggling with them. It was something to do with a voluble fulcrum (can't believe I wrote that). You had to be quick because the quantity of hessian sacks to be shifted was never ending.

We were under strict instructions to get the sacks cleared as fast as possible, (Jim was timing us – always watching), and we wheeled them across a lengthy mill yard to t'other side of t'mill. To add to the excitement, the barrows had to be pushed across greasy, worn cobbles. One particular day we'd moved several loads with the barrows and it had been raining. T'cobbles were very slippy and it was proving difficult to keep the sacks on the barrows. I was, as they say oop North, reaching the band-end. How anyone would choose to do that sort of work for a living I couldn't fathom, but in retrospect perhaps they had little choice. It was probably either that or knocking up thousands of felt slippers in Peter Black's shoe factory. Hobson's Choice.

As I struggled across the mill yard, yet again an accursed sack fell off the barrow and I struggled to get it back on there. Leaning on a nearby wall, watching, was an oldish sort of bloke, flat cap, waistcoat with chunky gold fob watch chain attached, smoking a pipe and watching me, with a definite smug expression on his weathered face.

The term 'mean spirited' describes him to perfection. The following conversation took place between us (*translation in Italics*):

Man: *(Sniggering)* Na then lad, 'avin a bit on a struggle ester? *(Having problems old chap?)*

Me: Yes, just a bit *(Bleedin' obviously)*

Man: What's to do then? *(What, in essence, is your problem?)*

Me: Well, it's these stupid bastarding cobbles, innit! *(The pathway is causing me a little technical difficulty)*

Man: Sither, there's no need for such foul language, lad! *(Is that sort of uncouth language really necessary?)*

Me: I'm sorry. No offence meant. (*Who's this pious old git?*)

Man: Any road, ah sed, what's up wint? *(What's the matter?)*

Prompted by his invitation to comment, I promptly went off on a rant:

Me: You'd think, wouldn't you, that if this particular aspect of the production line was key to the Mill's operations that a better system would have been devised for transporting these chuffing awkward sacks across the yard to the other side of the mill. It's time consuming and ridiculous.

Man: Oh aye. Bit of an expert are we then, lad? *(Really)*

He was getting angrier by the second, yellowed teeth firmly clamped on and puffing away furiously at his pipe. There were enough smoke clouds and sparks coming from the bowl of his pipe for someone to think that a mill chimney had caught fire – and summon the fire brigade. Ignoring the warning signs, I continued:

Me: Why don't the idiots that manage this place pay out a few quid to get a bit of concrete or tarmac laid and help to smooth the delivery process out. It'd be much quicker and more efficient. They obviously haven't got a shagging clue.

Clouds of smoke were emanating from the man's pipe by this time, as he puffed away furiously, his gimlet eyes glinting. By this stage I cared not a jot, I had nothing to lose.

Man: Does tha know about such matters, young 'un? (*Distribution expert then?*)

Me: I know enough to see that with a bit of common sense and by spending a few quid this could easily be sorted and improved.

Man: Well son, if tha dun't like it, tha nos what tha can deow! *(You need to consider your options)*

Me: What do you mean?

Man: Get thissen ower to t'main office and get thi cards! Tell them I sent thi! *(Your services are no longer required)*

Me: Ah right then, I'll do just that. Er – and who should I say sent me? (*Caring not a jot*)

Man: Just tell 'em - one of t'mill owners.

Me: (*Sensing defeat*) Ah, right! Consider it done.

Harumph! Didn't he realise that I was a Lance Corporal and Guardian of the Nation, working covertly at t'mill! I left the huge sack of wool on the floor of the yard with the sack barrow abandoned forlornly at its side and set off for t'main office, defiant to the last.

Man: Young 'un! Afore thi goes, tha mun tek yon sack ower to t'other end of t'mill. *(Before you depart, just pop that wool over to the Combing Department, will you)*

Me: Tha mun shove thi sack – and t'sack barrow - where t'monkey shoved its nuts! *(That's not going to happen)*

I marched off towards the mill office, still caring not a jot. Furiously, he called out to me:

Man: Sither lad, ah sed, what about yon sack and t'sack barrow? *(And the technical equipment?)*

Once again I advised him what he could do with both items, sack and barrow, (which would have affected his walking for a few days) and strode off into the sunset, head held high. Luckily I didn't need the job and really life was too short to be wasting my time there. As far as I was concerned, in my ignorance, they were living in the dark ages. It was an interesting experience though (and I do miss the Overlooker, Jim – not). When my Mother, who worked at the same mill, got home that night I got my feet sharpened because I'd caused her much embarrassment. I'd been t'talk of t'spinning. "Hey sither, Maureen Cavender's lad told t'boss where to shove his job!" For that is who(m) the old geezer was – one of t'bosses. He held the power of instant dismissal over his workforce, which is what had quite probably saved him from many a severe larruping over the years.

The beloved Mater said, "I have to work there when you've gone, lad!" She could also have lost her job. I hadn't considered that and so apologized profusely to her. For every action there's a reaction. When my Dad got home from work and heard about it all I expected fireworks but he just smiled and said, "Ah bollocks to him!" causing my Mother to go very thin lipped. She did not approve of the use of foul language in front of the children! My leave was running out and it was time for me to get back into uniform. Afternote: My Mother told me that a few months later, apparently, the yard at t'mill was concreted over, so if nothing else I had achieved that. It might have made life a little easier for the poor sod that replaced me.

AND SO –
'BACK TO THE JUNIOR LEADER'S REGIMENT RCT'

Now, a relatively quick resumé of my continuing military career. I was posted back to the Junior Leader's Regiment RCT, Taunton where I had been 'claimed' by my younger brother John, who was serving in the Regiment at the time. In one of those strange little historical coincidences, he'd also been the Drum Major of the Boys Band. Rather amusingly he was eventually 'invited' to leave the Regiment after a slight altercation with the Mayor of Taunton's somewhat pompous son, whom John had levelled on the Rugby field after an unnecessarily mean foul. My brother, a little upset by the foul, had severely rearranged the bones of the miscreant's nose, who then had to repair from the field of battle to the local hospital to have his sneck straightened.

The Commanding Officer, a friend of the Mayor, was, apparently, spitting feathers and to make amends ordered that my brother be removed from the Regiment without further ado. Bit of a travesty there because the lad, a loudmouthed bully, got what he deserved. He had picked the wrong person to tangle with. I knew nothing about this as I was attending a Senior Military Qualification Course (SMQC) at Buller Barracks in Aldershot. One evening a cheeky little face popped itself around the barrack door, my bro. He explained what had happened. He had, as a consequence of his on-field activities, arrived prematurely into adult service and was parked at the Depot RCT prior to being posted to BAOR (British Army of the Rhine) in West Germany. He called for me the next night and we went out for a drink. He had a highly polished and fully fuelled army staff car at his disposal, parked at the back of the accommodation block and we swept around several Hampshire watering holes in unabashed luxury for the evening. I didn't ask him where the staff car came from and to whence it was returned. I applauded his initiative. A splendid evening.

The Junior Leader's Regiment used to move én masse annually from Taunton to Penhale Camp in Cornwall for 'Summer Camp.' Penhale Camp is a fairly old camp consisting of lots of 'spider' accommodation, sited near Newquay in Cornwall. Whilst there, the Junior Leaders themselves would be engaged in all sorts of exciting activities throughout the day. We of the Permanent Staff would be thrashing around doing various supervisory tasks which for me meant doing normal administrative work.

I don't recall there being NAAFI facilities there for the 'grown-ups,' but there was an opportunity for access to alcohol and mischief, there being a pub at the bottom of the hill at Penhale Camp and we, the junior members of the Permanent Staff (i.e. Corporals and below) would repair there each evening for a glass or two of ale. The 'Junior Bleeders' were confined to camp for their own safety. The Warrant Officers and Sergeants had their own Mess facilities, as did the Officers, we all had segregated accommodation blocks according to our status (or lack of it).

Penhale Camp, near Newquay, Cornwall

Amongst our number was a most marvellous character called Phil Bradford. 'Bradders.' Bradders was a Lance Corporal employed as the CO's driver and as such was always treated with great respect.

Like all staff car drivers, he always knew what was going on and had the main man's ear. The CO, incidentally, was the same bloke who had arranged for my brother to take his leave of the Regiment.

Bradders was the proud possessor of a deep, sonorous baritone singing voice and at the drop of a hat would burst into song, usually something from an opera that we'd never heard of. One particular evening we, the lads, partook of an ale or two in the local hostelry, leaving there shortly after closing time. We had to be fairly quiet on our return to barracks because the little Junior Bleeders were tucked safely in and were asleep in their cots, it was after 'Lights Out.' They hadn't to be disturbed. It also meant that we had to tip-toe past the darkened Officers' Mess as the Officers had also retired to their pits for a decent night's kip in order to prepare themselves for the following day's strenuous activities. It was all as quiet as the grave.

Just as we reached the Officers' Mess, which we had to pass to reach our billets, some mischievous tit said "Go on Phil, give us a song!" whereupon Bradders burst into "Be My Love," bellowing like a bull moose and sounding not a patch like Mario Lanza had when he'd sung it. A light came on in the upper regions of the Officers' Mess and a sash window slid open.

A cultured and definitely officer-like voice bawled, "You chaps down there, what the bloody hell's going, eh? Don't you know that it's 'Lights Out!'" Lord love a duck, it was the CO himself and we could see that he was in his jim-jams. We'd disturbed his beauty sleep and we knew that inevitably there'd be hell to pay. He was a very clean living, God fearing officer whose word was law. We had transgressed and knew that there'd be a price to pay. Why couldn't Bradders have sung something quiet, like 'Whispering Grass?'

Bradders, unbeknown to us, was carrying a starting pistol in his pocket. He was assisting the Regiment's Physical Training Instructors (PTI's) with some sporting activities and had been tasked to take the starting pistol down to Summer Camp. He apparently carried the weapon on his person as he didn't trust the armoury facilities at Penhale Camp. He pulled the pistol out of his pocket and shouted "Fuck off - you knob!" before firing two very loud shots into the air. The CO, rearing back with shock at the sound of the starting pistol, smacked the back of his head rather fiercely on the window frame, groaned and then gracefully slid out of view.

To say that we legged it at a great rate of knots would not be much of an exaggeration. We scarpered, heading for the safety of our accommodation block. We got undressed as quickly as we could and then leapt into our respective pits, pretending to be asleep, knowing full well that it wouldn't be too long before the 'Wrath of Khan' in the shape of the RSM, would descend to find out who the disturbers of the peace were. He would want to know who had been out drinking – and more importantly, who had fired the pistol at the CO. We would all, inevitably, be invited to appear before the beak for a disciplinary interview the following morning with the distinct possibility of a hefty fine being thrown into the mixture. Bradders cared not a jot, he'd had a spiffing evening and thought that it was all highly amusing. We would all deny knowing anything about the incident and after a few days things would quietened down and returned to normal.

As we'd all thrashed into our billet, there'd been a loud shriek and a rather svelte, stark naked girl leapt out of one of the beds. Everyone froze for a glorious moment whilst everything stopped wobbling. A Lance Corporal, who shall remain nameless (he knows who he is), had been 'entertaining' one of the local maidens and they'd been indulging in a spot of horizontal jogging. Lance Corporal 'Nameless' was a much envied very tall, handsome, bronzed, muscular Physical Training Instructor (PTI) who hadn't been with us at the pub that evening because he'd made alternative entertainment arrangements. He was well into complex process of making sweet music with the fair maiden in the regulation single army cot with itchy issue blankets. He'd pulled her earlier that evening whilst out walking along the beach, kicking sand in lesser being's faces. We'd returned noisily and prematurely to the billet and spoiled things for him.

The young lady quickly and disappointingly covered herself with a large army blanket to preserve what was lefty of her modesty. We quickly explained what had happened and that the RSM and Provost Staff were probably on their way. The PTI person grabbed the wench and her few bits of clothing before hurriedly hiding her in the bunk at the end of the room. There was only one bunk in each room and this one had been allocated to a corporal cook. The young lady was a bit of a corker and there much envy amongst the troops. I say young, I should point out that she was 18 years old and knew what she was about. Unfortunately the bunk was occupied by a very fat and gay military cook known to us all as 'Gorgeous Geoff' (name changed). 'Gorgeous' was outraged that someone of the opposite sex should be thrust into his private space - after all, he had his reputation to think of. 'Gorgeous' was threatened with violence, told to behave himself, hide the girl and keep his gob shut until things settled down, whence she could be removed from the billet and smuggled out of the camp.

If she had been discovered, her Lance Corporal escort would have been in serious trouble on two counts. He had allowed an unauthorized civilian onto camp and had entertained her in the billets.

We, meanwhile, had all hurriedly changed into our pyjamas and leapt into beds various, pretending to have been asleep and therefore could not possibly have been involved in any mischief. It was all very silly looking back as we were adults not Junior Leaders! The Junior Leaders were probably having more fun and games than we were. Why couldn't we have a couple of drinks and get involved in a bit of mischief? You're only young once.

Shortly after we'd hit our beds, as expected, there was a great deal of clattering and banging of ammunition boots outside the billet as the Provost Sergeant and his Staff arrived, accompanied by a furious RSM. The rooms lights were switched on "Stand by your beds, you bastards!" was the hearty cry. It was all quite ridiculous, we were adults! We got out of our beds, hair tousled and pretending that we'd been asleep, probably not fooling the RSM one jot, after all – he'd been young once, hadn't he?

Us: Summat wrong sir?

RSM: Shut fecking hep!! *(Translation – "Be quiet, there's a good chap)*

Fortunately the corporal chef 'Gorgeous' had locked his bunk door and although the enemy tried the door handle, found that it was locked and fortunately left it at that, assuming that Geoff was out on Duty Cook or something. 'Gorgeous Geoff' must have been cacking himself, but our threats of violence guaranteed his silence. Meanwhile, Lance Corporal 'Nameless' remained under the bed covers and refused point blank to get out of his pit. The seething RSM pointed a trembling pace stick at him and snarled:

RSM: Get out of bed, lad, now!

Lance Corporal: I'd prefer not to sir, if you don't mind.

RSM: If you don't get out of bed NOW I'll get Provost to tip you out – now move your idle, festering body!

Lance Corporal: Yes but…

RSM: Out - Now!!

Lance Corporal: OK Sir, but I warned you.

Lance Corporal 'Nameless', (the one who hadn't been with us at the pub that night), eased his way out of bed, sans his Army issue jim-jams i.e. he was stark bollock naked and sporting what can only be described as the most thunderous erection. He had absolutely nothing at all to be ashamed of in that department and would have made Wales (!) proud. Both he and his appendage stood rigidly to attention at the bottom of his bed, his manhood pointing straight ahead of him. Thinking back, it was not a pretty sight. The Provost Staff Sergeant sniggered, the RSM was for once bordering on speechless. He turned puce with rage and stormed out of the billet, leaving matters in the hands (metaphorically speaking) of the Provost Staff Sergeant.

RSM: Provost – sort these bastards out – find Mario Fuckin' Lanza and get that disgusting Lance Corporal covered up!

Provost: Yizzah! Corporal – get back into your pit and cover yourself up!

The Lance Corporal leapt back into his pit and thankfully covered up his pride and joy. The Provost Staff Sergeant paced up and down the centre of the room whilst the remainder of us stood at the foot of our beds, not daring to snigger.

Provost: Now then you lot – which one of you is Mario Fuckin' Lanza then?

Deathly silence was the reply. 'All for one and one for all!'

Provost: I want to know the name of the cowboy who fired that starting pistol! The Boss is spitting feathers. He's got a lump the size of an Easter egg on his fucking bonce, so somebody here is in deep shit!

We all pleaded innocent to any mischief. It was obvious that no-one was going to 'cough' so we were eventually ordered to return to our beds. The Provost Staff Sergeant stumped off with his entourage, muttering threats of impending doom and destruction for the following morning when justice would be done.

As things eventually quietened down, the nubile young lady was recovered from the bunk and escorted on her way, sobbing, by Lance Corporal 'Nameless' who by this time had regained his dignity and was fully clothed. I remember her saying, plaintively to him, "I only wanted to see the inside of an Army billet!" Yes, of course dear. The cook, 'Gorgeous Geoff' never really fully recovered from the shock of being in the same room as a naked woman (the last and only other time had probably been when he was born). Geoff put his papers in and left the Army shortly after the Regiment returned to Taunton from Summer Camp. The drama's had all been too much for him.

Come the morn, we were all interviewed individually by the RSM, but closed ranks and denied knowing anything of the phantom opera singer/gunman. The RSM gave us the 'evils' but could do nothing about it without evidence. Apparently the CO was still seething and thirsting for revenge, particularly as he'd given himself a hearty crack on the back of his head when he'd performed a reverse nut on the window sash and was unable to wear his beret. We'd seen Phil Bradford at breakfast and asked him if he regretted causing injury to his boss, but oozing sympathy for the CO he was not. Tucking into his bacon and eggs, he grinned, shrugged and said "Ah, bollocks to him!" The lower decks of the Permanent Staff were confined to camp from that moment on and given extra-duties for the remainder of the Summer Camp (which still didn't stop us from sneaking out on covert drinking and wenching missions). He who dares – wins.

Whilst at Penhale Camp we were required to carry out the duties of 'Duty NCO.' Part of one's 'Duty NCO' responsibilities, which started at six o'clock in the evening and finished at six o'clock the next morning, was to go around the Sergeant's Mess and waken the Warrant Officers and SNCO's so that they would be up for breakfast and wouldn't be late for work. It transpired that one of the younger Sergeant's, who was follically challenged, wore a toupeé. It was such an excellent hairpiece that no-one knew of its existence until one fateful morning when the Sergeant got his early call but failed to respond to a knock on the door. The Corporal doing the early call made the mistake of enthusiastically ruffling the sleepy Sergeant's hair in an attempt to rouse him from his slumbers. Unfortunately as he did so, the toupeé slid off the Sergeant's head and adhered to the Corporal's hand.

The Corporal shrieked with horror and legged it out of the Sergeant's Mess trying to shake the toupeé off his hand, closely followed by the Sergeant, hand on bald bonce, hysterically demanding his hairpiece back. Eventually the 'rug' was retrieved, restored to its rightful place and the Corporal sworn to secrecy. The secret remained safe only until the Duty NCO reached the Cookhouse where he could hardly wait to share the information with us all over breakfast where, I'm ashamed to say, we had a rattling good snigger.

All in all though, I had a brilliant time whilst at the Junior Leaders Regiment and t'was whilst there that I met my future wife Maggie. After a romantic courtship we eventually tied the knot and settled down more than happily as 'pads.' Incidentally, it was one of the vagaries of military life in those days that I had to seek written permission from the Commanding Officer to get married. Had I not sought his formal approval, I would not have been entitled to a higher rate of pay nor get access to a married quarter. One was obliged to kiss arse. Somewhere I've still got my written application with "Approved" stamped on it. Aye, we were poor but we were happy.

Our wedding day – Taunton

Thankfully, after an acceptable period of time, our daughter Sara came along and we were happier still. There wasn't a lot of money around then, but I managed to splash out 15 quid on a little old car that I'd purchased from a fat Medic. It served us well, but was so ancient that it didn't have indicators, it had those arm things that used to lift out from the vehicle like bat wings – Trafficators. The electrics in the vehicle were a bit iffy and wires hung down from below the steering wheel in a gorgeous array of colours. If I wanted the Trafficators to work, Maggie occupying the co-pilot's seat, had to reach out and touch two wires with exposed ends together in order to get an electrical connection. There would then be a spark and then the relevant Trafficator would pop up. Needs must when the devil drives. Not many young soldiers had cars in those days. I remember a snooty Captain chatting to another officer, saying – "Humph, you know what Biffy, even the Corporal's have got cars these days." How very dare we.

We decided to undertake the marathon drive in our little Austin from Taunton up to Keighley in West Yorkshire and visit my relatives. It was no mean task in those bygone days as the roads were crap. Everything went swimmingly well until we reached a large hill on the outskirts of Bristol where even the largest trucks were passing us as we spluttered along in the slow lane. It was patently obvious that we weren't going to reach the top of the hill, the car was totally lacking in 'oomph' and was belching blue smoke from a rattling exhaust. We decided that it would be much safer to turn around and return to Taunton and perhaps try for Yorkshire another day.

Baby Sara was sleeping blissfully in the rear of the limo, firmly wrapped up in blankets and tucked away in the latest plastic yellow bath (I break into a cold sweat just thinking about it), but it was all that we could afford back then. We had plenty of laughs with that vehicle until it finally gave up the ghost and expired at the side of the road. I got more for scrap than I'd paid for it initially.

It was eventually time to move on and I left Taunton as a full Corporal, accompanied, naturally, by wife Maggie and our brand new beloved daughter Sara. We would 'serve' with a variety of units in the years ahead, starting with:

8 Regiment RCT, Munster, West Germany (as a Corporal)

Where I worked in the Orderly Room of the Headquarters at Portsmouth Barracks, Munster. A busy but fun place. As usual I got involved with a bit of theatre and staged several pantomimes in the cracking old theatre (which was situated at the rear of the cookhouse). I can't remember what its history was but I know that Tommy Trinder appeared there one year in a Combined Services Entertainment (CSE) Show. We staged a pantomime there one particular year, (Robin Hood), where one of the participants became a little over-enthusiastic (aided by copious amounts of Dortmunder Pils) and instead of using a 'prop' sword in a fight scene that we'd had made, he borrowed a proper sword from one of the officers. The end result was, yes you've guessed it, he ran 'Little John' through his gizzards! There were gallons of claret everywhere. To give the victim his due, he finished his scene and then was carted off by waiting ambulance to a nearby local hospital to be repaired. The audience loved it and comment upon how realistic the sword fight looked and all that stage blood. Little did they know! The German Doctors at the 'Krankenhaus' were mightily impressed as it gave them an unexpected and rare opportunity to see and treat a sword wound. "Ach, you haf been dueling, mien herr?" "Yerst mate," replied Little John, " I've been run through by the Sheriff of Nottingham!"

'There's a Ghost in the Cellar – what am I gonna do?'

Back to 'now' for a moment. We had recently acquired a VW camper van and my wife and I decided that we'd use it to visit a few old haunts in Germany. You know the sort of thing, just go for a wander around visiting the places where we'd served when part of HM Forces. A trip down Memory Lane. One of the places on our visits list was Portsmouth Barracks in Munster, Germany where we'd been with 8 Regiment RCT before the Iron Curtain collapsed and whilst Munster was still in West Germany. The Regiment had had a very important role supporting the Americans, who kept some very nasty nuclear weapons up their sleeves in order to keep the Russian hordes at bay. Anyway, we went and had a look at Portsmouth Barracks, which by then had had all of the metal railings/gates that had surrounded the camp removed and was now accommodation for 'Auslanders.' It looked so very strange and insecure. The Headquarters building was situated next to what was the rear entrance to the barracks, so we just walked in and had a look around. Seeing the building reminded me of a 'happening' when I had worked there in the Headquarters.

I lurked within the Headquarters of 8 Regiment RCT, eventually having received my third 'stripe' and as a Sergeant worked as the ORS - Orderly Room Sergeant, a very important role specifically designed to keep the Russian Hordes at bay. Portsmouth Barracks was an old Hitler Barracks, of which there were many throughout Germany, a few still in use at that stage to house the Brits although we are about to return every lock, stock and barrel back to the Germans. As I write this, what remains of our troops there are preparing to return to the United Kingdom, just in time for the latest tranche of redundancies.

The Commanding Officer (CO) of 8 Regiment RCT at the time was Lieutenant Colonel A (Alan) J Simmons RCT (whom I was later to meet when he was a Brigadier). The CO was – and still is – the epitome of a British Officer and Gentleman – who was much respected by his troops. He was known, respectfully, as 'Daddy' Simmons. A natural leader of the old school who was thoroughly British to the core and who looked the part, sporting a bristling moustache, the envy of many. Anyway, it transpired that a noxious smell was emanating from the cellars of the Headquarters building which had distressed the Adjutant, a delicate fellow, so the Regimental Quartermaster (RQM) was instructed to investigate. A small part of the wall in the cellar had to be removed to effect entrance. Apparently the cellars had been sealed since World War 2 as no-one had needed to gain access there. So it was opened up to see of the niff could be traced.

The CO, intrigued, decided to have a peek in the cellar, accompanied by the Regimental Sergeant Major (RSM), during the course of one of his weekly barrack inspections. Hearing that the dynamic duo were going to have a look in the cellar I thought to myself - opportunity for a bit of sport here. I contacted the Medical Centre and borrowed their teaching skeleton. Then, through various local contacts, I obtained a German steel helmet, some bits of old German Infantry uniform and a decrepit old rifle. The skeleton was then 'dressed' and tucked in a dark corner of the cellar, in a seated position, clutching a cigarette in its bony fingers, the rifle laid across its lap. You can see where I'm going with this…..

The CO and the RSM duly arrived at the newly revealed entrance to the cellar, the RSM carrying a torch. I was lurking around a corner so can repeat, roughly, the conversation that took place:

CO: Right RSM, let's have a look in the cellar. The Quartermaster tells me that apparently it hasn't been opened up since the end of the War! Probably find Adolf in here! It's a bit whiffy, what!

The RSM laughed dutifully.

RSM: I've brought a torch, Colonel. There's no lighting, so it's bound to be a tad gloomy in there.

CO: Good man, RSM, switch the bloody torch on then and let's have a good scout around eh!

RSM: Yes Sah! After you…. Cor, it's a bit whiffy, sir!

The CO eased himself through the smallish hole, followed closely by his ever loyal RSM.

CO: The RQM was telling me that the cellar's supposed to be haunted, RSM!

RSM: With respect sah, that sort of thing's a load of old bollocks! How do we know it's haunted if no-one's been down here since the war?

CO: Lots of funny noises and those foul smells, apparently.

RSM: That'll just be the drains playing up, sah!

CO: Oh I don't know old chap. Some strange things went on around this area during the War. Let's crack on then.

Thus began the inspection. All went swimmingly well until they were deep into the cellar, turned a corner and the weakening beam from the RSM's torch alighted upon the skeleton, whereupon there was a fearful bellowing from the CO.

CO: Aaaagh!..... It's a damned German, and he's got a bloody weapon, RSM!

RSM: Bleedin' Hell! *(Aside)* Bollocks to this, I'm off!

CO: Me too RSM!

There followed an unseemly rush when they both sprinted back to the opening of the cellar, where a desperate struggle took place between the CO and RSM in order for them to effect an exit via the relatively small hole. All propriety went out of the window as they struggled. Knees, elbows and a bit of rank pulling went on. Notwithstanding, the Colonel exited first, which was only right and proper.

They both, apparently, thrashed back to the CO's office for a glass or two of medicinal sherry and a calming down session prior to continuing the inspection, but this time studiously avoiding any mention of the cellar. That would now be left for the Quartermaster to deal with. In the meantime I recovered the skeleton and removed all traces of it before the Quartermaster got to the cellar. The Quartermaster reported back to the CO that there was nothing in the cellar and that he must have been imagining things. From that incident grew the story of it being haunted. Eventually the name of the person responsible for the skeletal outrage was leaked and I was summoned to the 'presence' had my feet sharpened and received several extra duties from the RSM for my wheeze.

We had a good time with 8 Regiment RCT and rather nicely for us Maggie's brother Richard had joined the RCT and been posted to Munster, so we were all able to spend a bit of time together. Richard eventually courted and married Renate, a Nurse, who is from Munster and we all lived happily ever after.

Once again, it was time to move on, this time to:

65 Squadron RCT, Bulford, Wiltshire (as a Sergeant (Chief Clerk))

I was posted from 8 Regiment RCT in West Germany to 65 Squadron RCT at Bulford in Wiltshire. I absolutely hated Bulford, the place, not the Squadron. Life there was so miserable that that Maggie and I decided that it was time to leave the Army and try something else. I do recall a couple of light-hearted moments at Bulford though.

The Squadron's Administrative Officer at that time was a dapper Captain Reg Tozer RCT. Reg had come up through the ranks, he was a cracking bloke and a great character. I always thought that he was the double of the 'Carry On' stalwart – Kenneth Connor. Reg had a television in his office and used to watch horse-racing throughout the day. There'd be great whooping and shouts of "Come on you bastard – run!" that sort of thing. He had a virtual direct line to the bookies and was never off the 'phone to him. I received a salutary lesson in the art of military letter writing from Reg. I used to draft letters for him and then take them in for his approval and signature. He called me in one day and said – "Chief, your letters are a bit too flowery. Spot of advice my son – Never say faeces when you can say shit!" From that day onwards my letter writing reflected his sage advice. A true character.

'BREAKING AND ENTERING'

The Squadron was 'crashing out' on Exercise (Manoeuvres) from Ward Barracks, Bulford Camp, just up the road to Salisbury Plain, turning fully tactical as we exited from the main barracks square. It was a very cold November but we were well prepared for that sort of thing. All went well for a couple of days until one particular evening when the Officer Commanding, let's call him Major Rupert Fartingbum-Smythe, decided that we would have a bit of soldierly fun so had organised a night attack where we would all be fully kitted up, camouflage cream slapped all over the place etc.

We, the RCT, would be 'Friendly Forces,' whilst the REME Workshops and a few non-RCT personnel, spare Water Scorchers (ACC) and Blanket Stackers (RAOC) etc would act as 'Enemy Forces.' All this action would take place somewhere on Salisbury Plain.

The fun and games commenced at about 2100 hours when it was nice and dark and very cold. I had been nominated to accompany the Officer Commanding throughout the exercise, this was standard procedure for someone in my lowly position i.e. 'Bodyguard/Male Escort/Bag-man.' We lay in the grass at the camp perimeter. Naturally my personal weapon, the Self Loading Rifle (SLR) had a blank firing attachment fitted to it, so I could let rip and make some suitably fearsome noise once the fun and games began. As the OC laid there in the grass we heard a rustling. Rupert FB-S turned to me and whispered, "Here they come, Chief." He loudly cocked his weapon, a Sub Machine Gun (SMG), immediately revealing our location to the 'Enemy Forces.' Big mistake. One of the enemy emerged from the dark, wielding a long stick, which he then used to give the Major a couple of meaty thwacks on the back, not realising that he was knocking seven bells out of the boss man. The assault caused Rupert to splutter with rage, he said, "Ferk it, he's hitting me, Chief! Do something!"

I was in the process of cocking my weapon, (a technical manoeuvre with the SLR, not a sexual deviation), when it decided to jam. In the time honoured fashion I placed a finger (mine) inside the breech of the weapon and tried to clear the jam. The OC was receiving further beatings about the back, neck and ears and enjoying his discomfort I started to snigger. At that precise moment for some reason the breech block of my SLR slid forward, without any warning whatsoever, and trapped my finger. After an agonising few seconds and a bit of foul language, I managed to extract the throbbing digit from the breech block. All sniggering stopped instantaneously. I turned to the OC and whispered something along the lines of, "Sorry, bit of a problem with my finger, sir!" The OC was not in the least interested in my finger as currently he had a large, manky army boot placed on the nape of his neck, grinding his face into Salisbury Plain. A very butch voice said, "You're dead mate!" I remember thinking to myself, "Yes, and so are you when you find out who it is that you've been giving the good message to."

Enemy Forces, an oaf of an REME Artificer Sergeant Major (ASM), a Warrant Officer Class One, had thought that it would be a good idea to take a long staff (that's a wooden staff, not a tall staff sergeant) out on the night attack, weighted at one end with a piece of metal, to use as a weapon. Why a man in such a responsible position would make such an illogical and irresponsible decision I still cannot comprehend, but he did. It was that implement that he'd beaten the OC with. As I'd turned to make my comment to the OC, the ASM decided to let me have a bit of grief as well and aimed a blow at me with the staff. I saw it heading straight for my face and just had a split second to hold up my hand to protect my eyes before it hit me full in the face, chipping my eye socket and breaking my thumb. I would have undoubtedly lost an eye had I not had my hand there to deflect the blow.

So there I lay in the dark, dazed, thumb broken and eye socket chipped. Within seconds my left eye had swollen so badly that I couldn't see properly, I thought that I'd been blinded. The OC called an immediate stop to activities and I was speedily transported off to the nearby Tidworth Military Hospital for treatment. The ASM by that time realised that he'd knocked seven bells out of the OC and the Squadron Chief Clerk – but cared not a jot, after all – he was an unassailable Warrant Officer Class One.

When I eventually reached Tidworth Military hospital I was taken straight to the Accident and Emergency Department for treatment. I was in a bit of a state, covered in mud, blood pouring down my face from the eye socket wound and a thumb the size of a Wall's pork sausage dangling uselessly at my side. I sat in a chair waiting for the arrival of the Duty Medic, feeling very sorry for myself. I saw with my good eye that sat opposite me was Captain Arthur Lambert, who had been the Regimental Sergeant Major of the Junior Leaders Regiment RCT when I'd been serving there as a Corporal. Arthur, now commissioned, deservedly so, as he was a brilliant bloke, was in the hospital that night with one of his injured soldiers. He looked at me and said "Bleedin' hell, Sergeant C, what have you been up to – and why are you wearing those crappy non-regulation pattern boots?" (I was wearing a pair of zip-up military style but Gucci fur-lined boots that we'd all worn in Germany, purchased at our own expense. As usual the issued kit was crap). So there I was having been severely thrashed but being bollocked for wearing the wrong sort of boots. Ah, you can take the man out of being an RSM – but you can't take the RSM out of the man. Don't you just love the Army!

The Army Medic arrived. "Come with me Sarge," he said and rather blatantly minced off towards the treatment room. I made my farewells to Captain Lambert and tottered off to the treatment room. The medic was filling a sink with warm water and said, "Oh dear, Sarge, you do look a mess. Whatever have you been up to! Let's ease your poor little thumb into this warm water and get it cleaned up. I think that we've broken it, don't you? Let's give it a bit of a tidy up then I'll get it splinted for you." He proceeded to very gently bathe my face thumb (suddenly the joke about having more hammer than a blind cobbler's thumb made eminent sense) and started to get me patched up. "Oh, you poor thing, Sarge. How did it happen then?" I explained that I'd been attacked by a thuggee with a weighted stick. "Well he should be prosecuted, dear!" said the Medic. A Doctor came and sorted out my damaged face, tutting but saying little before disappearing off to bed. The Medic did a magnificent job and I was fully repaired. Inevitably by that time I was feeling what squaddies describe as being "shite." I looked at myself in the mirror over the sink and saw the Elephant Man looking back at me. "They pay to look at me!"

I thanked the very professional Medic profusely and left to get the transport back out onto Salisbury Plain. On my way out of the hospital I passed Captain Lambert. "I won't shake your hand Sergeant Cavender!" he said, then smiled and winked at me, "Oh and Sergeant C," "Yes sir," I replied – "Get those fooking boots sorted, son!" I attempted a smile, winced theatrically, then departed.

Military Hospitals - an aside. I was once an in-patient in the Queen Elizabeth Military Hospital at Woolwich. Each morning there we had Matron's rounds and news spread like wildfire when she was on her way. I was, I think, in something like a six man ward. For Matron's inspection the walking wounded were required to get out of their beds and stand at the end of them whilst she (a Lieutenant Colonel – Hattie Jacques lookalike) came into the ward and inspected both us and the state of the ward with beady, experienced eyes. In one bed in the far corner of our ward was a very ancient Chelsea Pensioner, a Cockney, who had been admitted after having had a fall. Drink had been involved. The Pensioner was as deaf as a post and had kept us all awake for most of the night singing hymns, "Who would true valour see, let 'im come 'ither!" "Onwards a-Christian So-oooldiers" etc.

Come the dawn we were all at our wits end, I think that he'd bellowed his way through most of the New English Hymn book. We'd pleaded with him to go to sleep, but he couldn't hear us. Matron's rounds probably saved him from getting smothered by a pillow by some sleep deprived squaddie. The old guy remained in his pit and snored throughout the inspection. Eventually he was moved to a side room by the sympathetic nursing staff, which definitely improved his chances of survival.

Back to Salisbury Plain. When I reached Squadron Headquarters, in the field, the OC seeing the state of me decided to send me back to Bulford Camp. I wasn't fit for purpose and would 'hors de combat' for at least a week. I was ordered to go home to my married quarter and recover. The Squadron would remain on Salisbury Plain for another week or so, freezing their collective bollocks off. I picked up my kit and gratefully limped off home.

Just before the Exercise began, my wife Maggie had taken our baby daughter Sara 'Ooop North' to visit my parents whilst I was away doing my duty, so I was returning to an empty house. No matter, I could still make myself comfortable and get some sort of rest and recuperation in. It was starting to snow as I was dropped off outside our married quarter. As the Landrover disappeared back out onto Salisbury Plain it suddenly dawned on me that I didn't have a door key. The spare had been left inside the house. The plan was that Maggie would be back from 'Ooop North' by the time the military exercise had finished and the cunning plan was that a spare key would not, therefore be required. "Oh dear." I stood there in the freezing cold, like the 'Little Match Girl.'

In explanation for what was about to happen – bear in mind that I was exhausted, feeling a bit dizzy and everything was hurting. My mental facilities were at a low ebb, which I think goes some way towards explaining why I decided to gain entry through a small side window of the house, located in what had once been the coal-house. It had its own door which was usually left unlocked, leading to the kitchen door proper, which was always locked and bolted. I knew that a 'quarter light' window was always left open in the coal-house, so I decided that I would wriggle my way through it with a bit of effort and that way gain access into the kitchen. I was a reasonable bodily size then and it seemed perfectly reasonable that I could manage it. Battering the door in was not an option because I didn't have the strength left in me – nor could I have afforded the repairs on my piffling wages.

Entering the coal-house I closed the outer door behind me to keep the snow and freezing wind out. I didn't want any of the neighbours seeing what I was about to undertake – not only that, every now and again a Royal Military Police (RMP) vehicle patrolled the area keeping an eye on things, especially as they knew that the majority of us were out on Excercise. I lifted the little window up and noticed that although I could easily move the latch to one side, there was a large piece of latch metal sticking up right on the centre bottom of the window that would cause me untold damage if I tried to wriggle past it. "No problem," I thought," I'll unscrew it with a small coin," which I did. It took ages to do but I did it. It was a magnificent achievement and I was rather proud of myself. I looked at the window and realised that it was going to be a 'damn close-run thing' getting through it. I should have just kicked the door in.

A light came on in my befuddled brain and I decided that I would stand a much better chance of wriggling through the small window if I removed all of my bulky military clothing and effected entrance wearing just my growlers (underpants). Now, this is where the sheer brilliance of my actions came into play. I took all of my military uniform and pushed it through the small window, thinking that I could sort it out once I got through. As a consequence I was left stood there in the freezing cold, wearing just boots combat, military socks and a pair of growlers. The foolishness of my actions gradually sank in. What was I to do if I couldn't get through the little window? I realised at that precise moment that I was destined to become a commissioned officer.

There was no going back now. I had to rise to the challenge and get through the window. I dragged our dustbin across to just below the small window and balanced precariously on top of it. Having done a bit of caving in Boy Service I knew that the best chance I had of getting through such a small space was by imitating Superman in flight i.e. one arm straight ahead of me, the other one tucked into my side, thus reducing the size of one's shoulders. So I put the arm with the broken thumb through first, followed by my head and the battle commenced. I wriggled and sweated and strained, managing to get half of my upper body through the gap. After the initial surge, I hung there exhausted, one half of my semi-naked body, turning blue, hanging on the coal-house side of the kitchen window, the cold wind whipping around my nether regions with the other half of me hanging in the kitchen. I paused for a moment in order to get my breath back, beads of grey, freezing sweat lining my top lip, resting like a side of beef in a butchers 'fridge.

To my abject horror, I heard the sound of an approaching RMP Patrol Vehicle, a very distinctive sound. Had one of my neighbours 'phoned them to report suspicious activity at Number 27 Canberra Drive? I had to do something and it had to be done quickly before they arrived. I couldn't be discovered hanging there in my growlers. I decided to make one last effort to gain entry, counted to five and heaved the rest of my body across the unforgiving lintel of the window. The pain as the entire front of my body got scraped was indescribable. I hit the kitchen floor with an ungainly thud, landing like a sack of spuds, thoroughly exhausted. My growlers had been ripped off and my shins were bleeding but I cared not a jot, I had gained safe haven and also escaped the attentions of the mean minded Redcaps. There I sat, face, body and broken thumb throbbing, naked apart from my socks and boots. Not a pretty sight.

As the Memsahib was up in Yorkshire and the house was left unattended, there was very little scoff left in the 'fridge so I decided that I would have to go and get some food and milk from the shops. No car, so it would have to be done on foot, walking from the married quarters area down to the shops in Bulford Camp square. Not a long way normally, but a bit of a hike considering my reduced circumstances. I got washed and changed into civilian clothing and hobbled from the house, this time by the front door. It was snowing and I felt as if I was in a scene from 'Dr Zhivago' as I trudged off to the NAAFI Shop in Bulford Square.

As I tottered down to the shops I attracted several nervous glances from those walking past me, women with children were crossing themselves and crossing the road to avoid meeting me. I eventually made it to the shops, bought what I had to then started to walk back home again. I bumped into Colonel Danny Cardle, the Commanding Officer of 27 Logistics Regiment RCT, our superior Headquarters. He asked me what on earth had happened to me – had I been in a car crash or something? I explained what had occurred and he was absolutely furious. He sent for his staff car and had it take me home, which was a relief as I was, by this time, bordering on useless. Once home, entering by the front door this time, I made myself a pot of tea, switched the gas fire and television on and slumped into the uncomfortable army issue 'G

Plan' chair - (with Disruptive Pattern Material cover).

A couple of weeks later I was told that Colonel Cardle had ordered Major Fartingbum-Smythe to instruct the brute of an ASM to come and apologise to me, either that or formal disciplinary action would be taken against the ASM. He never did and the subject gently died the death. Warrant Officers Class One did not apologise to mere Sergeants, under any circumstances. I eventually recharged my batteries and looked stunningly average by the time my family returned home. Our plans to return to 'Civvy Street' continued.

Major Rupert Fartingbum-Smythe moved on to pastures anew and his replacement arrived. We were all tasked by a new Officer Commanding to find a suitable motto for 65 Squadron RCT, by doing so, we would establish a Squadron identity and morale would be raised accordingly. I suggested 'Take A Dive With 65,' which wasn't received in the spirit that it was intended, and went down like a lead balloon. The 'new' OC used to bring his dog, a puppy, into the office daily, which then proceeded to shite everywhere (at least I think it was the puppy). The OC came into the Orderly Room one day and said to me "Chief, get one of the clerks to get the dog shit cleared up from my office, will you." I was outraged and refused point blank. I told him that it wasn't the clerk's job to do that, it was the owners responsibility. He said something like, "I'm the OC, do you expect me to do it, eh!" "Well," was my reply, "it's your dog, sir." Things got awfully tense as we stared at each other but thankfully he left it at that. Things were a bit icy for a few days.

There was much joy a couple of weeks later when the said OC signed out a classified file (Secret) from the Headquarters and quite illegally left it on top of his office desk whilst he nobbed off somewhere doing a spot of socializing. The puppy, locked in and left alone in the office, chewed the classified file to bits and, much to our delight, did a splendid re-shatting exercise all over the file itself. The OC was summoned to the Colonel's presence to explain why the file had been damaged and worse – left insecure and unattended. Happy days. Eventually, as I was about to depart for Civvy Street, the Squadron was notified that it was going to Northern Ireland (NI) for a three months Emergency Tour. I told the OC that I was happy to go on the tour and then leave the Army, but he decided to bring in a replacement.

In those bygone days it was standard procedure then that when you went across the water, you took everything military with you, including office furniture. So everything was prepared for the move, even down to 'G Plan' desk legs being unscrewed ready for dissembling and packing etc. One day our CO, Colonel Danny Cardle, a flinty Jock, wandered into the Orderly Room, ordered his Labrador to sit under the desk whilst he sat on to of the said desk, his legs swinging. He'd come to see how the preparation for NI was going. "Oh bollocks," thought I – "Do I tell him that the desk legs aren't screwed on?" He was chatting away and was not the sort of man to whom an interjection would have been well received. I could smell disaster looming. The desk was going to collapse beneath him and hell would break loose.

I extracted myself from the impending situation, sliding out of the office and going down to see an old mate of mine, Sergeant Tony Griffiths who was Chief Clerk of another RCT Squadron at the other end of the building. I was half way down the passage when I heard a thunderous crash, a dog howling, followed by a huge selection of ripe Scottish curses. The Clerks told me that the desk had collapsed, the Colonel had been deposited on the office floor in an unseemly pile, his dog, unharmed but scared had crapped itself and legged it out of the building howling like a banshee, followed by its furious, thin-lipped master. There were no repercussions though, Colonel (later Brigadier) Cardle was a good man and eventually, a few years later, saw the humorous side. I wasn't particularly bothered either way as I was just about to leave for Keighley as Mr Cavender. Eventually the Cavender family departed Bulford and travelled 'Ooop North' to Keighley where we'd managed to wangle a house out of the Council. Seeing Bulford disappear into the distance was a sheer delight.

'LEFT THE ARMY FOR A WHILE'

So, I'd left the Army, skipping merrily out of Bulford, hoping never to see the place again. I got a job working with Securicor at Keighley, just to keep body and soul together. Towards the end of my service I'd taken a resettlement course at the Catterick Resettlement Centre where I and several others were prepared to sit the entrance exam for the Civil Service. We were lectured 'at' by a withered and dry old stick who normally taught at one of the Universities in the area. It was quite obvious that he considered squaddies to be the lowest form of intellectual life and spent the entire month of the course talking down to us. He was one of those teachers who mumbled to the class whilst writing on the blackboard, so that you couldn't hear a thing he said. One could only ask him to repeat himself so many times before just switching off and letting him get on with it. Bloody useless.

I eventually sat the Civil Service entrance exam in Darlington. It was an incredibly fraught occasion, those in charge of the proceedings had mill-boards with two stop-watches clipped to the top, everything was to be timed to the last second! The pressure was on. "You can turn your first papers over now – you have three minutes and four fifths of a second to complete the paper. You must stop when we tell you or you will be executed!" Hells bells, we only wanted a job in the Civil Service. Several people left the hall well before the end of the exam. Some left quietly, sobbing – their Civil Service dreams shattered, whilst others left in a blaze of glory, telling the examiners just what they could do with their examination papers and stop-watches. Testing lasted a full, taxing day. I stayed and continued to the bitter end but I wasn't too confident of the outcome. Still, nothing ventured, nothing gained.

A number of weeks later I was informed, much to my delight, that I had passed the entrance examination with flying colours and would be informed in due course where I was to be employed. The first job I was offered was in T'Labour Exchange at Bradford. "You're a big lad and we need someone like you to deal with our more difficult regulars! You can be on t'main counter." Oh no you don't, I thought, someone else can have the joy of that. In the interim period I'd been working on nights as a driver for Securicor. Terrible. I used to get the bus home after my shift and would often waken up back in Keighley bus station having done the full circuit – and then had to pay for another bus fare to get home!

In all honesty I was missing the Army and, with my wife's permission, decided to reapply to rejoin. In my heart of hearts I didn't really want to be a Civil Servant, so I called into the Bradford Recruiting Office and did all of the necessary paperwork in order to rejoin the Army. Eventually I was signed up and summoned to the Depot RCT at Buller Barracks, Aldershot. On arrival there I was interviewed by a Retired Officer (RO), Lieutenant Colonel Smith. Old Smudger said, – "Right Sergeant Cavender, I'm sending you to one of the 17 Regiment RCT Squadron's at Marchwood. They need a Chief Clerk." "That's no good to me sir," I replied, "I need to get out to Germany and get some money together. I'm skint." "You'll jolly well go where you're told, Sergeant. Beggars can't be choosers!" "Well, this one can," I replied. "It's either Germany or I'm going back to Yorkshire." The Colonel sighed and said "Look old chap, come back tomorrow morning and I'll see what I can do for you."

I duly returned to see him and was told that I was to be posted to 2 Squadron RCT at Nienburg in West Germany, part of 1 Armoured Division Transport

Regiment RCT. I was rather pleased about that – (that is until a few months later when I heard that the Squadron in Marchwood I had originally been destined for was to be moved to Cyprus). 'Hoist by your own petard' I think is the phrase. Still, I was perfectly happy with a posting to Germany.

2 Squadron RCT, Nienburg, West Germany
(Part of 1 Armoured Division Transport Regiment RCT, Liebenau)
(as Sergeant, Chief Clerk)

Yahoo! - back in the thick of it. Lots of military exercises (manoeuvres) and a chance to make new friends/acquaintances. Back into the 'Meat and Two Veg' of the RCT and delighted to be there. Memories of the dastardly Bulford had faded. One particularly good mate who made life great fun was the then Staff Sergeant Peter McGrath (a.k.a. 2Lt Rodney Warrington-Mynge, the 5th Ranjipoor Rifles) of British Forces Broadcasting Service (BFBS) fame. We soon discovered that we shared a keen sense of the ridiculous and had many, many laughs and got up to a lot of mischief and silliness. Peter is such a colourful, humorous and pleasant person, a vibrant man now living the life of Reilly with his wife Jacquie, somewhere in Greece.

The Officer Commanding (OC) 2 Squadron RCT was Major J P (John) Mordant RCT, who despite a fearful and fierce demeanor, once you got to know him, was a great bloke, a one-off. Unfortunately I lost my Father to lung cancer and my Grandfather to a heart attack in the space of two weeks. I was in a slough of despond. Major Mordant was brilliant, compassionate and very supportive officer and, along with my beloved wife, helped me get through that particularly bad patch. Everything happens at once. I'd been in hospital myself during that time having damaged a vein in my throat from shouting on stage (pantomime) so was at a low ebb. As usual, those around me pulled everything back together. That's something that our Wives and the Army handles brilliantly.

The Administrative Officer (AO) there was Captain R (Ron) Lettington RCT, a character in his own right and a thoroughly upright chap. Captain Lettington was a very tall, eloquent and likeable individual. His only fault as far as we could see was that he always had an exceedingly smelly cheroot hanging from his lips. Peter McGrath and I could easily emulate Captain Lettingtons voice, which was very plummy and distinctive. Peter and I caused much mischief and mayhem in the Squadron Headquarters by shouting ridiculous orders and telephoning instructions using Ron's voice. The Sergeant Major was WO2 (SSM) G (George Packer) RCT, whom I'd known when I was a Junior Leader. He had been a full corporal in the Gymnasium there, again, a lovely bloke and salt of the earth was George.

Eventually Major Mordant and Captain Lettington were posted and replaced by Major G L (Larry) Kevans RCT and Captain C (Chris) Hawkey RCT, both of whom I'd served with before in different capacities at Bulford. Ron Lettington is no longer with us, which is very sad. He has left behind some very happy memories. The last time I saw him was when I was a Warrant Officer Class One (Superintending Clerk) at Headquarters the RCT Training Centre in Aldershot, when Ron popped his head round the door to say hello, still smoking one of his foul cheroots. He wanted to scrounge a lift to Aldershot Railway Station, so I got the Brigadier's staff car to drop him off there. I remember him with great fondness.

There are many, many stories I could tell about 2 Squadron RCT, post Mordant and Lettington, but that would require a separate book and would undoubtedly involve me in some form of litigation, so I'll let sleeping dogs lie. We had some great lads in the Squadron and a lot of them still keep in touch to this day via the miracle that is 'Facebook.' The Squadron went to Northern Ireland for an Emergency Tour. Lots of adventures there, again - stories for another time. Towards the end of that tour I was ligging around in the Ops Room at Moscow Camp, Belfast when a signal came in stating that I was to return home a few weeks earlier than expected. Deep joy, I was returning home to my beloved wife Maggie and baby Sara. Not only that, I was being promoted and posted within Germany.

2 Squadron, 1 Divisional Transport Regiment RCT (Nienburg an der Weser, West Germany) - (Pre 'OP BANNER' Tour 1976)

So, towards the end of a lively, interesting emergency tour with 2 Squadron RCT in Northern Ireland and having been informed that I was to be posted as Chief Clerk to 38 Squadron RCT, Wrexham Barracks in Mülheim an der Rühr, West Germany, I packed my kit, handed over to my relief and legged it from Moscow Camp, Belfast to fly back to Germany. Back in BAOR, I had a few days off then handed over our Married Quarter before the three of us legged it to Mülheim an der Ruhr. I'd never heard of Mulheim and having read up on the place the only thing that I could find out was that the singer Engelbert Humperdinck had served at Wrexham Barracks as a National Service Corporal.

38 Squadron RCT, Mulheim an der Rühr, West Germany)
(Part of 28 Transport and Movements Regiment RCT, Dusseldorf)
(as a Staff Sergeant – Chief Clerk)

38 Squadron RCT (Main) was in Cyprus when I arrived, so I got myself up to speed with the Rear Party and was ready for Squadron (Main) when they returned. The OC was Major John White and the SSM was a fine Irish character, WO2 Danny Kaye. I gently familiarised myself with my job, under the guidance of the AO, Captain Roy Garside, another ex-ranker and gentleman of the first water. Eventually Squadron (Main) returned from Cyprus and then (Main) and (Rear) melded together nicely. Major White and Danny Kaye were both eventually replaced, in the natural scheme of things, by Major Noel Muddiman and WO2 Ray Bunting, both of whom I was destined to serve with again in the future.

There are some postings that are just a sheer delight from start to finish. 38 Squadron RCT was one of them. The sun always shone – and we really enjoyed ourselves during our time there. We had a great Sergeant's Mess and served alongside a fine bunch of people. Our Regimental Headquarters (RHQ), 28 Transport and Movements Regiment RCT was based far enough up the road at Dusseldorf, so that fortunately there was hardly any interference from there and we saw very little of them. There are myriad stories I could tell about our time at Mulheim, but I'll just mention this one.

We had a particularly pompous young Troop Commander at that time, who shall remain nameless to save his blushes. He was the proud possessor of a throbbing Triumph Stag sports car and used to go roaring around the place, speeding, posing and generally pissing people off. As it was approaching the 1st of April, I decided to compile a 'cod' letter purporting to be from the Royal Military Police (RMP) at Dusseldorf Station, full of military legalese, stating that this particular officer had been spotted speeding around Mulheim/Dusseldorf Station, in uniform driving his racy sports car whilst not wearing a crash helmet. The OC, Major Noel Muddiman, who was in on this wheeze, rather sportingly invited the Troopie to his office and revealed to him the contents of the letter, asking him why he had failed to wear the appropriate headgear.

The young subaltern, apparently, had spluttered, farted, blushed etc and denied knowing that he was supposed to wear a crash helmet whilst driving an open topped sports car in uniform. The OC told him, in no uncertain terms, that ignorance of BAOR Standing Orders was no excuse and to sort himself out. It was common sense that some form of safety helmet should be worn by those driving open topped sports cars and that as a professional transport officer he should have had more sense. Not only that, he was setting a bad example to the lower decks. The Troopie, duly chastened, made the appropriate ingratiating apologies to the OC, then proceeded to drive around in his Triumph Stag wearing a crash helmet, (Army issue green, motorcycle style) for about a week or so, looking for all the world like a first class nobber. Soldiers were seen to be applauding him when he drove past. Eventually he was tipped the wink that someone had been taking the piss and that I had been heavily involved.

He was a hefty lad and, spitting feathers, came gunning for me. It was only Army disciplinary traditions that saved me from being hammered. He hadn't taken it at all well, calling into my office and stating, through clenched teeth, cheeks puce and veins in his head throbbing, that he would definitely seek some form of physical revenge, i.e. knock seven bells out of me, when the opportunity presented itself. He warned me that - "You'd better watch your fucking back, CHIEF!!" before exiting stage left. Alas, the joke had fallen flat and as far as he was concerned I was about as popular as a fart in a space suit.

We were at a Squadron Barbecue a couple of weeks later where much drink had been consumed. The young Troopie decided that that was the time to wreak his revenge and confronted me, ham like fists bunched. I whispered two little words, "Court Martial," whereupon much to my relief he unclenched his fists and decided to leave it at that.

Whilst with the 'Fighting 38th,' at Mulheim, I wrote and presented several pantomimes and also did a lot of stuff for the British Forces Broadcasting Service (BFBS) down at their Cologne studios, writing and voice-overs etc. I co-wrote the pantomime 'Jack and the Beanstalk' with a talented and amazingly funny character, Staff Sergeant Tom Balch. Tom also played, brilliantly, the role of 'Idle Jack' in the unit pantomime. Tom and I frequently drove down to BFBS to tape some voice-overs/promo's for road safety and stuff like that. There was lots of laughter and 'corpsing' going on. I recall that we had to do one promo about a football team arriving at Düsseldorf Airport by 'Service-air' who were to be met by a welcoming committee of German and Scottish footie fans, singing competing songs and trying to outdo each other.

As part of the promo, that Tom and I had written on our way down to Cologne, Tom was required to sing a segment of 'Edelweiss' and much to our amusement he sounded a bit like Minnie Bannister from the Goon Show. I was doing the Scottish bit, "Haste Ye Back" – or trying to. When the taping started we laughed that much that he and I were put in adjacent studios to record the rest of the one minute promo, just so that we wouldn't have to look at each other. It didn't work. The laughter and hysteria spread around BFBS like wildfire until everyone in the production team joined in. The somewhat fey sound engineer kept tutting at us in the special way that 'creative' fellows have, which only made things worse. It was a quite a while before we got the promo finished. Rattling good fun and lots of laughs. That particular session was taped and added to a compilation of BFBS 'out-takes', but I suppose it has now been lost in the sands of time. It would be fun to hear it once more.

I had a young Brummie clerk working for me as part of the Orderly Room team in 38 Squadron. Let's call him 'Smithers.' Not the sharpest tool in the box, but nevertheless a hard working, decent lad. He lived with his wife near to the barracks in a married quarter and they toddled along quite happily. Eventually as Christmas approached, his name was plucked out of the hat (that's how they did it then - none of your careful calculations based on leave card percentages) and he was informed that if he wished, which he did, he could return to the UK for a spot of leave. His only problem was that his wife wouldn't want to go back to the UK because it meant leaving their cherished family pet, a budgie, behind. His Troop Commander ('Troopie'), a recently married young Lieutenant, kindly offered to look after the budgie during their absence, an offer that was gratefully accepted. Their leave was approved and travel plans set in motion.

The day before the family 'Smithers' was due to depart for RAF Gütersloh to catch their air trooping flight to England, the budgie and a hearty supply of 'Trill' budgie food was delivered in a bird cage to the Lieutenant's married quarter and with great ceremony, handed over into his care. Mrs Smithers was bordering on suicidal and in floods of tears at the thought of leaving her budgie behind with strangers. However, a calming pot of NAAFI Tea was brewed, assurances proffered and something approaching normality was resumed. Eventually the family Smithers toddled off back to their married quarter, sans budgie, in order to finish their packing etc. All seemed to be going well.

At twelve o'clock-ish that night the doorbell rang at the married quarter of the young Lieutenant and his wife. He answered the door in his dressing gown - a strange place to have a door – (old pantomime joke). He opened the door, wondering what on earth anyone would want at that ungodly time of night/morning. There on the doorstep stood Driver and Mrs Smithers, Mrs Smithers gently sobbing. The Lieutenant, fighting to stay awake, said:

Troopie: Smithers old chap – it's gone midnight – what's the matter? Is something wrong? Has there been a family bereavement?

Smithers: *(Nonplussed)* No sir, nothing's wrong, like.

Troopie: (*Getting a bit pissed off by now*) Oh. Do you realize just what time it is, Smithers?

Smithers: Yes sir, sorry about that. Our packing took a bit longer than we expected. Those army suitcases don't hold much though, do they.

Troopie: Look, I don't mean to be rude old chap – but what do you want?

(Concerned Troopie's wife's voice from upstairs):

Troopie's Wife: What is it darling? Is there an Active Edge? - *(Alert Exercise)*.

Troopie: No dear, it isn't an Active Edge. It's Driver and Mrs Smithers!

Troopie's Wife: Eeeeough, I say, really - what do they want?

Troopie: I'm just trying to find that out, darling. I'll deal with it, you go back to bed.

Troopie's Wife: OK, then. Nighty night Mr & Mrs Smithers.

Smithers: Nighty night, ma'am.

Troopie: *(Losing patience)* Look, Smithers, what do you want?

Mrs Smithers: We've just come to say goodnight to the budgie, sir.

Oh, before we leave Mulheim, just remembered. We had a chap, let's call him Corporal 'X' - who was a professional debtor. He was always in deep shit in relation to his finances, owing money to everyone. His personal file was as thick as the new English Bible and try as we may we could never quite manage to get his head above financial water. Every time we thought that we'd got him sorted, another debt letter would appear in the post. We even got a threatening letter from a Jewish money lender based in Cologne who was threatening to send in the heavies if he didn't get at least some loan repayments. We kept a personal file on Corporal X's complex financial activities so that we could make some sense of them. Jokingly on the bottom of his personal file I wrote in large black lettering "**VOLUME 5.**" That little jape would later come back to bite me on the arse.

I was to be posted from 38 Squadron RCT on promotion to Warrant Officer Class Two and sent to the Junior Leaders Regiment RCT, located at that well known spelling mistake, Azimghur Barracks, Colerne in Wiltshire. I was chuffed to bits about returning to the Regiment where I'd started out all those years ago as a Junior Leader. To return there as a Warrant Officer was the icing on the cake. Our time with 38 Squadron RCT was amongst the happiest and most rewarding of postings. We were sad to leave there but, as ever, onwards and upwards!

I had been Regimental Chief Clerk at the Junior Leader's Regiment RCT but a couple of months when I received a 'phone call from the then OC 38 Squadron RCT, Major G G Hardaker RCT (who, years earlier, had been a Troop Commander when I was with 55 Air Despatch Squadron RCT in Telok Paku, Singapore) but I don't think that he remembered me.

Major Hardaker: Ah Mr Cavender (*followed by the usual pleasantries*) Wonder if you could help me? Do you remember Corporal 'X' the bad debtor?

Me: Indeed I do sir. The Pay Sergeant, me and the AO spent many hours trying to help him get his financial affairs sorted out but he was a bit of a lost cause.

Major Hardaker: Well he's got into a lot more debt and we just can't control him, so I'm washing my hands of him and applying for his discharge. He's his own worst enemy. The Brigadier has read Volume 5 of his personal file and was mortified. He asked me why on earth we'd let things go on for this long. Anyway, I think that Corporal 'X' will probably be discharged from the Army.

Me: Bit of a shame really sir, he's not a bad lad in himself. Anyway, what can I do for you?

Major Hardaker: The Brigadier has asked to see Volumes 1 to 4 of the Corporal's personal files but we can't seem to lay our hands on them. Can you advise?"

Me: Ah, well sir, er, perhaps I should explain. It's like this ....

Volumes One to Four, of course, had never existed. They were just an 'in' joke between myself and the Admin Officer.

The mention of Major Hardaker has transported me back in time to when I was a very young Driver/Clerk serving with 55 Air Despatch Squadron RCT at Telok Paku, near Changi in Singapore. One particular morning I was delivering that days copies of Squadron Part One Orders around the Squadron lines, which included the troop offices. This had to be done by hand – it was pre-computer days.

When entering one of the Troop offices I saw, to my horror, the then Lieutenant Hardaker rolling around the highly polished linoleum, struggling fiercely with a Lance Corporal and with meaty blows being exchanged between the two of them. There were fists flying, teeth bared, fingers being bent, grunts, headlocks, farts, belches etc. I thought that I'd better try and help stop the altercation before it got any worse. A lower deck having fisticuffs with a Rodney, it went against all we'd been taught.

Mortified, I threw the Part 1 Orders to the floor and dived onto the soldier who was attacking the officer. I grabbed him in an all enveloping bear-hug. There then followed a hellish struggle between the three of us which went on for several long moments in the sticky Singapore heat. We rolled around the slippery floor, puttees unraveling, buttons pinging, stockings footless drooping, until Lieutenant Hardaker finally cried out in utter desperation:

Lieutenant Hardaker: Driver Cavender, will you bloody well get orft me! This chap's having an epileptic fit and I'm trying to stop him from biting his tongue! You're not bloody well helping matters!

I froze – normally Mr Hardaker would not have used such salacious language and I was shocked into inactivity. As the soldier gradually 'de-fitted' I blushed daintily, stood up, brushed off my starched shorts, dabbed my scuffed and bleeding knees with a grubby hanky, handed Mr Hardaker a copy of Squadron Part Orders, made my excuses and left him to his medical ministrations. I think I was called a "Fucking half-wit' or something along those lines by the trembling Lance Corporal, through his blood drenched teeth. Ingrate. I was only trying to help.

Meanwhile, back at the Junior Leaders Regiment:

The Junior Leaders Regiment RCT, Azimghur Barracks, Colerne
(as WO2 Regimental Chief Clerk)

We'd arrived at the Regiment and the work of setting up home and settling into a new job was progressing nicely. I had a good job and the area was lovely. The sun always seemed to shine, our daughter Sara was busy making new friends at a nice school and everything felt completely right. Bath was just a couple of miles just down the road, as was Bristol. We were in fine fettle.

One day I'd been shopping with the Memsahib in Bristol when I stumbled across a joke shop and bought a few items, one of which was a can of 'Instant Fart Spray.' The stench emanating from the tin was eye wateringly ferocious and I knew that I could have some sport with it. You know that when you buy a tin of WD40 that it has a small straw with it so that you can dispense the contents of the tin in a more accurate manner, well the 'Instant Fart Spray' had the same sort of appendage.

When I arrived in my office on the Monday I sat and worked out a cunning plan. Every now and again I inserted the small straw into the keyhole of the door that led into the CO's Office (right next door to me), then I coughed theatrically and gave the CO, Lieutenant Colonel 'Spider' Webb, the benefit of a hefty squirt of 'Instant Fart Spray.' I did this a couple of times, then secreted the can in my desk, waiting for something to happen once the foul stench had permeated the atmosphere.

The Adjutant at that time was a charming and erudite gentleman, Captain Graham Fitness. Graham worked in an office on the other side of the CO's so that they both had easy access to each other. I sat there listening when something along the lines of the following conversation took place as the CO swept into the Adjutant's office, eyes streaming with tears and coughing, (I may have overdone the fart spray a tad).

CO: Graham!

Adjutant: (*Jumping to his feet, trembling with enthusiasm*) Yes Colonel?

CO: Can't you smell it, man?

Adjutant: I'm sorry sir, smell what?

CO: There's an absolutely awful stench in my office. Come and have a whiff!

They went for a collective whiff.

Adjutant: Goodness me sir. Have you eaten something you ought not to have?

CO: It's not me, man! (*Brightly*) Must be the drains! Well I can't sit here all day with that stench assailing my nostrils! Do something about it!

Adjutant: (*Intelligent option*) Er, have you tried opening a window, Colonel?

CO: (*Not impressed*) Of course I bloody well have! Anyway, what's to say that the smell isn't coming from outside, eh!

Adjutant: (*Brightly*) Mmmm, quite sir. Well the RQM's on his way up here to see you, Colonel. Perhaps we should invite him to look into it?

Colonel: Yes of course, the Quartermaster. Good idea Adj, he'll know what to do. Well done!

Mmmmm, I remember thinking, this is going much better than I expected. Enter the RQM, Lieutenant Colonel John Atkinson RCT, a most marvellous character, a Mancunian of the finest water, oozing bonhomie:

RQM: (*To CO*) Morning Frank! How are you?

CO: Oh, morning John.

RQM: Morning Graham.

Adjutant: Morning Colonel. Er, we have a slight problem.

RQM: What's up?

CO: John, could you come and smell my office please. It's quite dreadful.

RQM: Oh, bit whiffy is it?

CO: Bit of an understatement there, John!

RQM: Let's have a look then.

CO: Adj, come and take some notes will you!

Off the three toddled into the CO's office, the Adjutant dutifully trailing behind taking notes. The RQM carried out a sniff test and they all hurtled back into the Adjutant's office.

RQM: Strap back, Frank, that's disgusting. Have you eaten a curry or something?

CO: Certainly not! It's not me!

The RQM looked accusingly at the Adjutant.

RQM: Graham!?

Adjutant: It's not me either, Colonel!

CO: What on earth could it be, John?

RQM: If it's not you two, it must be the drains! To be frank, Frank, it has to be said that there's a distinct whiff of ancient shite in there!

CO: (*Distasteful look on face*) Quite, quite. Faeces, definitely - and it's getting worse.

RQM: (*Dry Retching*) I'll get on to the PSA (*Property Services Agency*) Frank and get the drains around the Headquarters checked out. Probably just need flushing through. Doubt if they've been touched since the RAF left here.

CO: Well I can't possibly work under these conditions. Let's pop over to the Officers' Mess for Tea and Biscuits, John.

RQM: That's a cracking idea, Frank.

They made to leave.

CO: Adj, you stay here and hold the fort will you. Transfer all of my calls to the Mess – and take that handkerchief off your face!

Adjutant: Yes Colonel.

I made a policy decision there and then to keep very quiet about the whole thing and covertly dispose of the 'Instant Fart Spray' at the very earliest opportunity. I just couldn't resist one more squirt though and gave the civilian staff room a generous burst of spray on my way out of the building at lunchtime. The civilian staff who were in there eating their lunches complained bitterly about the stench and had to exit to eat lunch in their offices and cars. It wasn't my finest moment.

Later that day a team from the PSA arrived hot-foot with mountains of special 'Dyno-rod' style equipment, closed off the main road and started to rive up lengthy sections of paving outside the CO's office and along the front of the Headquarters. They then started replacing yards of sewage pipes. Gulp! Work in the building was severely disrupted because of the sound of jack-hammers and a noisy generator, so the civilians were sent home for the rest of the day. The CO was not known for having a keen sense of the ridiculous and I felt that it could have had a definite detrimental effect on my career had I mentioned 'Instant Fart Spray' and my involvement with it to him.

The RQM, John Atkinson, alas no longer with us, was an extremely nice man, who always had a smile on his face and a kind word to say to lesser beings like me. I once nearly took off the tip of his nose with an exploding cheroot at one of our Sergeant's Mess Summer Ball's. The cheroot wasn't intended for him but he nicked one out of a packet that was left on the table, lighting it before I could stop him. The cheroot exploded, leaving a blackened ring round his mouth. He looked at me, laughed and said, "Cavender – you twat!" I'm sure that he would've seen the funny side if I'd told him about the 'Instant Fart Spray' but I didn't take the risk. Colonel Webb would definitely have had a sense of humour failure. It would have been a career stopper. John Atkinson has now passed over the great divide and I know will be sorely missed by all who knew and loved him. Cheers Sir!

Incidentally, back when I was a full Corporal at the Junior Leaders Regiment RCT, pre-Colerne and when it was at Taunton, one day I'd tidied up my little office in the Headquarters and moved a few cupboards around. Behind one cupboard was a strange button on the wall, covered in cobwebs and obviously unused for a number of years. Intrigued, I pressed it and a bell rang through in the Adjutants office, coincidentally sounding just like his telephone. The Adjutant, (a certain Captain 'Spider' Webb), had a huge old Bakelite style telephone on his desk with lots of complex levers and buttons with which to monitor the incoming calls for himself, the CO, the Training Major and the 2IC etc. I decided to have some sport on the strength of my new discovery. I rang that bell day in and day out for about a week. The normally very placid and patient Adjutant was getting into a terrible lather pressing levers and swearing at the telephone as he tried to answer it, with little success. "Hello, Adjutant" click. "Hello, Adjutant!" click etc. It was such fun to behold.

Eventually someone put the bubble in and my name popped into the frame. The bell on the wall was disconnected and I was summoned into the regal presence of an irate Captain Webb, who expertly sharpened my feet and quite rightly gave me an icy adjutantal bollocking. Perhaps in later years when he was the CO of the Regiment at Colerne he might have recalled that particular 'bell' incident, which could have led him to the conclusion that I was responsible for the drains debacle and several other such wheezes? I never dared broach the subject of the 'Instant Fart Spray' with him or with anyone else for that matter. The cleaning and repairing of the drains outside the Headquarters must have cost an arm and a leg. 'Spider' would have had a definite sense of humour failure. I hereby confess.

Colerne was a magnificent posting. Lots of hard work, lots and lots of fun – which is just how it should be. The old adage – 'Work hard, play hard' describes it perfectly. Our Sergeant's Mess, the most exclusive club in the world, worked along very traditional lines and was a joy to be part of. We spent many memorable and happy hours there, quaffing ale, putting on shows and functions and generally enjoying ourselves. Working in the Headquarters was joyful. It was an eclectic mix of military and ever supportive Civil Servants. A great team. We had one wonderful lady there, a Mrs Ena Watson, who had an intense dislike of spiders and snakes and unfortunately let it be known. So rubber spiders and snakes were purchased from the 'Instant Fart Spray' Joke Shop and secreted around her office. Her fearful shrieks regularly echoing around the Headquarters as she discovered these items brightened up our lives immeasurably.

The Regimental Sergeant Major (RSM) at Colerne at that time was a colourful character, Warrant Officer Class One Dave Turner-Swift (imagine a combination of the actor Windsor Davis, the Sergeant Major in 'It Aint Half Hot Mum and the erudite actor Terry Thomas and you'll get a good mental picture of Dave). Dave had a party trick where he would sneak up behind you, bark like a dog then nip your ankle. It was always amusing to see someone hopping about thinking that they were being savaged by a dog. Dave did his 'Dog' trick on our most adorable Assistant Adjutant, Second Lieutenant Rachel O'Meara. Rachel was (and is) a very funny, bright and beautiful young lady. The epitome of a true English rose. Having seen it, Rachel was so impressed by the RSM's amusing dog trick that she decided to pull the same wheeze on the Adjutant, Captain Graham Fitness. Graham was at that moment out doing his adjutantal rounds. Rachel decided to hide herself under Graham's desk in their shared office, where she couldn't be seen and wait for him to come in and sit down before yelping like a dog and nipping his ankle. "Gosh, it's going to be such fun, Chief," she said to me, smiling and looking so innocent.

I should point out at this stage that Graham was forever thrashing around, madly enthusiastic, at 100 miles an hour in Basil Fawltyesque fashion, consistently on the edge of adjutantal lunacy. His was a very busy job. As his mind was constantly elsewhere, if you sneaked up behind him and said "Booo!" he would jump six foot into the air (which I often did, just for a spot of sport). I often had to duck a clout from him for being cheeky. Recognising that there was a whiff of potential disaster regarding Rachel's intentions and that her jape would probably go badly wrong, I decided to adopt an immediate low profile and continued with my clerical duties, leaving Rachael to enjoy a jolly spot of officer type larking about with the Adjutant. When commissioned officers decided to play silly buggers, it was always wiser to leave them to it because it inevitably ended in tears. It's known as the 'Kiss of Death' syndrome.

Graham eventually returned to his office – and I awaited the outcome of the wheeze about to be perpetrated by Rachel. "Miss O'Meara in Chief?"

Graham asked me. "She's around somewhere sir," I replied innocently. Rachel had been hiding under his desk for about thirty minutes by that stage, full marks for enthusiasm. Graham went into his office and sat at his desk. After a few moments I heard a little girlie dog style bark, followed by an "Aaaaargh!" a loud bang then a girly whimper. My office door swung open and Rachel came tearing in with blood pouring from her lips (I should mention that the poor girl had had her top set wired to help straighten her teeth, her mouth was full of sharp scrap dental metal).

As predicted, Graham had reacted very badly to having his ankle nipped and had, unfortunately, kicked out with his heavy leather, officer pattern silver stud shoe, the bulled toe-cap of which landed fairly and squarely on Rachel's gob. The loud bang was from where her head hit the underside of Graham's desk as she had tried, unsuccessfully, to avoid the adjutantal toe-cap. Rachel whimpered and pointed at her by now very fat, bleeding lips and lisped pathetically, "Chief! Look! The Adjutant hath kicked me in the lipth! It'th all gone tewibbwy wong." The Adjutant was mortified and was desperately trying to dab her lips with a large, spotted handkerchief, saying "Oh my God, oh my God I couldn't help it, it was an automatic reaction!!" "Weave me awone, you beatth" Rachel cried. Chaos reigned supreme.

I fell to the floor laughing. No sympathy there I'm afraid. "Ith not funny, Chief!" Rachel wailed. The CO was singularly unimpressed by the racket and popped his head around his office door to say something along the lines of "Settle down chaps and let's get some work done shall we!" He took the scene in at a glance, tutted and went back into his office totally unperturbed. Rachel was OK, eventually, once her damaged lips had deflated. Notwithstanding, she had a pair of smackers to die for, for quite a while. Some people pay a great of money to get a 'trout pout' like she was sporting. Just as a side issue, my wife Maggie, who worked on the base as a civil servant at that time, came into my office purely by chance during the midst of the mayhem. Favouring me with one of her accusatory stares she said, "What have you been up to Cavender!" but for once I was innocent. A damn fine gel, Rachel and a jolly good sport to boot, (did you see what I did there?) Oh how I tittered for the rest of the day. Whitehall farces had nothing us lot.

Rachel O'Meara & Graham Fitness

We, various members of the Colerne Sergeant's Mess, decided to enter a float in the prestigious Bath Carnival. We acquired an Army 4 ton truck (flatbed for truck aficionado's) and built a German 'Bierfest' scene on the back of the vehicle. We also managed to scrounge a couple of barrels of German beer and a quantity of beer steins then changed into our dirndl and lederhosen cossies etc. We'd also wired up a sound system to blast out German style Bierfest Songs. It was then just a matter of us all sitting on the back of the truck, swigging copious amounts of ale as we slowly trundled into Bath to join in the procession. The difficult part was not falling off the vehicle whilst it was in motion.

Arriving safely in Bath, we joined up with all of the other participants in the carnival parade, lining up in a local park to be judged by a local carnival committee who would then awarded rosettes for the best efforts. For those not familiar with Bath, it had a large Royal Navy presence there and there were lots of high ranking Naval officers lurking within its boundaries. As we were all sat on the back of the truck singing German songs, (one beer barrel had served its purpose and we were all semi-bladdered), a large black limousine pulled up at the side of our truck and out stepped a man whom we immediately recognised as being a very high ranking naval officer. His blue jacketed sleeves were covered in gold rings, the peak of his hat covered in 'scrambled egg' and he sported a dashing white goatee beard. This vision strode towards our truck, clutching a mill board and surrounded by an attentive entourage. We all sprang to attention, thinking that he was at the very least a Vice Admiral and that we mustn't let the honour of the Regiment down by appearing to be pissed out of our brains. "Morning Sah!" called out our nominated OIC Truck.

"Morning Ladies and Gentlemen (our wives had been coerced into joining in). There then followed the usual silly and stilted conversation that always takes place between senior officer and the lads, "And who are you chaps?" "Sergeant's Mess, the Junior Leaders Regiment RCT, Sah!" "Mmmm, I little long in the tooth to be Junior Leaders!" We slapped our thighs and laughed heartily, as one does when a very senior officer cracks what he thinks is a funny. We stood rigidly to attention, cheeks of our arses cracking walnuts in the approved fashion as the conversation continued and we were asked about our efforts to 'dress' the truck etc. Eventually when 'The Admiral' had finished marking our efforts and had declined our offer of a beer, he bade us a fond farewell, jauntily saluted, jumped into his car and was driven on to the next display. We found out afterwards that the gentleman concerned was in fact 'off the telly' who advertised fish fingers – 'Captain Birds Eye.' So much for the Royal Navy! We'd been, metaphorically, kissing the arse of the 'Fish Finger' man!

During the course of the carnival we managed to easily polish off the second barrel of beer as the carnival procession slowly drove around the streets of Bath, the good citizens throwing coins at us (in the nicest possible way) to be collected at the end of the Carnival and handed over for charity. The parade wound past city hall, where the civic dignitaries were assembled waving regally at the floats. We were by that time whooping and singing songs, loudly. To our abject horror, we spotted our Commanding Officer stood alongside the dignitaries; our Colonel was definitely giving us the evil eye. Obviously a chat with our Regimental Sergeant Major (RSM) would be looming in the not too distant future, but being fortified by vast quantities of the finest German ale, we cared not a jot, let tomorrow take care of itself.

What the CO didn't know, however, was that the RSM was on board the vehicle with us, dressed in his lederhosen (suspiciously tight leather shorts), wearing a jaunty cap with approved green feather and sporting a large Bavarian style moustache. His face was also hidden behind a huge bier stein, which fortunately saved him from being recognised by the CO. At the conclusion of the carnival parade we drove back to barracks along the very winding roads of Wiltshire, this time at a much slower speed than we had travelled down to Bath, everyone whooping and still clinging on for grim death. 'Elf and Safety' was not a particular consideration that day and our driver just wanted to get back home so that he too could have some of what was left of the beer (dream on)! We just wanted to get back to the Sergeant's Mess for a pre-prepared celebratory Barbecue and some more ale.

As the sun eventually sank beneath the horizon, so did we. A cracking day, plenty of fun and a nice amount of money collect for charity. What more could a chap ask for. Not only that, we'd met 'Captain Birds Eye.' Just as a little after-note, we did in fact get a "Jolly well done chaps" note from our Colonel a few days later - who had, apparently, been highly amused at our high jinx. I think it was Billy Connolly who said, "Life is a waste of time. Time is a waste of life. Get wasted all the time and you'll have the time of your life!"

We put together a variety show for the 'Wives Club' at Colerne, part of which was a performance by a skiffle group (for those of you old enough to remember skiffle) performing under the name of 'Foul Ground' (don't ask). Though I say it myself, 'Foul Ground' was rather good. A couple of singers playing guitars (Geordie Prady and Hughie Forsyth), me thrashing away on a converted tea chest, someone on wash-board, someone on mouth-organ and one lunatic person who kept thrashing around beating his head with a tin tray in time with the music (Tony Newton). We also had our very own Drummer, apologies but some of the names escape me. What we didn't know was that in the audience that night was the owner of a very large night-club located in nearby Weston-Super-Mare and he wanted to book us for the summer season. We were thrilled to bits.

In those days permission had to be given by the Commanding Officer for soldiers to take on additional employment not concerned with their military duties. We asked for permission to play at the night-club throughout the summer season, but he turned us down and said, rather sniffily, "I'm not having my Senior NCO's and Warrant Officers appearing in some shabby sea-side nightclub. It's unseemly." So that was the end of that. 'Foul Ground' bit the dust.

To cut another long story short, I was selected for an appearance on 'Blankety Blank' when Terry Wogan was the Presenter. Again I had to ask permission from the Commanding Officer to do it. Once again he was rather sniffy about it, once I'd explained what 'Blankety Blank' was. Much to my surprise, a few days later the Adjutant informed me that permission had in fact been given and I could go ahead. Apparently the CO had received a telephone call from our Brigadier who'd heard about it and was highly delighted. It was all very exciting and on the day of the show (they recorded two shows during the course of a day) I met so many interesting performers that I was nearly overcome with excitement. Performers like Beryl Reid, Tony Blackburn, Keith Harris and Orville (had a good chat with the Duck), Alfred Marks, Windsor Davis and Dame Barbara Windsor. There were some other luminaries there but time has clouded my memory – which is a good thing because the only thing I won that day was a 'Blankety Blank Cheque Book and Pen,' which I've still got. If nothing else, I'd had my 15 minutes of fame and was big in Bath for about a week.

It's hard to imagine an Army Barracks as being an entertainment hub, but it was at Colerne. Because it had been RAF Colerne before being conquered by the Army, there were several humongous aircraft Hangars on site. One particular Hangar was empty and proved to be an ideal facility to loan out to film companies for shooting movies/TV movies etc. It was an ideal spot because it was secure and well away from the general public, extraneous noise was not a limiting factor (both from them and from 'us') actors and crew could be fed and watered without too much difficulty and shooting could and did go on until late into the night. If you went into the Sergeant's Mess for Lunch (a 'Pie and a Pint'), as I often did, you never knew who you were going to bump into. I'll give you an example. There was part of a TV Movie being shot there called 'The Curse of King Tutenkhamun's Tomb.' I nipped into the Mess to tie on a nose-bag and in the main bar found myself alongside a group of very famous actors. These show-business luminaries were just sat chatting away and being completely normal. I shared a table with the most beautiful and effervescent Miss Eve Marie Saint who had been in the movie 'On the Waterfront' with Marlon Brando, a classic. She has had a long and illustrious career. Miss Marie-Saint was really sweet. We chatted about her various films, the local area etc and she was very patient with me.

Eva Marie Saint –
On the Waterfront (with Marlon Brando), North by North West (with Cary Grant), The 39 Steps, Exodus (with Paul Newman), How the West was Won

I also got to spend a bit of time with Harry Andrews – whose work I had admired for very many years, particularly his role as the RSM in that gritty film 'The Hill.' It's still shown on TV now and again and is in my humble opinion, a classic.

Harry Andrews - as 'Stubb' in the film Moby Dick
Also appeared in: The Hill, Ice Cold in Alex, Charge of the Light Brigade, Moby Dick, 633 Squadron, Watership Down

A couple of ladies of mature years who worked in our Headquarters were all of a twitter. Apparently an actor called 'Van Johnson' was filming on site. The ladies were bordering on hysterical, so I arranged with my boss to take them across to the hangar and watch a bit of filming and possibly also to meet their hero. Van Johnson was an extremely charming and erudite man who took a great deal of time in between takes to chat to these ladies and sign autographs etc. They were in swoon city. It was only afterwards that I managed to read up on Van Johnson (no Google then – so it took a bit of time) and was astounded to see that I had been fortunate enough to meet a man who was not only an immensely talented person but who had had such a key part in the entertainment industry. In his time he was a massive star:

Van Johnson
30 Seconds Over Tokyo, The Caine Mutiny. Battle of the Bulge, Brigadoon, I Love Lucy

I remember asking him if he'd served in the armed forces and he replied that he'd done "Thirty Seconds Over Tokyo' in 1944. I had romantic thoughts of him doing an 'Enola Gay' type mission, but it turned out that it was the title of one of his hit films. Totally missed the point there chaps. Sharing a plate of chips with Dame Wendy Hillier was also a memorable experience. She was totally 'without edge' and had you not known it you would never have guessed that she was an actress of great note.

Dame Wendy Hiller DBE
Pygmalion (with Leslie Howard), Major Barbara (with Rex Harrison)Murder on the Orient Express, Voyage of the Damned, The Elephant Man

All this was very exciting stuff for me, a film buff, particularly when I got to meet Raymond Burr -

'Chief Ironside.' Mr Burr was a rather private person, but was happy to chat away quietly in a corner of the Sergeant's Mess. He was temporarily being billeted in a house in the Crescent, Bath but really just wanted to finish filming and get back home to America. A very pleasant man and a massive star of film and TV in his own right.

Raymond Burr
Perry Mason, Chief Ironside, Airplane II, Love Boat

I won't go on too much more about those who I met at Colerne, but for someone like me, it was a dream come true to be able to meet these talented people and get to spend some time with them. I achieved temporary hero status with my daughter Sara when I managed to have her meet up and spend a few minutes with the 4th Doctor Who, Tom Baker, a rumbustious, fun-filled man who lit up the room with his enigmatic presence. He took the time to speak to Sara and some of her friends. He didn't have to, but he did.

Tom Baker
Doctor Who (4th Doctor in the series),

I can't recall any of these actors who wasn't nice and approachable, although I'm sure that being only human they would get fed up of the constant attention of their admirers. A small price to pay though, for the trappings of their success. Finally, I would just like to mention Lesley Crowther. He wasn't filming at Colerne but had given up some of his valuable spare time to come along to our charity fund-raising day. I managed to spend some time with him and we chatted for ages bout his time in the 'Flanagan and Allen' play in which he had the part of Chesney Allen, partnered by the comedian Bernie Winters who played Bud Flanagan. What a nice man Mr Crowther was and it was such a tragedy that he suffered badly in a car crash not too long afterwards and eventually died from his injuries. He was taken far too soon. A lot of you may remember him in BBC's 'Crackerjack' children's show.

Lesley Crowther
Bill Cotton Bandshow, The Back & White Minstrel Show, Crackerjack, The Price is Right, Stars in their Eyes

April the 1st was approaching, so I had an idea for a film type wheeze. I'd posted notices throughout the barracks that (a fictitious) film company, 'The Salty Sea-Dog' Film Company, would be coming to film part of a movie entitled 'The Last Voyage of Sinbad' in our 'film' hangar and that they were looking for extras to participate in the filming. Also, there would be a token payment for those involved. Anyone interested in being an extra in the film was required to present themselves at the 'film' hangar offices where they would be interviewed by members of the film company re their suitability. On this particular day, April the 1st fell on a Saturday. I thought that it would be a jolly good wheeze and those who fell for it would have a bit of a laugh and enjoy the experience.

I'd placed a series of signs on several office doors within the hangar on which it stated that applicants wanting to participate in the film had to pass through each office – of which there were many, until reaching the last office - where there was a large sign saying 'April Fool!' They would see that last sign and burst into laughter thinking, 'What a jolly wheeze, we've been had!" From flash to bang the process would take about five minutes before it was revealed to be a joke, or that was my intention. Needless to say, it all went Bristol's Uppermost (Tits Up).

In those days we used to work on a Saturday morning, so I was sat in the Headquarters sorting through the morning post when one of my mates breezed in and a conversation something along the following lines took place:

Friend: Hi Cav, if I were you mate I'd make yourself a bit scarce!

Me: (*Smiling*) Why?

Friend: I shouldn't smile mate, you are in deep shit!

Me: (*Gulp*). Why?

Friend: There are literally hundreds of people, men, women and children who have queued for hours up at the hangar, hoping to get extra work in the Sinbad film.

Me: Well it's only a joke for April Fool's Day innit! Bit of a laugh that's all.....

Friend: Not so funny when a lot of them have spent hours making costumes or have scoured Bath, Chippenham and Bristol to hire pirate costumes to better their chances of being selected. There's loads of kids in floods of tears, bitterly disappointed. Some of the young Rodneys have hired expensive costumes and are muttering death threats.

I hadn't meant for it to go quite this far and was so sorry, particularly, to have disappointed the children. As usual I hadn't thought the consequences through. Would I never learn?

Me: (*Gulping*). Shitty death! What am I going to do?

Friend: I should slide off somewhere and keep out of the way until after weekend. Things might have calmed down a bit by then.

I made my excuses and left, whimpering. Luckily come the following week people had seen the funny side of it and I survived, although I was flitting about like Jack 'O Lantern whenever I saw a group of wives walking around the camp with their children. Never again, I promised myself.

Not having learnt my lesson, the following year I decided to have another go at a 'wheeze.' I'd seen somewhere a letter stating that one day everything would be 'decimalised' and that there would be ten hours in a day, ten days in a week, ten months in a year etc that sort of thing. So I did a 'cod' written order that 'Decimalisation' would be introduced a few months later and distributed it throughout the barracks (this was pre-computer days). I thought that it was so patently ridiculous that no-one would fall for it and titters would be had throughout the workforce. Wrong. I had been warned by my wife Maggie that things would go 'Bristol's Uppermost'and she'd reminded me of the 'Sinbad' debacle, but I chose to blunder on regardless. The

Civil Servants were up in arms. There was talk of them going on strike because this 'Decimalisation' process would affect their wages, their leave, their promotion prospects (?) they hadn't been consulted 'blah blah' etc. The Civilian Admin Officer, a slightly deaf retired Major was thrashing around the barracks, bellowing and trying to restore law and order. Chaos reigned supreme. I was summoned into the Adjutants office, had my feet sharpened and slunk out of there like a whipped cur. Never again, I promised myself. I had been warned by my wife Maggie that this would happen. I should have listened to her.

'HMS EDINBURGH AND THE EDINBURGH GOLD'

I was sat in my office at Azimghur Barracks, Colerne, where I was earning a dishonest crust as the Regimental Chief Clerk of the Junior Leaders Regiment RCT. Throughout that particular day I kept hearing a series of explosions coming from the far side of the airfield. I wasn't too concerned by this because we'd been informed that an MOD 'specialist' had brought some old ammo/explosives onto the old airfield of what had once been RAF Colerne, and was detonating it in a very far corner of the place, well away from everything.

I met the 'specialist' a Doctor Sidney Alford and we were chatting over a cup of coffee one day. It transpired that Dr Alford had been on board the ship that was part of a salvage consortium, raising the gold stored in the HMS Edinburgh that had been sunk in World War 2. Dr Alford was there on board the salvage ship on behalf of the Ministry of Defence to advise on the ammunition and explosives (he is an acknowledged expert on these matters) that lurked beneath the waves in the shipwreck, some of which was lifted onto the recovery ship whilst the gold was being raised from the sea-bed.

Later on that day Dr Alford very kindly presented me with a bullet (the expended part i.e. the round that had been extracted from its shell casing) which had been part of a consignment that was lifted from the Edinburgh and was now in the process of being destroyed because of its instability – ergo the window rattling explosions emanating from the deepest, darkest corners of the airfield.

Man of mystery - Doctor Sydney Alford

Why I was particularly interested in the raising of the gold from the HMS Edinburgh was that I knew Keith Jessop who was the boss of 'Jessop Marine' - the outfit that had raised the gold from HMS Edinburgh (some 431 gold bars valued at today's costs something in the region of £142 million). Keith, like me, was born and bred in Keighley, West Yorkshire and I'd met him when we were both much younger at a party at my Mother's house one Christmas. Keith's son Graham was at that time engaged to my sister, Gail. Keith invited me to become a part of his 'treasure hunt' consortium when it was at the very early planning stages. He didn't mention gold, and told me that he was looking for copper ingots. If only I'd had some money to invest in his dreams, but I didn't so missed a 'golden' opportunity.

The late Keith Jessop (Jessop Marine)
Treasure Hunter and Adventurer

Keith was a fine man, a hard working, imaginative entrepreneur who managed to reap the rewards of his efforts. Keith had also had a distinguished career as a Royal Marine.

I was at that time taking a career break from Her Majesty's Service and was living with my family in Keighley, working for Securicor as a driver whilst waiting the results of my Civil Service/Diplomatic Corps Entrance Exam results. I didn't have a pot to piss in or a window to chuck it out of – as they say – at that time of my life so couldn't afford to take up Keith's offer. Keith wrote the full story of the travails of finding and raising the gold in a brilliant book called '**Goldfinder**.' If you can get your hands on a copy – it's well worth the read. If you can't, I'll lend you mine, but I want it back!

Anyway, the bullet that Doctor Alford had kindly presented to me I had mounted on a small plinth and it was tucked away on a window ledge with my 'Blanket Blank' cheque book and pen and other bits of militaria, gathering dust.

Many moons later when I was gainfully employed as Captain Cavender, the AO (Administrative Officer) of 617 Tank Transporter Squadron RCT in Hamm, West Germany, I was attending a Regimental Dinner in Hamm Station Officers' Mess and was seated next to the then Commanding Officer of 1 Battalion Royal Scots and Hamm/Werl Station Commander, Lieutenant Colonel (later General) Mark Strudwick. The Colonel was telling me that he was attending a Regimental Lunch later on that week and would be hosting some RN officers from the crew of the current 'HMS Edinburgh.' I told him the story about Keith Jessop, Doctor Alford and the bullet and said that I would be happy to give him the bullet, metaphorically speaking, and he could then present it to the ships officers the Dinner.

Colonel Strudwick was delighted and liked the idea. It was the sort of quality wheeze for which the Royal Scots were well known. I remember being very privileged to be invited to one of their Regimental Dinner Nights, which was something accorded to the rare few. At the conclusion of dinner, I repaired to the facilities in order to ease my bladder. Whilst stood at the urinal I noticed that there was a fairly large picture of Lord Mountbatten mounted, (when I say mounted I mean hung on the wall), directly over one of the urinals. I said to a Royal Scot's officer standing next to me that it seemed rather a strange place and a slightly disrespectful one to hang a picture of such a luminary over a urinal. He looked at me through bleary eyes, just sort of "Harrumphed" and replied, "We don't talk about it, old chap." Not wishing to cause offence, I made my excuses and repaired to the bar. What had Lord Mountbatten done? Never did find out - sorry.

Major General Mark Strudwick CBE, Chief Executive Prince's Scottish Youth Business Trust (who as Lieutenant Colonel – Commanded 1st Battalion the Royal Scots)

Many years later when I'd retired from the Army, I was lurking up in Scotland, visiting my son-in-law, Ian Langthorne, who invents things and runs a very successful business. I was in his Glasgow based office when I noticed a familiar signature on the certificate that adorned his office wall. The certificate had been signed by none other than Major General Mark Strudwick. Ian had been a successful participant of the Prince Charles Scottish Youth Business Trust Scheme and had crossed paths with the high and mighty, including General Strudwick. He also bumped into:

HRH Prince Charles chats with Ian Langthorne regarding his recent award from the Prince's Scottish Youth Business Trust

I told Ian all about the 'Edinburgh Gold', Doctor Alford, the bullet, and 'Colonel' Strudwick etc. He said that it was an interesting series of coincidences and that if I ever wrote a book I should include it in there. So I have - make of it all what you will.

Like many other members of the Permanent Staff, Military and Civilian at the Junior Leaders Regiment RCT, at Colerne, I worked very hard and for many long hours. Work hard, play hard and everything will be OK. Eventually I was selected for promotion to Warrant Officer Class One (WO1) the top rank of the non-commissioned tree. What an achievement that was, I was thrilled to bits. As a reward I was posted to Aldershot.

HQ the RCT Training Group, Buller Barracks, Aldershot
(as WO1 Superintending Clerk)

Author as WO1 in Antwerp on a fact-finding tour

It was something of a déjà vu experience for me, returning to Headquarters The Training Group RCT (HQ Trg Gp RCT) as a WO1, particularly as I'd started off my adult military career there many moons before as a young Private doing menial clerical tasks. It was a jolly Headquarters with a happy and closely knit staff. One chap there, who was great fun, was John Cleese look-alike, Captain Jonathon Knowles. Had many a laugh with him. We were both always getting bollocked for stretching the Friday lunchtime break (which usually involved beer) to some unacceptable hour in the afternoon. Different days, different standards. Imbibing was not without risk. Our 'Glorious Leader' - the then Brigadier, would sit in his office, scouring the barracks using his binoculars and it seemed that we were always spotted by him as we sneaked back into the office, belching lager/beer fumes. Slappings were administered.

An old mate of mine is John Heward, who had a successful career in the Army and was eventually commissioned, leaving the Army as a Captain. We worked alongside each other in HQ The RCT Training Group, John as the Chief Clerk of one of the Branches and me as Superintending Clerk. One of our tasks at HQ RCT Training Group was to organize the funerals of the great and good of the Corps at the Garrison Church on Queens Avenue, Aldershot. On one occasion one of our Generals, who had reached high office, had, unfortunately, shaken off his mortal coil rather unexpectedly and was to be 'laid in state' overnight at the Garrison Church prior to his funeral taking place the following day, attended by the great and the good. My task was to get the 'Orders of Service' compiled and printed then laid out on the church pews.

On receiving the 'Orders of Service' from our Graphics Department, I went along to the Garrison Church, accompanied by John Heward. John was, unusually for him, on edge. I asked him what the matter was and he said something along the lines of, "Do you mind if I don't go in the Church, sir, I haven't seen a dead body before." I replied, rather snittily, "Well you're not going to see one now, John – he's in a coffin! Now get in there!" John bit the bullet and we entered, respectfully, the very quiet and empty Church then started to place the 'Orders of Service' on the pews. Everything had to be perfect as we'd been informed that there were Royals and some very senior officers attending the Service.

I noticed that John kept himself to the very far side of the Church, as far away from the coffin, (which was laid on a trestle by the altar), as possible. I stood next to the coffin and said, "John, come over here for a minute!" He hissed back, "I'm not coming over there!" "Get yourself over here now, Sergeant Heward!" Military discipline came to the fore and he came and stood next to the coffin. He was not comfortable. I said to him, "Can you hear anything, John?" "My God sir," he whispered, turning white, "No ah can't hear owt!"

Unseen by him I'd slid my hand beneath the coffin and gave it three sharp raps. I have never seen a man move as fast in all my life. John was out of that Church and sprinting along Queen's Road back to the Headquarters faster than Sir Roger Bannister could ever have managed it. When I eventually returned to the Headquarters, John was sat in his office, a rictus grin on his face, doing his best to drink a mug of coffee without spilling it. All military discipline forgotten, he then called me some very unsavoury names, quite deservedly. John Heward - a good man to have at your side (unless you were in a coffin).

As usual, all good things come to end. My job and a couple of others in the Headquarters were written out when the Inspectorate of Establishments (I of E) 'Gestapo' descended on us to inspect our jobs and try to get rid of them. These teams were mean-minded miserable bastards who made their living out of causing misery. They always asked a series of seemingly banal but mega-sly questions, which was totally unnecessary as it was plainly obvious, as usual, that they'd made their decisions about who would be getting the chop before arriving there. "Yes Brigadier, I've managed to cut several posts from your establishment. Haven't I been a good boy."

My job as Superintending Clerk bit the dust. Superintending Clerks were becoming a thing of the past. As it would have been innately foolish to get rid of a man of my obvious qualities, modesty being one of them, the leadership decided there was no other option but to send me just across the road to:

HQ The Depot and Training Regiment RCT, Buller Barracks, Aldershot - (as WO1 Staff Assistant)

There, magically, a vacancy for a WO1 Staff Assistant had arisen. This was good for me and my family because it meant that we wouldn't have to move married quarters and schools etc. A not particularly enjoyable time was had at the Depot Regiment RCT. Life was only made bearable by the Adjutant, Captain Jeff Little, (eventually Brigadier), who worked himself into the ground on a daily basis supporting a very colourful character, the CO, Lieutenant Colonel Larry Brown. Colonel Brown had presence and was a brilliant, colourful officer, often described as that magical beast - a 'man's man.' He'd had a large truck wing mirror screwed to the corner of his desk so that he could see out of the window that was sited behind him. When squads of Women's Royal Army Corps (WRAC) marched down the road from the main square and past his office window he would shout out – "Tit Alert!" and we had to nip smartly into his office and make appreciative noises. Horrible really, but it happened. Different times, different standards. The clerks in the Headquarters were great lads, one of whom was Sergeant Stevie Biles, a quality act and charming, efficient young man, who went on to get commissioned and become an Officer and Gentleman. It was very, very hard work there and I spent many long, demanding hours working under pressure, which fortunately culminated with me being commissioned.

There was a programme on BBC TV at that time called 'Songs of Praise' and we were informed that a segment of it would be filmed at Buller Barracks, Aldershot. I was nominated to assist with the day to day administration of the 'shoot.' The 'Presenter' was Sir Harry Secombe, who had served in the Royal Artillery during World War 2 so everything had to be tickety-boo for this much-loved performer. The day of filming came and I was nominated to look after Sir Harry, which I happily did, duly trailing around catering for his and his support staff's various whims. At one stage Sir Harry, who (with respect) was knocking on a bit, started to feel the cold, it was snowing and chilly, so I loaned him my military Parka whilst I dutifully froze. He was a very nice man, totally unaffected by all of the fuss and continually cracked jokes and blew raspberries – as made famous on 'The Goon Show.' He was a very nice and amenable bloke, with no edge to him whatsoever.

I recall that during filming a sequence near the newly installed ski slope at Aldershot, with lots of soldiers dotted around to make the place look busy, someone in Sir Harry's managerial entourage sidled up to the RSM of the Depot and Training Regiment RCT. It was still snowing and bitterly cold. The RSM, as they do, was also keeping a beady eye on things. One of Sir Harry's assistants, long haired, fey and rather self-important, spoke to the RSM, saying something along the lines of:

Assistant: I say old boy, instead of just standing around, do you think that some of your chaps could give Sir Harry's Rolls Royce a bit of a wash and polish whilst the filming's going on?

The RSM of the Depot, who was old school and definitely not to be tampered with - and also had the troop's interests at heart, gave him the 'evils' and a not too diplomatic, but succinct reply:

RSM: Firstly, if you haven't noticed mate – it's snowing and it's freezing cold. And secondly you can fuck off and take Sir Harry's jam-jar to the car wash like I have to. The lads aren't here to wash fucking cars! Is that fucking clear?

Exit one blushing Assistant. One particular joy for me was seeing the comedian Arthur English doing a skit for the TV programme about a soldier on guard during World War 2. Can't remember where it was performed but l know that it was in some draughty hall (shed) in Aldershot with an audience of cold and not particularly enthusiastic squaddies. Mr English was knocking on a bit by then but for me it was such a privilege to see him doing a segment of his act and the audience loved it.

After also having served in the Army throughout World War 2 1949 Mr English became resident comedian at the Windmill Theatre in London and performed much other stage work. His radio work began with the BBC series. 'Variety Bandbox' using as always his own Aldershot accent. His usual persona was a stereotypical wartime 'spiv,' and he became known as The Prince of the Wide Boys He'd tell long rambling shaggy dog stories ending with the catch-phrase: "Play the music! Open the cage!" Another popular catch-phrase was "Mum. Mum. They're laughing at me!" He began to appear on British television in mainly comedy roles in the 1970s but will probably be remembered mainly for his character of the bolshy maintenance man, Mr. Harman, in 'Are you being Served?' For those of you with a football bent, Arthur had been president of Aldershot Town FC. Their club badge depicting a rising phoenix was designed by Mr English. We also had the privilege of hearing Iris Williams sing in that same cold hall. A beautiful Welsh lady with a heaven sent voice. Just as an aside, I saw her performing on a cruise ship last year and she was as lovely, talented and professional as ever, once again singing 'He was Beautiful.' (I just knew that she was looking directly at me when she sang it). It was a privilege to listen to her singing and whisked me back in time to that freezing cold day at Aldershot. I saw Miss Williams, alone in the Restaurant before the show. I was going to say hello to her, but she looked so serene and peaceful that I decided not to disturb her. Sadly Sir Harry and Mr English have now departed for that great theatre in the skies.

'THE COMMISSIONING MEDICAL'

Word was received from the Throne Room at Buckingham Palace that I was to be commissioned. There followed the usual faffing about getting new uniforms, badges of rank etc undergoing a gruelling medical examination (where you had to be 100% perfect or everything ground to an immediate halt). It was always such a relief to get the results of one's X-Ray as that was the final part of the medical process.

The Medical Officer who carried out the commissioning medicals was a bombastic retired Brigadier. When I'd finished being examined by him I felt like a prime piece of horse-meat, such was his disdain, apparently he treated everyone like that. He knew that he could get away with being obnoxious because it was vital that one passed the medical examination, the last hurdle to becoming a commissioned officer. So, I'm stood there, divested of all garments apart from a nice pair of Marks and Spencer growlers (underpants) after undergoing a very thorough and comprehensive medical inspection, when the Brigadier said:

Doctor: Right Mr Cavender, take your spectacles off, cover your left eye with your right hand, read the letters on the optical chart and tell me what you can see.

Me: *(Removing spectacles etc)* Nothing sir.

Doctor: Right Mr Cavender, cover your right eye with your left hand and tell me what you can see.

Me: Nothing sir.

Doctor: What do you mean nothing!? Why can't you see anything, man!?

Me: *(Losing patience and not bothered about being an officer anymore)* 'Cos I haven't got my fucking glasses on, sir!

Doctor: *(Snarling)* That'll do! Get dressed!

The Brigadier refused point blank to tell me there and then if I'd passed the all important medical inspection and said that I'd have to wait until he sent a letter to my unit with the results. Must have got his rocks off on the strength of that. Those were the days, my friend.

The medical report duly arrived stating that had passed and that the commissioning process was completed. Getting commissioned would lead, with much relief, to my eventual escape from Buller Barracks. There's a great deal of fierce competition in the ranks for those wishing to get a commission in the armed forces and it is undoubtedly something of an achievement when you are successful. Of course not everyone that applies makes the grade, but that's a fact of life.

I remember that when I was told that I'd been successful and was to be commissioned (sounds like a ship) I went to the Sergeant's Mess for a celebratory pint or two. Stood at the bar was another Warrant Officer Class One who had been considered by the same board but hadn't been selected. He was in the depths of a deep depression and sucking lemons. It was, understandably, something of a disappointment, particularly when everyone knew that you hadn't made the grade on that occasion. Notwithstanding, he was very gracious and congratulated me on being successful. I asked him if he would be applying to the commissioning board again and he said, with a touch of bitterness:

"No mate, I rather be 'King of the shit than be shit of the Kings."

The intimation being that he'd rather be at the top of the pile in the Sergeant's Mess than at the bottom of the pile in the Officers' Mess. Oh well, if that thought kept him happy. It did put a bit of a dampener on things that day though.

I was eventually informed that I was to be posted to West Germany, which was a joy to me. One Friday I was a WO1 – on the following Monday I was a Captain. It was as easy as that (not). I morphed from being a lower deck into being an Officer and a Gentleman over the weekend. Oh I forgot, several of us 'Retread Newbies' had to complete a four week commissioning course in Aldershot which included things like being instructed about the correct way of writing official letters, how to eat peas orft a knife, never to call portraits 'pictures,' key objectives like that. There were only four of us on the commissioning course and we made the best of it, surviving all that they threw at us and then we're ready to be let loose.

Number 17 RCT Commissioning Course
(Outside Buller Barracks Officers' Mess, Aldershot)
Rear: Author, Captain Mike Jones
Front: Captain Peter Stableford, Captain Neil Fyfe

(*Remind me to tell you about the speech test when one gets commissioned from the ranks*)! O.K. - seeing as how you've asked, I'll tell you about the speech test. In the Army, to qualify for a commission from the workhouse floor and become an Officer, a key part of the lengthy and complex procedure is to pass a speech test in order to prove that you will not embarrass yourself or the 'chaps' once joining the refined circles of the military gentry. The test, usually conducted by a senior officer, goes something like this:

PRE-COMMISSIONING SPEECH TEST (FOR EX-RANKERS)

Tester: (*A 'proper' officer*) OK old chum, now for the 'Speech Test.' Please repeat the following words, after me.

Me: (*Enthusiastically*) After me!

Tester: Er no, perhaps I didn't explain it properly. I will say a word and then I want you to repeat it back to me. OK? *(Smiling gratuitously).*

Me: (*Thinks to self, "not going well*) Er, of course sir, sorry.

Tester: Not a prob, old bean.

Me: Not a prob, old bean.

Tester: No, no, Mr Cavender, please, we haven't started yet. Here we go – now, please say 'Air.'

Me: Air.

Tester: Hair.

Me: Hair.

Tester: Lair.

Me: Lair.

Tester: (*Rubs hands together*) Right, that's spiffing, first class! Now link those words and say them all together as a sentence.

Me: Air, Hair, Lair.

Tester: (*Imagine Lesley Phillips*) 'Oh Hellooooo.' – Jolly well done! You've passed!

It will help you, dear reader, to understand this very old joke if you repeat the above segment out loud – and before you ask, no - one doesn't have to pass a speech test, but that little chestnut was too good to leave out.

Any road up, it was off back to Deutschland for me and my beloved family. The family Cavender didn't leave Aldershot without one final drama though. We'd boxed up all of our goods and chattel, which had been collected by a removals firm and we were due to drive to Germany (in our new duty-free car) the following day. Exciting times. All we had left in the front room of our married quarter were two manky old deck chairs, to be binned when we left and an upturned Military Forwarding Organisation (MFO) packing case with an old table-cloth placed over it. It was just for one night. Our land-line telephone had been disconnected (no mobiles in those halcyon days).

During the course of the night my wife Maggie decided that a visit to the Lavatory was a vital necessity and trotted off to the heads. I should add that as our duvets etc had been packed and sent off, that particular night we were each sleeping in an Army issue sleeping bag. Anyway, during the course of the night, my beloved had departed for the 'facilities' without wearing her spectacles (blind as a bat) and upon exiting the lavatory, mistook the top of the stairs for our bedroom door and hurtled down the stairs, bouncing off every step until landing at the bottom of the stairs in an undignified heap and with a sickening thud.

I was awoken by the noise and commotion and thought that we were being burgled. I saw that Maggie wasn't at my side and went immediately into the protective mode. In the hurry to exit my sleeping bag, the zip jammed. I couldn't reach my spectacles (blind as a bat) so hopped to the bedroom door looking for all the world like a large squinting caterpillar. I peered down the stairs, saw a rumpled heap at the bottom and quickly realised what had happened. Maggie had done one of her 'spectaculars.' Savagely I ripped the sleeping bag's zip wide open and thrashed down the stairs, wearing only my shreddies. Maggie was laid in a heap at the bottom of the stairs, groaning, dazed and not quite sure what had happened to her. It was a very dramatic tableau. I gave her a quick examination to check for spinal injuries etc then carefully carried her into the front room, manoeuvring her gently into a deck-chair before covering her with an old, threadbare picnic blanket (also due to be binned). She was badly dazed and I was worried that she might have concussion. I lit the gas fire, thrashed back upstairs, threw some clothes on and hurried to our next door neighbours to 'phone for an ambulance.

I rapped on my neighbours door. Their landing light came on and the lady of the house thrashed downstairs at a great rate of knots, sensing that there was something untoward going on. She'd been woken by the racket of Maggie tumbling down the stairs and knew that something was amiss. By the time our neighbour reached the bottom of her stairs and opened the front door, unbeknown to her, her breasts had slipped over the elasticated top of her night dress and were displayed for all to see. I now had to prioritise the actions to be taken. I asked her if I could use their telephone and then indicated that it might be better if she were to tuck her mammaries away from public view. She turned puce with embarrassment, quickly tucked the offending articles away and then led me into their front room where I 'phoned for an ambulance and returned to our house to wait for it to arrive.

It was a cold, misty night and the ambulance men eventually arrived, having been delayed by the inclement weather. They examined the Memsahib then put her on a stretcher to load her onto the ambulance and then take her to the nearby Cambridge Military Hospital. As they wheeled her out to the ambulance, the Medics gazed around our front room, which was cold and virtually empty – apart from the two old deck chairs and an upturned box – one tutted and said, "It's disgusting the way they make our lads live!"

As the Cambridge Military Hospital was just up the road from where we lived, we didn't have too far to travel. Whilst Maggie was being dealt with by the medics, I had to do the relevant paperwork and was interviewed by a very suspicious Doctor who thought that I'd caused her injuries by being violent and knocking seven bells out of her. He took some convincing that it had all been an accident. Better to be on the safe side I suppose. Fortunately, after a series of X-Rays and examinations, it was confirmed that no serious harm was done to my beloved, nevertheless she was bruised and battered. She had her arm placed in a sling, sported a shiny black eye and had a rather large bump on the back of her head. We then returned home. Maggie was declared fit to travel, although very delicate, and we set off in our car for Hamm in West Germany later on the following day. We arrived at our new unit in Germany with Maggie looking as if she'd done seven rounds with Mike Tyson and with me getting lots of suspicious glances from those around me.

617 Tank Transporter Squadron RCT
(Cromwell Barracks, Hamm, West Germany
(Part of 7 Tank Transporter Regiment RCT)
(As a Captain – Administrative Officer, then Quartermaster)

Yes, joy of joys, back out to West Germany this time serving with 617 Tank Transporter Squadron RCT in Hamm. I was extremely fortunate to ultimately be able to spend five years there, half of the tour as Administrative Officer then for the remaining time as the Quartermaster. I took over as Quartermaster from a colourful character called Captain Joe Sadler, a very nice bloke. As well as military staff I controlled several members of the Mixed Services Organisation (MSO), which included a German Carpenter, a Polish Sign-writer and a one-legged Italian Cobbler (don't ask). I was also responsible for a group of others employed around the base who came from all over the place, Lithuanians, Estonians, Germans, English, Scottish etc.

The majority of the MSO though consisted of Poles who had been with the British Army since the end of World War Two. Unfortunately for them, at that time, they were unable to return home as the Communists had them all down as persona non grata. It was such an honour to serve alongside them and they were a fine body of men. Ladies and Gentlemen, Boys and Girls – 617 Squadron was another truly marvellous posting where once again we worked hard, played hard and had the time of our lives defending the Nation from the Communist hordes. Never to be repeated joys. There were a few awkward and difficult periods, but those tales are for another time. Here, though, to give you a flavour, is a true story from that time.

'THE WRATH OF GRAPES'

After a couple of years of being the Admin Officer, I had been appointed Quartermaster (QM) and was Commander in Chief of all I surveyed within the Quartermaster's Department, 617 Tank Transporter Squadron RCT. It was a delightful little number, with a relatively large, enthusiastic staff.

I hadn't been in the job for more than a couple of weeks when I was informed by the Squadron OC that we were to be visited by our Director General (DG) who was to visit several of the Royal Corps of Transport (RCT) units in West Germany on his annual 'Wine Tasting and Seeing How the Troops Were Rubbing Along' type of visit. He wanted to call into Hamm on his way to Bielefeld, to meet up with some of his old Mixed Services Organisation (MSO) chums and have a look at the latest developments in the hardy world of Tank Transporting. I was told that the General had not yet had the opportunity to examine one of the 'new' 24 hour Ration Packs and would like to do so at some stage of the visit, if we could oblige. As QM I was tasked to ensure that a brand spanking new 24 hour Ration Pack would therefore be available when called for. "Aha," I thought "an opportunity for a bit of sport here."

One the day of the visit, pre-arrival of the DG, I had one of my loyal staff members pop across to the NAAFI and purchase some fresh grapes. The General's 24 Ration Pack was then cunningly opened from underneath and the black, juicy grapes carefully placed in the box – which was then resealed. Oh what a jolly wheeze this was going to be. I forgot to mention that the DG was a little crusty and not renowned for having a sense of humour. Careers had been known to founder at his whim. As I'd recently been granted a Regular Commission (Late Entry) and was relatively secure, I wasn't particularly concerned about that. I was sure that he'd see the funny side of my little jape. Ah, the crassness of youth.

Example of a 24 hour Ration Pack

The visit progressed nicely and the DG eventually arrived at my department, accompanied by the usual elongated line of millboard laden nodding flunkeys. After a spot of badinage with the chaps along the usual lines of "Wife in Quarters?" "Getting your LOA?" "Food alright?" etc, the DG mentioned the 24 hour Ration Pack to the CO, who mentioned it to the OC, who nodded in my direction, I nodded at the SQMS who sent a Corporal for the Ration Pack. The 24 hour ration pack duly appeared up the supply chain as if by magic. "Just happen to have one here, sir." The smug look on the OC's face clearly intimated that he was thinking something like – "I love it when a good plan comes together." He thought that things were going swimmingly. 'Watch and shoot...'

The 24 hour Ration Pack was handed to the DG, who then handed it to the accompanying Brigadier – "Open that up, 'Smithers' (*name changed to protect the innocent*) there's a good chap!" he commanded. The Brigadier, sweating profusely at this unexpected and complex task, finally managed to prise the box open and handed it back to the DG. The DG lifted the lid of the box and proceeded to have a good root around inside it. He paused momentarily and then, a la Paul Daniels, produced from the innards of the box a bunch of black, glistening, juicy grapes. "I say, how jolly clever – how do they manage to do that? Are they frozen or something?" he said. The DG looked questioningly at the Brigadier, who turned to the CO, who looked at the OC – the OC, with a fine bead of grey sweat adorning his upper lip, looked (rather furiously I thought) straight at me. "Quartermaster?" he said. Deathly silence for a very long minute whilst I thought of a career saving and brilliant riposte, but couldn't.

Suddenly, like a ray of sun breaking through the now stygian gloom, the DG smiled, something suspiciously phlegm-like rumbled in his chest then he began to guffaw heartily. "Captain Cavender, you're such a wag!" he said and continued laughing. The accompanying Brigadier, sensing that all was not lost, threw his head back, slapped his thigh, braying like a donkey, whilst the CO encouraged everyone else to join in the merriment. I was saved. As the party eventually departed for the Workshops, much to my relief, the Brigadier was heard to say to the OC, "Actually, old boy, just how do they manage to keep the grapes fresh?" ……

Later on that year I was instructed to organise a Lunch for the 'new' Brigade Commander, Brigadier Rupert Smith (eventually Lieutenant General Sir Rupert Smith KCB DSO OBE QGM) who was visiting the Squadron for the first time. We had to get this one right as you only get one chance to make a good first impression. The Brigadier's reputation preceded him, he was a brave and brilliant officer, well liked by all, approachable and all that sort of thing, but you had to be on your toes. He was known for asking pointed questions. I organised the Lunch with great care, a first class menu, good wine, chatting through everything with the Officers' Mess Manager etc. Lunch was to be held in the 'special' dining room of Hamm Station Officers' Mess, with vast quantities of good quality wine available ("Grapes picked from the south side of the NAAFI sir!"), the Dining Room knee deep in highly polished regimental silver, finest sparkling crystal, crisp red and white serviettes (Squadron colours) etc.

The Officers' Mess Manager had recently employed a couple of new members of staff who had been thoroughly briefed by him on the complexities of 'Silver Service' when serving food on auspicious occasions such as this. The Brigadier arrived, was welcomed into the Mess and after chatting with the Squadron's officers we all repaired to the Dining Room and sat down ready to tie on a nose-bag. Wine was taken, there was polite chat for an inordinate amount of time, then the Officer Commanding flashed me a steely glance, tapped his watch and nodded discreetly at the kitchen door indicating that I should go and see what the delay in serving the food was. I slipped away from the table and into the kitchen to investigate.

Juxtaposition is a very nice word and fitted the situation admirably. From the genteel chat and ambience of the Dining Room I entered a scene from Dante's Inferno; there was hell on! The Mess Manager's face was puce with rage and he was bordering on hysterical, hissing abuse at his staff. "You bunch of bloody incompetents! You'll never work in an Officers' Mess again!" stuff like that. I said something comforting along the lines of "Everything OK?" – which it clearly wasn't. He looked at me and said, "Sorry for the delay, food's arriving now, sir!" He nodded across to a hatch in the wall containing the Silent Waiter that was creaking its way down from the kitchen, situated directly above the dining room. The hatch to the silent waiter slid open to reveal – absolutely nothing. Like Mother Hubbard's Cupboard, it was bare. The Mess Manager went an ever deeper shade of puce, gibbering "I'll sort it, I'll sort it! Fucking useless cooks! Excuse me sir!" and thrashed off up to the kitchen at a great rate of knots.

I returned to the dining room, exuding a confidence that I didn't feel and whispered to the OC that lunch would be served very shortly. The Brigadier was having a rattling good old chat with the chaps and pretended that he hadn't noticed anything was amiss. After a few minutes, thankfully, the dining room door swung open and one of the new members of staff, a delightful young lady, entered the dining room carefully balancing a large silver platter containing copious amounts of sliced, juicy beef. At last, something was happening. The OC beamed with delight, crisis averted

As was the custom, the Brigadier being the senior guest, took priority and was served first. The young lady, whose very first 'Silver Service' Lunch it was, swept regally down the side of the dining table to where Brigadier Smith was sat, by this time smacking his lips, then grappled with a spoon and fork and expertly lifted a large juicy piece of beef, dripping with gravy (sauce if you went to Sandhurst) and placed it delicately directly onto the Brigadier's place mat. Alas someone had forgotten to put out the dinner plates. The young lady gazed at the place mat in abject horror, realising that she'd committed a faux pas. There was a stunned silence as we all sat there, agog. Now what?

The Brigadier looked around the table quizzically, then started to laugh. We all joined in. The poor girl scraped up the beef, gravy and placemat and exited stage left, puce with embarrassment. Seconds later, the Mess Manager rushed in with a replacement placemat and some plates, dealing the plates out swiftly like a pack of cards. Both order and dignity were restored, Silver Service resumed and a jolly good lunch was eventually had by all. The best laid plans of mice and men...... Notwithstanding, the Brigadier enjoyed himself immensely and much to our relief, nothing was said afterwards. The young lady recovered from the drama of her first 'Silver

Service' and went on to become a key member of the Officers' Mess staff.

There was one other occasion when we had a particularly good laugh, albeit it a bit school boyish. The current German Chancellor, Angela Merkel, when she was a much lesser but still important functionary, visited the Station Officers' Mess one day and we had a 'Gucci' Lunch laid on for her in the very impressive ballroom of the Mess.

German Chancellor, Angela Merkel

A small band was thrashing out German military style tunes up in the rather splendid minstrel's gallery above the ballroom throughout the meal, in honour of the occasion. Everything went swimmingly well until after lunch when the speeches began. Frau Merkel was welcomed into the Mess by the Station Commander and he said a few kind words. Frau Merkel gave a return speech that went down rather well. Unfortunately as she was speaking, the Padre, who was sat opposite her on the top table, swivelled around on his well polished leather dining chair and there followed a sound that can only be described as someone cracking off a long, ripe and mortifyingly juicy fart. After a momentary pause by Frau Merkel, possibly not believing her ears, then she continued speaking. The Padre oblivious to the lavatorial sound he had made, once more moved around in his chair and let out a further seemingly tremendous rasper. "Where 'ere you be, let your wind blow free. In church or chapel, let it rattle." Good old Padre.

Lesser beings, like me, who were sat at different tables in the Dining Room, had heard all this and of course hysterical sniggering broke out. We were trying our best to be polite and not laugh out loud, doing our utmost to appear to be listening raptly to Angela Merkel - but the Padre kept fidgeting in his seat and making fart-alike noises. Frau Merkel had gone to the trouble to learn an English joke and confidently told it. It was a great relief to us that she did so because we were able to laugh hysterically at it, which gave us an excuse to laugh out loud without causing offence and avoiding a diplomatic incident. She was delighted at the response to the joke's punch-line and everything else went swimmingly. Boys will be boys.

One incident, worthy of a mention, if only for historical purposes. Before World War 2, Hamm Station Officers' Mess had previously been an Annex of a larger German Army Officers' Mess. That particular Annex had been used by senior German Officers during World War Two and apparently had had a brothel attached for the use of their senior officers. They certainly knew how to do things in those days.

The Annex, apparently, was a favourite haunt of and had been visited by almost all of the Nazi hierarchy, Adolf, Heinrich, Hermann etc at one time or another just before and throughout the war. It was an impressive place. Solidly built, with a lovely ball-room, a dining room, a minstrels' gallery, huge windows and a magnificent crystal chandelier as a centre-piece to the ballroom. A delightful place that reeked of past Germanic 'glories.' The huge chandelier in the dining room could be easily lowered electronically for light bulbs to be replaced. In England we would have used a forty foot rickety ladder.

Late one particular evening, at the conclusion of a sparkling Ladies Dinner Night, we had all repaired to the main bar for post Dinner refreshments and were stood there bar in our respective finery i.e. mess kit for the chaps, flowing ball gowns for the ladies etc. A military Band was tootling away in the background, red and white candles (our squadron colours) fluttering in heavy silver candelabra, whilst white jacketed waiters flew around replenishing drinks, that sort of thing. Stood in the group at the bar was an oldish civilian male honorary mess member who had brought along his 'squeeze' for the evening. The lady was German, bordering on pissed, and although by now in her sixties and something of a stately galleon, had obviously been a bit of a looker in her time. She was dripping with sparkling jewellery and holding court, people paying her polite attention. In the Mess that evening were several Polish Officers' who were part of the Tank Transporter Squadron world, many of whom had served valiantly in World War 2. Frankly, there was still not a lot of love lost between the Poles and the Germans.

So, picture the German lady stood talking at the bar, with the British Officers and their ladies listening politely, Poles bristling on the periphery. For the purposes of the story, let's call the German lady – 'Brunhilde.'

Brunhilde: (*Tapping the bar with a liver-spotted, pudgy, bejewelled hand, in time with the military band that was playing something like 'Berliner Luft.'*). Ach, this is so wonderful boys! Ze dress uniforms, ze medals, ze decor, undt der ambience. It takes me back to the war. So many happy memories.

Officer: (*Feigning interest*) Oh, you were here during the war then, Brunhilde?

Brunhilde: Ja, Ja. I was much younger then of course but meine husband and I used this Officers'

Mess frequently. We had many wonderful nights here undt met many interesting people. For instance, I had the honour of being presented to der Fuhrer here on one occasion.

Officer: The Fuhrer. Oh really.

Brunhilde: Ja, you see my husband, Heini, was the Head of Gestapo here in Hamm.

Conversation in the bar petered out and silence descended as we all was sensed that this was going somewhere where it ought not to. Brunhilde was, meanwhile, drowning in distant memories of the Third Reich, a beatific smile on her face.

Brunhilde: My Heini was in charge of the (*pause*) - 'Jewish' problem. You know, that sort of thing, the Poles and all of the others that passed through Hamm during the war. That was of course before your RAF destroyed the rail yards. All that is behind us now.

Needless to say her comments were not well received, particularly by the Polish officers All thoughts of bonhomie rapidly disappeared from the bar area. Brunhilde had become about as popular as a fart in a space-suit. The Polish contingent were, shall I say, not best pleased and I sensed that violence was in the offing if Brunhilde didn't zip it, rapidly. Oblivious to the rapidly cooling atmosphere – she continued holding centre stage, failing to note the steely glances that she was attracting from our gallant Polish allies, and continued to dig herself deeper into a trench from which there could only be one escape.

Brunhilde: Meine Heini is, alas, no longer with us, but he took care of me and made sure that I had property and plenty of money to survive after the war. I'm sure you know what I mean,

Chentlementz! (*winking and tapping her nose with a beefy finger*).

By now a deathly silence descended had across the bar room. Our CO was stood at the bar listening to all this. Seething, he leant across to me and hissed through clenched teeth:

CO: Captain Cavender, get rid of that fucking creature. She is to leave the Mess immediately and the buffoon that brought her here is no longer a Mess Member! Remove them both!

Me: My pleasure, Colonel.

Delighted to do just that, I firmly clutched one of Brunhilde's bingo wings and without further ado escorted both her and her highly embarrassed paramour off the premises, she paused momentarily to collect her mink stole. As she swept out of the Mess, Brunhilde cried out:

Brunhilde: But I haven't finished my champagne, Herr Hauptmann! Ach, this would not have happened in ze good old days. Cherman officers knew how to behave in the presence of ladies!

Me: (*Easing Brunhilde and her paramour out of the door*) Well I'm not 'Cherman' and you're no lady! Ta Ta then. Oh – and er, don't come back here. Either of you!

Brunhilde and her highly embarrassed cohort disappeared into the night, never to darken the doorstep of Hamm Station Officers' Mess again. Order and dignity was restored although it took a little time for the Polish officers to calm down, their feathers had been well and truly ruffled. Brunhilde had reminded them of darker times. She shouldn't have been there in the Officer's Mess that night, but we had not been made aware of her background.

One of the Squadron officers, an old friend of mine, the legend Captain David Capper, decided one evening whilst we were sat at the bar in Hamm Station Officers' Mess having a few ales, that it would be a jolly spiffing wheeze if he went up to the room above the main bar, secured an abseiling rope to the central window supports and then swung down it entering into the bar, theatrically, through a large double window (open of course). He would then, Tarzan-like, land on the floor in front of the bar and quaff and ale whilst basking in the admiration from his fellow officers, mightily impressed at his derring do. Dave, very sports orientated and a fine golfer, had been organising some adventure training for the troops and had a suitable abseiling rope in his possession.

Copious amounts of the grape had been taken by this stage, which had a definite detrimental effect on Dave's logical thought processes. Undeterred off went Dave into the night and we waited in the bar to see what would happen.

Officers of 617 Tank Transport Squadron RCT
(Left to Right)
T C, Superintendent Kelvin Williams, Major Gerry Boyle, Lieutenant Stephanie McGowan, Captain Paul Baker, Captain David (Tarzan) Capper

The rope uncurled past the window, there was a loud Tarzan like yodel, we held our collective breath, a pair of feet appeared just below the top of the window and then down the rope slid Dave. There was a shriek of pain as he continued down the rope at speed, disappearing from view. He had forgotten to wear protective gloves and in the process of carrying out a daring abseil he had removed most of the skin from the palms of his hands. Dave returned to the bar later on that night with blistered and throbbing hands bandaged, to howls of laughter from his brother officers. What a good sport he was.

We didn't have British Forces Broadcasting Service (BFBS) Television in those days and had to make our own entertainment. Dave was a constant source of fun, laughter and games and is now enjoying a well earned retirement somewhere in Spain, hands fully recovered and no doubt clutching golf clubs on a daily basis. What a player!

When I was the Admin Officer at 617 Squadron, the Post Room NCO was Lance Corporal Robbie Robinson. Robbie was a most likeable character and a bit of a cheeky chappy. On one particular morning in the Headquarters he was getting a bit too lippy so I told him to go to the Guardroom and place himself in close arrest. Off he went and I thought no more about it. I was sat at home later on that evening, enjoying a beer, when the telephone rang. It was Robbie's wife Kim. She said that as her husband had been in the Guardroom all day, was it possible that he could come home now? Well, A: I had forgotten all about it - and B: I didn't imagine for one moment that Robbie would place himself in close arrest. I was mortified and without further ado I nipped around to the Guardroom, had him released and sent on his way rejoicing. Gulp! Robbie and Kim have settled locally here in East Yorkshire and he now works as a much respected Driving Instructor at the Defence School of Transport, Leconfield. I often bump into his wife Kim when out shopping and we laugh about it. I genuinely never meant for him to Jail himself though!

'WEST BERLIN'

I was fortunate enough to be given the opportunity to visit West Berlin with a 'train' of some 14 Tank Transporters, delivering tanks to Brook Barracks in Berlin. This necessitated travelling along the Berlin Corridor. The task was made more complex by the Russians who jealously guarded the border and closely scrutinised all of the complex paperwork and written authorities that were required for us to be allowed free passage. The Russians were difficult and obtuse and would unfailingly do their utmost to find errors in the paperwork so that they could deny us access to Berlin. Naturally we ensured that absolutely nothing was wrong with our paperwork and that we could proceed along our merry way accordingly. It was always a testing moment though.

We left Hamm and drove along the autobahn in a mightily impressive military convoy of 14 fully loaded Tank Transporters, a back-up 4 Tonner (REME) a Land Rover and me leading the charge in a glorious white Ford Escort, heading for Braunschweig. Our lads were professional and proficient drivers and I felt proud to be working alongside them. The lads were old hands at the game and worried not a jot, it was just 'another day at the office' for them. At Braunschweig, in accordance with standard procedure, we booked into an RMP post for the standard briefing regarding the complexities of travelling along the Berlin Corridor, had our paperwork thoroughly and efficiently checked then overnighted ready for an early start the following morning. The briefing and checks were key elements to our reaching Berlin, and designed to help avoid any confrontation at the border crossing post with the Russians, whose prime aims it appeared to be was to make things as difficult, complex and long winded as possible.

The following morning we 'First Paraded' our vehicles, ensured that the men had breakfasted and were OK, then carried out our radio checks. Radios were carried in both the leading and rear vehicles in the event that there was some sort of delay caused by mechanical breakdown etc. The bright young man manning the rear vehicle was Staff Sergeant Gaz Merrills, so we were definitely OK there. A breakdown would have delayed the arrival of the convoy in Berlin, which would have delighted the Russians no end as they could then cause a mega-fuss. We set off for the border crossing post. On arrival there we were placed into a lay-by whilst our paperwork was closely scrutinised by an eagle eyed Russian. The Russian Adjutant rolled up in some sort of clapped out jeep, belching fumes (the Jeep, not him), accompanied by his interpreter. We then exchanged ferocious military salutes and I answered the various questions that were fired at me, which I had been well briefed about and fielded accordingly.

The Russian Adjutant did his best to confuse me and put me off my stride but only succeeded in looking as if he was some knob from central casting in some 1950's movie. He pretended that he couldn't understand a word of English, but it was patently obvious that he could. He would address his interpreter in Russian, which would then be translated into English. I then replied back to him through the Interpreter. A long winded process. I could see the Adjutant reacting to my replies before they were translated back into Russian. It was typically sly and Slavonic. I was eventually informed that all of our paperwork was correct and that we could progress along the Berlin Corridor, but not until his Commanding Officer, a Colonel, had appeared and given us the final nod. Whilst we were waiting for their Colonel to appear, all of the British Military personnel were counted several times over, their ID's checked and rechecked. We waited impatiently for a further 30 or so minutes until another Jeep hove into view containing the Russian Colonel and his driver.

The Russian jeep roared to a stop in front of my gleaming white Ford Escort. There was much saluting as the Russian Colonel stomped around. I recall there being a distinct whiff of alcohol on his breath, the heels on his shoes were slightly worn down and there was a grease mark along the neck of his greatcoat. A bit seedy looking and not very impressive. There followed several semi-shouted conversations between Colonel and Adjutant (it seemed to me that the Adjutant was really the one in charge of the proceedings and that the Colonel was in fact his subordinate). Further salutes were exchanged and we were then allowed to proceed along the Berlin Corridor. I remember looking at the Border Guards who were, apparently, specially selected Russian soldiers. They were all six foot tall or so and immaculately turned out. The principle being, apparently, that as they were some of Russia's finest, they wouldn't leg it over the border to West Germany and its freedoms. As we passed them we waved, smiled and winked. We had no argument with them and it was an opportunity to prove to them that we were friendly. They were not allowed to respond in any way, to do so would have meant their immediate removal.

We were required to stick to a precise speed throughout the drive and had to arrive in Berlin at a specific time or questions would be asked by the Russians. Presumably this was in case we stopped to drop off several spies along the way. We arrived in Berlin without any fuss or bother, picked up our German Police escort and then swept through the city to Brook Barracks to deliver the tanks.

On arrival at Brook Barracks, I ensured that the tanks were delivered and off-loaded, the chaps were adequately billeted, fed and watered, then went across to the Officers' Mess where I had a room reserved. I won't name the Regiment, but the Mess Sergeant was very snooty and it was quite obvious that he didn't really want a mere transport officer despoiling the atmosphere of his Officers' Mess. He was patently used to much classier beings. I cared not a jot, I held the Queen's Commission and that was good enough for me. He took my overnight bag from me as if it contained some unmentionable medical specimen and escorted me to my room. "Will you be joining us for Dinner, sir?" he enquired. I informed him that I wouldn't. I'd been invited out for a drink with my chaps. "Anywhere nice, Sir?" he asked. I took great pleasure in telling him that we were going for a jar or two in a nightclub called the 'Mon Cherie' in Charlottenburg (know to the troops as 'Grotty Charlotty'). He sniffed, somewhat disparagingly and deposited my bag in a room the size of a broom cupboard where I was destined to spend the night. He then he departed back to the palace kitchens and into history without so much as a glance in my direction.

Ah, the 'Mon Cherie' night club, a name that is well known to the troops. Dressed in casual attire I leapt onto the 'U' Bahn and sped off to shady Charlottenburg. I entered the club to meet up with the chaps. What a seedy dive it was, but it oozed character. I sat at the bar and ordered a beer, costing the better part of a smallish mortgage. There was a small stage at the front of the club upon which there was unmentionable activity taking place between a jaded young couple (not too much detail here, my daughter will be reading this). I sat at the bar chatting with one of my Staff Sergeants who had promised to keep a beady eye on the troops throughout the night. As I sipped my beer I noticed that strangely I was surrounded by six foot Korean Transvestites, all looking exactly alike and wearing silver pop wigs. It was all very surreal but fascinating. I gripped my beer stein and began to wonder if it was a wise move me being there.

The young couple left the stage to a smattering of impolite applause and then there was a ten minute or so pause in activity before loud pop music began blasting through the speaker. The stage lights came back on – and to my amazement a large piece of the stage, right in its centre, lifted up like a lavatory lid, revealing a foam filled bath. I was intrigued. The troops were wildly excited by this time and were, whooping, cheering and applauding etc. A naked young maiden appeared onstage, waggled her bits at the audience and then slid into the foam, smiling seductively at the troops.

A volunteer was called for from the audience to join her in the bubble bath. We had a mega-butch Australian Sergeant attached to us at the time and he had his kit off within seconds, elbowing all of the other interested parties out of the way, sprinting down to the front of the nightclub to the foot of the stage. He was stark bollock naked and covered in butch tattoos. Jumping up onto the stage to much cheering from the troops, he dove manfully into the bath - to further enthusiastic cheers from the by now mightily pissed audience. Several of the British troops who he'd beaten to the stage put their clothes back on and returned disappointedly to their seats.

There then followed a cleverly devised game whereby the young maiden slid around the bath, taunting the Australian Sergeant, who did his utmost to try and enter her hallowed portals. Such was her expertise though that he didn't stand a chance as she tormented him to distraction. The troops applauded wildly, cheering him on. There was flashing coloured lights, loud pop music, foam and bare flesh everywhere. You couldn't write it (but I'm trying to). Eventually the Aussie cornered the girl and his huge, bare Aussie tattooed arse rose from the soap suds, ready to plunge forward and do the dirty deed. At that precise moment, enter stage left another naked maiden, clutching a beer bottle.

She leant across the bath, leered at the audience and then proceeded to tickle the Australian on a rather sensitive part of his body where the sun didn't normally shine. He shrieked with outrage and took great offence, turning around and smacking her straight in the mouth with an Aussie fist as big as a bunch of banana's. She was sent spinning and fell into the bath, sinking majestically beneath the waves. At this, all hell broke loose. Several very mean looking bouncers, male and female, appeared and a massive fight broke out. Chairs and tables going over, struggling bodies, swearing, meaty blows were exchanged – for all intents and purposes it was just like something out of a 'Wild West' cowboy movie. It was brilliant, highly amusing, colourful and memorable.

I was sat at the bar sipping my beer and thinking that perhaps it was a bad idea for me to remain in this dubious establishment for very much longer. My lads were all big enough and old enough to enjoy the remainder of the evening without my presence, so I finished my beer, ducked the odd flying bar stool, blew several theatrical kisses to the Korean transvestites and departed into the night, making my way back to Brook Barracks, admittedly with a great sense of relief.

The 'Mon Cherie' Night Club- Charlottenburg, Berlin

The following morning I held a working parade at about 0900 hours, just to check that all my lads had returned safely, which fortunately they had. They were stood there on the parade square sporting black eyes, fat lips and various bruises but all present and correct, much to my relief. Later on that day we readied ourselves for the return journey home, via the Berlin Corridor, which was – Ladies and Gentlemen, not to be without incident.

Our convoy rolled up to the Berlin RMP post, where we were issued our instructions, paperwork and two new types of radio. I had a radio in the lead vehicle and Gaz Merrills in the rear vehicle of our convoy had the other. We carried out our various radio checks, picked up the German police escort and headed off into the wild blue yonder. I should point out at this stage that we were required to carry out radio checks with the Royal Military Police (RMP) over in the West, throughout the journey along the corridor. We were unable to do that because once we'd got a few kilometre's along the corridor, the radios malfunctioned. We couldn't really stop because of the time constraints so continued along as best we could.

Halfway across the corridor we were met by an RMP vehicle containing a driver and a simply fizzing RMP Major, face puce with anger, who halted the convoy and asked me why I hadn't contacted his HQ by radio. I told him that the radios weren't working. "Ah," he said "Not the old – the radio's aren't working ploy! You are not complying with procedures and have caused a major incident between us and the Russians." I told him to stop talking bollocks, which didn't go down too well. I repeated that although the radios weren't working we were precisely on time and would have been at the border crossing in short order. He grabbed at the radio in my vehicle and said that he would carry out his own radio check, obviously disbelieving me.

My driver, Corporal 'Spy' Hummel, had eaten a ferocious curry the night before and the inside of my vehicle stank of garlic. As the RMP Major put his head inside the vehicle he visibly blanched. I'd made Spy drive for the majority of the journey with his head stuck out of the window because he stank so badly. His breath would have blistered paint. After the Major had farted around with the radio for a few minutes, trying to contact his Headquarters in the West for a radio check, he found that like me, he couldn't raise a squeak out of it. He then noticed that a vital component was missing from the radio – the ariel. A gleam of triumph spread across his face, "You haven't got a fucking ariel on the radio, man," he said icily.

I replied that I didn't know that we had to have that type of 'fucking ariel' on the radio and couldn't be expected to know that. It was a new piece of equipment and it hadn't been mentioned when we collected the radios from the RMP post in West Berlin that a particular ariel was required. At the start of our journey I had carried out a radio check between me and the rear vehicle, as per standard operating procedure. The radios had worked just fine. We had then tried to carry out the series of required radio checks with the RMP as we progressed, but couldn't do so. It wasn't possible to turn the convoy around and return to West Berlin, so I decided that we would continue and complete the journey in the time allowed.

"Right!" Major Basil Fawlty barked, "I'll have the bastard's bollocks who issued you these radios. Who was it?" he enquired. "Your Adjutant!" I replied. He blushed bright red and mumbled something along the lines of, "Right, fucking right, he's in deep shit! Get your convoy to follow my vehicle and I'll escort you back to the West!" I gently reminded him that he was addressing a fellow commissioned officer, that I did not like his attitude and would be reporting him to my Commanding Officer once I returned to my unit. We departed for the West an air of doom and gloom hanging over us. I made Spy Hummel drive with his head out of the window again because he was making me feel ill.

On arrival at the RMP post in West Germany, once again we overnighted there before setting off for Hamm the following morning. I ensured that the troops were properly billeted, fed and watered etc before retiring to my cubby hole. Later on in the evening I was sat, brooding in my room when a knock came on the door. It was an RMP Sergeant. He threw up a magnificent salute. "OC's compliments sir, he would like to see you in his office." "OK," I replied. The Sergeant stood there expecting me to drop everything and accompany him there and then. I instructed him to bugger off and that I'd make my own way to the OC's office when I was good and ready. He blushed delicately, took a pace to the rear, saluted once again and minced off. I'd had enough of being mucked about by the Redcaps.

After a respectable pause I made my way to the OC's office, expecting yet another bout of his un-officer like shouting and rudeness but I was to be pleasantly surprised. He couldn't have been nicer, offering me a glass of whiskey and giving me a guided tour of the facilities on the post, which included showing me the special telephone that he assured me had a direct link to Downing Street. We became best buddies and I assured him that I wouldn't be speaking to my Commanding Officer about our previous confrontation, (I'd had no intention of doing so anyway). The following morning we prepared to set off for Hamm and back to normality. The RMP Major was up and about to wave us off, smiling benevolently as we departed. Lots of saluting going on. The sun was shining and my spirits lifted. The perfect end to a perfect weekend.

I returned to Berlin the following year with my wife Maggie and a couple of our friends. This time though, we travelled there on the Berlin Military Train. Because of the Berlin Military tattoo, (a parade not an adornment), accommodation was at a premium and we were obliged to stay at a place called the 'Hotel Gribnitz,' which was undoubtedly on its last legs and appeared to have remained unchanged, including the sheets, from World War Two. We were allocated rooms right at the top of the hotel, requiring the use of a very slow and creaky elevator. It was just like something out of a 1950's spy film.

We did the usual touristy things in Berlin culminating with a visit to a nightclub (not in Charlottenburg I hasten to add). We stood outside the famous 'Kit Kat' nightclub where the film Cabaret was made and decided that because the entrance fee was inordinately expensive, disappointingly decided that we'd have to give it a miss. At that moment, however, a bus full of Japanese tourists drew up and lots of Japanese leapt off it, forming a queue behind someone gesticulating with an umbrella and were then waved towards the entrance of the nightclub. On the spur of the moment we cheekily tagged on behind them and astoundingly got in for nothing. Terribly British. We were shown to a premier table at the side of the stage, handed a bottle of champagne, nicely chilled in an ice bucket, and settled down to enjoy the cabaret. Drinks and small eats kept arriving at our table and we had a spiffing night, which included being invited up onto the stage and doing the hokey cokey with a group of very gay dancers. So much for being low profile.

We finished of the champers and made our excuses, leaving before the Germans realised that we weren't in fact Japanese and had blagged our way in to enjoy a most memorable 'freebie.' In retrospect, they probably presumed that I was a Sumo wrestler with friends? Well, after the last 'nastiness – '39 to 45' the least that the Germans and Japanese could do was provide us with an evening's entertainment and refreshment at their expense. One up for my Dad and his mates.

At the end of the evening we returned, replete, to our rooms in the 'Hotel Gribnitz' and hit our respective sacks. We were unable to get to sleep for quite some time because there were two males (either that or females with very deep voices) hard at it, whatever 'it' was, accompanied by lots of bed creaking, accompanied by guttural German gasps and groans, 'Mein Gott schatzie, das ist gut, neh?" "Jawhoul meine liebchen!" that sort of thing. It didn't paint a pretty picture and went on for far too long until eventually my wife Maggie lost all patience and hammered on the wall of the adjacent room, shouting, quite unintentionally, "Will you two buggers (!) shut up and get to sleep!" Silence descended throughout the hotel and we drifted off into der Land of Nod.

The following morning at breakfast, everyone was sat in the dining room of the Hotel Gribnitz, scoffing a full European, nodding and being exceedingly polite to each other. Two German males were sat at their own table eating their breakfasts.

Maggie went across to their table, doing her frighteningly accurate Miss Marples impression, and said something along the lines of, "You were very inconsiderate last night gentlemen, decent people were trying to get some sleep, you know!" They looked puzzled, but nevertheless apologised for being noisy and guiltily continued eating. I did the nodding dog act, adding some theatrical "Hear hear, outrageous!" comments as I sat dipping my soldiers into a lightly boiled egg. It was evident that, fortunately, the Germans clearly hadn't any idea what Maggie was talking about and we sat there blushing profusely when their wives came into the breakfast area and joined them for a spot of scran. Wrong guys. When we left we gave them lots of nice smiles and several 'Auf Wiedersehens.' Goodness knows what they thought. If you're reading this, meine freunds, sorry about that little misunderstanding. Ah, another memorable weekend in Berlin.

My wife Maggie and I drove over to Berlin last year for a long weekend, just to see how things had changed since the 'Wall' had been torn down and the Russians had departed. It seemed rather strange being able to drive straight into Berlin without out all the drama's of over-excessive documentation checks, border posts and sinister looking Russian border guards. Also it seemed equally strange being able to drive freely into East Berlin without that feeling of being watched over all the time. The air of gloom and depression had lifted, palpably. There was a great deal of rebuilding going on and the city was well on its way to being reunited. Check Point Charlie had, however, turned into just another trashy tourist spot, which was disappointing.

Notwithstanding, we had a very pleasant stay, the Berliners making us feel most welcome. I recall though, that when we booked into our hotel, not the 'Gribnitz' this time but something more salubrious in the 'Zoo' area, my wife Maggie went across to the very smart and efficient looking female hotel receptionist and enquired, politely, in German, "Excuse me, do you speak English?" The lady drew herself up to her full height, stared at Maggie and said, icily, "Of course I speak English!" They'll be back.

We had a really pleasant stay in Berlin. It was nice being able to walk completely around and through areas like the Brandenburg Gate unhindered, when in the 'old' days it would certainly have attracted rifle fire had you attempted it. Berlin is a brilliant place to visit and 'Grotty Charlotty' is still there peddling its mischief. I suppose that every large city in the world has an area like it. I'm sure that we'll go back for a further visit.

'GAY PARIS'

Being travellers of international repute, we decided to visit France, taking in Paris, which as we all know boys and girls, is a beautiful city and should be visited whenever you get the opportunity to do so. I've been there several times with the Memsahib and each time it was tremendous fun. There's always an air of the exotic about Paris and always something to do or see. My very first visit there was a few years ago with my wife Maggie, accompanied by my brother and sister-in-law. We had a brilliant time in the Loire Valley in a truly ancient and beautiful Gite then proceeded on to Paris for a couple of days at the end of the holiday, wrapping things up nicely.

An Army colleague of mine had mentioned to me that there was a superb Officers Club in central Paris and that we should make the effort to go there for an overnight stay on our way home from a week or so of ligging in the Loire Valley. Sounded like a good idea and rather a nice way to finish our holiday off, I thought. Kindly, my amigo volunteered to book us into the Officers' Mess as he'd stopped off there several times and thoroughly enjoyed the experience. We received a message from him that the actual Officers' Club in central Paris was fully booked that particular weekend, but 'Nil Desperandum,' he'd managed to reserve accommodation for us in the Annex of the Officers' Club, still in central Paris and sited near Montmatre. Montmatre, if you don't know, is a little like London's Soho, but we didn't know that at the time.

We left the delightful Loire Valley after a having had a great time looking around, meeting the locals and supping copious amounts of wine, then driving sedately into Paris. Meandering through Paris is an adventure in itself , but my brother is a superb driver and we eventually arrived at the Officers'

Club safe and sound. When we pulled up outside the Officers' Mess Annex, which was tucked away down a non-salubrious side street, I volunteered to go and get us booked in etc. After all, I was a serving officer and as it was an Officers' Club I thought that it might ease our passage. I entered the building, oozing confidence, and sashayed over to the reception desk. Sat behind the desk was a swarthy little gentleman attired in full Arab dress. Quite naturally, as Paris is very cosmopolitan, I thought nothing of it. In cruelly strangled, schoolboy French, I introduced myself and asked about the availability of our rooms.

The Arab gentlemen looked at me, fluttered his rather long eyelashes, pursed his lips and then answered my query in rather fey English:

Receptionist: "Bonjour Monsieur le Capitaine, hai speek h'English. Chest a leedle moment."

He ran a forefinger, his, down a long list. He had rather long finger-nails and too many rings for a chap I thought, but – hey-ho, this was Paris.

Receptionist: Ah oui, we 'ave rooms book-ed pour vous.

For some strange reason I then morphed into Noel Coward speak.

Me: Oh, that's quite excellent. Is there somewhere for us to park our limousine?

Receptionist: Certainement! Leave her outside by le pavement. Everything weel be er kay. Please bring in the remainder of your partay and ai weel process your passports etc. Oh Monsieur - bon pantalons! *(Nice trousers*)

As gay as a blade (him not me). Still, it takes all sorts. I got the others from the car and we entered the establishment, hefting our suitcases. I had been informed that:

Receptionist: Unfortunately, Monsieur le Capitaine, there is hay shortage of le staff and you will 'ave to carry your own loogage oop le stairs, n'est-ce pas?

Me: (*Miffed*) Well then, we'll just have to manage, won't we.

Receptionist: You 'ave rooms on the top flair. I'm afraid that we do not have le elevateur in the annex.

We were then handed our room keys and pointed in the direction of the stairs. Still, we were in Paris, on holiday (albeit the last few days) and were in fine fettle and could easily manage a couple of stairs. So off we toddled to the stairs and started to climb. As we got higher, the stair carpets gradually turned from lush rich red into threadbare matting and then finally, faded linoleum. Eventually we reached what must have been the attic of the Officer's Mess annex and found our rooms.

As I stood fiddling with our room key, a door directly opposite ours opened and out stepped a French officer and, I kid you not, he was dressed in some sort of formal Legionnaire style dress uniform. He looked for all the world like Peter Sellars in some wild scene from a Pink Panther movie. I glanced into his room and saw that it was furnished in what I can only describe as being something like you would imagine a late 1960's knocking shop style. Lots of purple chaise longue and heavy curtaining, seductive lighting, that type of thing. He nodded in our direction and said 'Hair Lair', then turned and called into his room, "Au revoir, ma petit fleur!" A gravelly voice replied "Au Revoir, mon Colonel!" Now, just between ourselves, the voice that replied from the depths of the Colonel's bedchamber was rather on the gruff side (obviously a heavy smoker) and gave us pause for thought. Did the Colonel dance from the other side of the ballroom? Mon Colonel lit a smelly Gauloise cigarette, winked at Maggie, closed the door and marched off down the stairs.

This was all turning into something rather unusual. We eventually managed to get into our room, which was, to say the least, a little on the seedy side. We weren't too bothered as it was all part of our holiday. The Memsahib checked the bed out, as they always do, noting that the bedspread was a little threadbare and had several cigarette burns, although the bedding was clean. There was the odd bit of well worn carpeting on the floor and, the window wouldn't open but hey – we were on holiday and it was all a bit of fun. Maggie said to me, "What's this at the side of the bed?" I looked and saw a small metal box with a slot for coins. That'll be for the TV, I suppose, I replied knowingly. So I was instructed to fire the TV up and we could perhaps catch a bit of news whilst we were unpacking.

I slid a few centimes (those were pre-Euro days my friends) into the box and switched the TV on. Of its own volition, the bed started to shake, at first rather slowly and then at a fair rate of knots. "What on earth...." Maggie looked at me, I gave her a Gallic shrug and opined that it was probably a device to help one sleep. Our room was decidedly seedy, the windows grimy and there was just a suspicion of damp – (but enough of the mattress). In essence It felt like we were appearing in a scene from 'Day of the Jackal.'

Wife: Bloody hell, where have you brought us? This can't possibly be an Officers' Mess. What's your brother going to think!

Me: Make the best of it my treasure. We're only here for one night and we're in central Paris – and it's not overly expensive.

Wife: It's a bloody knocking shop, that's what it is! I suppose we'll just have to make do. I'm booking the hotel next time!

There was that special sort of silence that lasted for a few minutes as we got showered and changed, met up with my brother and sister-in-law, then proceeded down le boulevard looking for a decent restaurant. The H'Officers Mess Annex was not serving food that evening because of le staff shortages, although if we wished, they could probably knock us up a couple of le sandwiches. The Receptionist smiled a coy smile and said something about 'Le Rosbifs' which we ignored. Knowing our luck there would quite probably have been horse-meat involved.

We declined the offer of sarnies and went out into Montmatre seeking some decent scoff. For those that haven't had the chance to visit there, Montmatre is very colourful with lots going on and we easily found a nice restaurant, where we had a lovely meal, washed down with copious amounts of edgy vin rouge. The staff there were really attentive and pleasant and the cost of the meal and wine was not at all bad. We were expecting to be ripped off as it was central Paris, but it was quite the opposite. Eventually we tottered off back to the Officers' Mess Annex for what we hoped would be a decent night's kip, before setting off the following morning for Angleterre.

To our immense disappointment, we'd been informed that:

Receptionist: There is ner breakfast to be 'ad, Monsieur le Capitaine. Alas, staff shortages - and also it is le weekend (*lots of Gallic style shrugs*).

We cared not a jot, we could always 'mange' something en route. Off we tottered to our rooms, lots of jokes about Sherpa Tensing and the climb up the south face of Mount Everest. Screaming for oxygen and lathered, we eventually reached our rooms where we hit the sack. I decided not to put any more centimes into the magic metal box and we drifted off into Le Land of Nod. The following morning I informed my Mistress that I would go down to reception, recover our Passports, settle the bill and book us out, whilst she finished packing her suitcase, (which was the size of a small sideboard).

I left to make the epic journey down the several flights of stairs carrying my suitcase. As I maneuvered my way around the corner on the last flight of stairs, things went slightly awry. I had failed to notice previously that on the wall there was mounted a large full length mirror. Mistaking what was my own image and thinking that someone was coming up the stairs, I moved to one side, lost my footing and crashed down the remainder of the steps, followed closely by my suitcase, tumbling in a most ungentlemanly fashion, base over apex, into the reception area cursing like an SS Storm Trooper.

Everything on my body was stinging and I was a little embarrassed and ashamed of my dramatic entrance. A French family, avec several enfants, stood at the reception desk in shocked silence as I stood up, brushed myself off and pretended that I wasn't injured. I smiled and inexplicably said those immortal lines:

Me: Morning everyone, er, pardon my French!

I blushed and joined the queue. It was patently obvious that the children were now very afraid of this strange, sweating Englishman and drew closer to the bosom of their Mother. She made it quite obvious that not only was I a lunatic but that my breath obviously whiffed of garlic or stale wine (which it probably did) by furiously waving a handkerchief under her nose. I tried not to breathe on anyone. The French family booked out, les enfants looking at me as if I was going to kidnap them and sell them into slavery. The stinging from my fall reduced a little, but there was definite swelling in several areas and I knew that my knees had been skinned (lino burns). It was not a particularly good start to my day.

The fey receptionist, who never seemed to sleep, looked at me and smiled, delicately:

Receptionist: Ah, Capitaine le Cavandier, you 'ave enjoyed your stay in Paris, oui?

Me: *(Waspish – reverted to Noel Coward speak again)* It's Cavender, actually, and yes, it's all been most memorable, merci beaucoup.

Receptionist: And your rooms?

Me: What about them?

Receptionist: They were, er, satisfactory?

Me: *(Caring not a jot by this stage)* Passable, I suppose, Monsieur. We've stayed in better.

Receptionist: Bon! A moment and I will get your Passports from le safe.

Me: Oh, and our bill please.

Receptionist: Ah, but Monsieur le Capitaine, that has already been settled.

Me: *(Puzzled)* Really, when?

Receptionist: When your rooms were originally booked. I personally took the reservation and payment. Your friend sounded very nice, a Scottish man I think.

Me: Oh I know who that was. Well, if that's all sorted, we must fly.

Receptionist: Ah, you are driving to the h'airport?

Me: No, no, it's just a phrase.

Receptionist: A phase?

Me: No, no – a Phrase! Oh, look, just hand me our Passports and we'll get out of your way.

Receptionist: Certainement, Monsieur le Capitaine.

The remainder of the h'English party had arrived at the reception desk from the upper regions. They too were overhung and lathered.

Receptionist: Good moaning Ladies and Chentlemen. I trust that you 'ave 'ad a good stay? - any complaints before you depart le h'Officers' Mess h'Annex?

Wife: Yes, you might want to get a bloody lift installed in this flop house! Those stairs are treacherous.

Receptionist: But of course, My Lady, actualement that is in 'and.

The military friend who'd reserved the rooms for us had obviously paid for them at the same time, which was rather nice of him. He and his wife were supposed to be meeting up with us in Paris for an evening's festivities, but his unit in Germany had been 'Active Edged' and he couldn't make it to Paris. I never did work out if he'd deliberately booked us into the French Officers' Mess Annex as a wheeze. I wouldn't have put it beyond him as he had a wicked sense of humour. We placed the suitcases into our limo and left for the coast, traversing several times around the centre of Paris on the accursed, lengthy and unfathomable 'Peripherique'(the French version of the M25) before finding le correct escape route, and seeking out along the way somewhere where we could obtain a reviving breakfast. So it was 'Au revoir Paris until le next time!'

One of my many additional roles whilst serving as the Unit Quartermaster of 617 Tank Transporter Squadron RCT was what was described as 'The Budgie Strangler.' In the event of the Russian hordes descending on West Germany, Cromwell Barracks, Hamm in particular, the military families would have to be evacuated rather rapidly from Hamm by railway train. This would be done by transporting them to the nearest railway station in Hamm, where specified trains would be waiting to take them to Europort or some other similar port of departure.

In the meantime I had in my stores a cunningly designed mobilisation destruction kit consisting of a sledgehammer, a Jerrycan full of petrol and a box of waterproof matches. The sledgehammer was to be used to destroy any vehicles left in barracks – presumably by knocking seven bells out of the engine blocks, it was also to be used to destroy anything useful in the billets like lavatories, water supplies, electrical equipment etc. The matches were to be used to set fire to anything that would burn, to deny any use to the enemy (curtains)?

Destroying the lavatories was particularly cunning. Having no cludgies would cause terrible inconvenience to the Russian hordes. Me and my loyal staff also had the potential terrible task of having to destroy any family pets that had been left behind, dogs, cats, rabbits, budgies, goldfish, horses etc. It was important that we prioritised and didn't destroy the lavatories before getting rid of the goldfish because we could then just flush them away, at least giving them a bit of a chance. These things are important morale factors in war. Luckily the Russian decided not to invade whilst we were there so the barracks, vehicles, families and family pets remained safe.

Maggie and I called into the grounds of what was the beloved Hamm Station Officers' Mess whilst passing through Hamm last year only to find that it is now being used as a civilian hospital. There were hospital beds in what was the bar area, leading through to what had been the ballroom. Could have been worse, Cromwell Barracks had been virtually levelled and was being used for parking buses. Another precious memory bubble burst. They say never to go back.

We did, however, go and have a look at our old married quarter, which is still there, although it's now occupied by three local families! Whilst there we recalled an occasion when we'd been invited to Dinner by our immediate neighbours. Living next door to us at the time was a highly polished and erudite Major of, I think, the Blues and Royals and his lovely wife. They were very top drawer, (his God Mother was the Queen Mother), so goodness knows what they thought about living next door to a vulgar Corpsman.

A really nice and approachable bloke, he kept inviting us to go to his house for Dinner which, to be perfectly honest we did our utmost to avoid, ducking and diving because we thought that we might be a bit uncomfortable and out of place mixing with people from that level of society (well I did, my wife Maggie fits in anywhere). We were asked once more and not wishing to offend, decided to go for the dreaded Dinner.

On the appointed evening, we dressed appropriately and meandered next door. His Officers Married Quarter (OMQ) was furnished beautifully throughout with lots of antique and obviously very valuable furniture. Their dining room table was laid out with solid silver cutlery (with family crest), the finest crystal, wine decanted into Queen Anne silver wine jugs and suchlike. The little circular butter dishes filled with butter had been impressed with the family crest. Everything was quality. We were bordering on panic but shouldn't have worried, as we were made to feel extremely welcome and enjoyed ourselves. After a sumptuous Dinner the ladies 'repaired' to the front room, whilst the chaps, me and the Major remained in the dining room for a bit of 'When I' and a glass of port whilst the Major puffed luxuriantly on an expensive and very smelly cheroot. He then invited me to "come down to the cellar and view my model railway set", which rather suspiciously I thought might be a euphemism for something else. Of course, his intentions were entirely honourable.

Down in the cellar, which was rather large, was laid out a huge train set stretching the length of his house. It was brilliant, all of the signals worked, all the sounds were realistic and there was smoke everywhere. He'd even had holes cut in the skirting board so that the trains could pass through unhindered. A lads dream - and we played with it for as long as we dared. It was time to depart. In the Majors front room was a beautiful Queen Anne table (Queen Anne had a lot to answer for) upon which were displayed several exquisite and delicate antique snuff boxes and some pill boxes, a couple of which, apparently, were Fabergé.

As my wife Maggie turned to leave, the bottom of her dress flared out, I panicked and I thought that the delicate items were going to be swept from the table and destroyed. Leaping forward to prevent her dress from brushing the items, I inadvertently kicked the lip of the table and all of the very expensive and delicate artefacts hurtled into the air. Time stood still and everything went into slow-motion as we all made a grab for them. Fortunately all were caught and replaced on the table. The Major and his wife thought that this was really hilarious and were hysterical with laughter. They cared not a jot. We were lathered and once we got home and calmed down, aided by a stiff drink, saw the funny side. How the other half lives! They were a lovely, kind and generous couple and we felt fortunate to have been invited.

One more little tale from Hamm. The local Stadt authorities had decided that the cobbles outside the front gate of the Cromwell Barracks needed repairing which meant that entrance and exit to the barracks via the main gate would not be available to us for about a week. There was, however, another gate at the rear of our camp that we could use but which led through a German Medical Unit's, (our immediate neighbours), barracks. We had a meeting with the Germans to seek their permission to use the rear gate and pass through their barracks until such time as the road repairs had been completed and things could return to normal. Chairing the meeting was the German Commanding Officer, a full Colonel. He was tall, authoritative and the epitome of what you would imagine a German Colonel to be.

During the course of the very correct meeting a German Major asked me, in my capacity as Quartermaster, if it had been ascertained that our Commander Tank Transporters would fit through the rear gate. I hadn't checked that particular aspect as I thought that it would have fallen into the remit of our Transport Control Officer, who wasn't at the meeting. So I replied, sounding more confident than

I felt, "Of course they will!" He then asked me if I was certain, whereupon the German Colonel slapped his hand onto the desk and the room went very quiet. The Colonel shouted, "Major, if ze Quartermaster says they will fit – zen zey vill fit!" That ended the conversation.

At the conclusion of the meeting and when no-one was watching, I sneaked over to the rear gates with my Squadron Quartermaster Sergeant (SQMS), Staff Sergeant Alan Hayward, who had obtained a tape measure. We measured the width of the gates versus the width of one of our Commander Tank Transporter's and were relieved to find that we had four inches to spare on each side of the vehicle. Phew! - 'Bullshit Baffles Brains.' And that, Ladies and Gentlemen, is why we won the war.

My joyful times with 617 Tank Transporter Squadron couldn't go on forever though and eventually I was posted to the Army School of Mechanical Transport (ASMT), later the Defence School of Transport (DST) at Normandy Barracks, Leconfield, East Yorkshire, an old RAF base.

Army School of Mechanical Transport/Defence School of Transport *(as a Major – Officer Commanding the Licence Acquisition Division)*

I was appointed Officer Commanding the Licence Acquisition Division of the Driver Training Wing, responsible for hundreds of driver training vehicles, some 'green' the others, in the main, Ryder Truck Rental hire-fleet.

It was certainly a totally different life to that experienced in the much missed world of Tank Transporters. At Leconfield I was tucked away in a miserable little office, situated in a gloomy Hangar and seeming to spend most of my life attending interminable meetings to discuss riveting issues like mileages covered by training vehicles, fixed master variable something or other and the like. Sorry chaps, important as it all was, it did not fire my rockets. I didn't like it and knew that in my heart of hearts it would probably be my last posting. My enthusiasm had definitely waned, although hopefully I never allowed that to show in public. I was still receiving the 'Queen's Shilling' and being paid a good wage. I always tried to give it my best shot.

Fortunately for me, at Leconfield I was surrounded by a magnificent bunch of men and women, both civilian and military, helping me to survive various traumas and days of crashing boredom until decided to hang up my well stretched stable belt and call it quits. I knew that the end was nigh one day when the latest instruction filtered down from the Headquarters directing that we had to start working out how many miles we could get out of the different types of tyre on our many different types of hire vehicle. You yawning yet? I was. Stultifying. It wasn't what I had been put on this earth to do and I decided that it was therefore time for me to head into the sunset. I applied for the redundancy package that was being dangled before us at the time and was fortunate enough to be selected for the first tranche. My military days were definitely numbered.

One's last day in military uniform was spent inspecting the huge morning working parade. I was accompanied throughout the inspection by a damn fine friend, cavalry officer Major Don Willson, who was also, like me, departing on redundancy. We inspected the hundreds of students who were there on the parade and then stood on the back of two trucks before being driven at a funereal pace with great drama and received a rousing three tear-jerking cheers from the assembled troops, out of the aircraft hangar that was Driver Training Wing. Whenever I see a military parade on TV from North

Korea it reminds me of it. Once outside the hangar we transferred to a white Rolls Royce (Don Willson and I paid for it out of our own pockets) and then did a couple of circuits around the base, waving regally like two old queens. We asked our chauffeur to drive us past the Headquarters a couple of times where we both joyfully fired off a series of 'Reverse Churchills' at the building before departing to the Officers' Mess for a spiffingly nice late Breakfast – our duty to Queen and Country finally and honourably completed. A sad day but one that comes to all of us. One day – 'Mr Importance,' the next day – "Didn't you used to be ...."

'BEYOND THE DST'

I'd joined the Army at 15, that's 15 years, not 1915, (committing myself to a 22 year engagement, scratchily signing the paperwork at Bradford Recruiting Office with quill and ink when I was a mere stripling of some 14 and ¾'s) and had had, as a result of my Dad's foresight and a great deal of hard work and good fortune, a respectable career. Can you say 'had had?' My Dad, a wise old bird and an ex-Serviceman himself, had insisted that I join the Royal Army Service Corps (RASC). When I asked him why the RASC, he'd said – "I'm not having you walking to war, son!" His memories of the failed Norway expedition presumably coming into play.

I'd had a spiffingly good time in the Army, made a lot of friends along the way, met a fair few lunatics (they know who they are), a few enemies (I know who they are and I haven't forgotten them) and served with plenty of fair-weather colleagues. Best of all though, early on in my career I met my lovely wife (Maggie) and we'd had (rather Maggie had had) our beautiful daughter (Sara). By the time I was tottering towards the end of my time with the Army, our little team had been all over the world and we thought that it was high time to do the decent thing and settle down in one place. So that was precisely what we did - and why we were washed ashore initially in Hull, before moving on to the delightful little market town of Beverley in the East Riding of Yorkshire.

Throughout my Army career, I'd always been involved writing, producing, directing and participating in variety shows, pantomimes, unit smokers, also did quite a bit of voice over work and scripting adverts for the British Forces Broadcasting Service (BFBS) Cologne whilst in West Germany and things like that. I even appeared on 'Blankety Blank' (a somewhat circuitous and sly route which enabled me to get a look inside the BBC at London) – and before you ask – it was hosted at that time by Terry Wogan who was a nice bloke.

At the BBC I got to spend a memorable afternoon with people like Dame Barbara Windsor, Windsor Davies, Tony Blackburn, Miss Beryl Reid, Dame Zandra Rhodes, Alfred Marks and most impressively of all ..... Keith Harris and Orville – beat that! It's funny the people one bumps into. After the show when we were in the 'Green Room' for some very small cans of beer and curly BBC sandwiches, I attempted to strike up a conversation with Barbara Winsor but she was rather distant. She did speak to me, however, and when I told her that I was in an Army Warrant Officer she relaxed and became very chatty, saying, "Sorry for ignoring you love, I fought you was a fucking screw!" (Prison Officer) and then doing that annoyingly braying laugh that she still does. Her then husband, Ronnie Knight, having had a spot of trouble with the law, had been banged up at one of Her Majesty's guest houses and when she'd visited him there she hadn't been treated particularly well by the 'Screws' ergo her apparent dislike for them. Notwithstanding, the then Miss Windsor was very bright, bubbly and nice and it was a pleasure meeting her.

I sat in my office at ASMT, Leconfield bored out of my skull. I gazed out of the small window at some hundred or so of 'my' trucks thinking that 'there must be more to life than this,' important to the safety of the realm as driver training was – and still is. I was relatively young at that stage and could have continued serving before the mast had I wanted to do so. The prospect, in all honesty, appalled me. The moment had definitely come for me to draw stumps and do something else. It was about that time that the 'R' word – Redundancy, hove into view. I decided to apply for Premature Voluntary Release (PVR) and leave the Army with a modicum of dignity and perhaps a few quid to help me get a new start in civvy street. I'd done my bit and also it was high time for my wife Maggie and daughter Sara to be able to settle down and do what they wanted to do.

A telephone call came through from the Kremlin (Headquarters ASMT) wherein lurked our Commandant, the Brigadier, a tough, feisty Irishman, who shall remain nameless as I value my knee-caps. His PA summoned me to the regal presence. Thrashing up to the Headquarters, I tapped lightly on the glorious leader's door, before marching smartly in and throwing up a crisp salute. The Brigadier, without looking up instructed his PA to get us both a cup of coffee. "My God," I thought, "Coffee, I'm in deep crap for something!"

The Brigadier eventually put his pen down, glared at me then picked up a large and well stuffed red plastic folder, waved it under my nose and snorted – "I suppose you know what I've got here, Major?" he said. "Er, 'This Is Your Life,' Brigadier?" I replied, rather wittily I thought. I was rewarded with an evil glance from my leader. "Don't be flippant, man! Sit!" I sat down. 'No – in the chair,' he said. I sat in the chair, crossing my legs in the usual laconic officer-ish style with just the right amount of stocking top showing, waiting to find out what this was all about (OK, I knew really, but I'm building up the suspension so that you'll want to read on).

The red folder that the Brigadier was clutching in his meaty paw contained the official notification from the Ministry of Defence that I was to be made redundant in yet another round of swingeing Armed Forces cuts, (now apparently an annual occurrence), cunningly designed to wreck, sorry trim, the Armed Forces and eventually morph them into a Home Defence Force. I had previously decided to leave the Army anyway, but kept my powder dry after hearing that 'they' wanted people to leave anyway. The redundancy route would ensure that I received a ludicrously small lump sum of money which would obviously be more than I would have had, had I left under normal circumstances.

Anyway, to cut a long paragraph short, the boss told me that I had indeed been selected for redundancy and that he was actually very sorry to see a man of my obvious qualities and professionalism not 'soldiering on.' He smiled and asked me to reconsider my application, saying that it wasn't too late to withdraw it and that he could resolve the issue with just one telephone call. I said that I had made my mind up to leave. He then said he was going to throw the red book into his waste bin and I replied that it made no difference, I really wanted to retire. He smiled in an avuncular fashion, said that he fully understood then shook me warmly by the throat. He didn't really, I made that up to add a bit of drama. He was charming, erudite and fully supportive of my decision to retire from the fray. He said that he was sorry to see me go though and looked as if he meant it.

I then had quite a few months to plan what I wanted to do once returning to life as a civilian. This would be my one golden opportunity to have a go at doing something I really wanted to. So there I sat in my little office, boldly flicking through the local telephone directory, because that's what officers are trained to do, idly flick. I wanted to find a local theatre company who would be willing to take a genius onto their books, both of us benefitting from our combined knowledge. When I look back I smile whimsically at the route I took, which in one way was a complete and utter waste of time, but at the same time was something of a memorable experience. You can't just slide into a job in the theatre, unless it's selling programmes or ice-cream. It's sheer ignorance to assume otherwise.

I'd read in the local newspaper, the 'Hull Daily Mail,' that a Hull based theatre company, 'Remould,' was presenting a community play called 'Vital Spark.' It was an opportunity for members of the community to get involved in a massive theatrical project about Hull's heritage fishing industry (when it had one), and would eventually be staged at Hull's prestigious City Hall. I saw this as being my window of opportunity to make some contacts and I volunteered my services, eventually being offered the part of a rich, arrogant Ship/Trawler owner and also John Prescott MP. 'Remould' was run by Averil Coult and Rupert Creed, two of the most enthusiastic, patient, humorous and talented people that one could ever wish to meet. The play 'Vital Spark' was written by a clever and erudite individual, Jon Oram. I got to know many of the people involved in this play, a lot of whom would later become woven into the fabric of my life.

Somehow or other ITV got wind of the community play project and I (*along with several others participants*) was followed around at work by a TV crew to show how those in the community play earned a crust. They filmed us as we rehearsed etc preparing for what was to be a very major production. It was great fun and we all knew that it was going to be something special. Eventually we were as ready as we were ever going to be and decamped en masse to Hull City Hall where the play was to be presented for about, if I recall, some ten days. During its relatively short run a lot of famous people came to see the play. One is now a Knight of the Realm, the other now a member of the House of Lords and a third a definite Queen. Such esteemed company.

'Vital Spark' was a most marvellous experience and a steep learning curve for me – because Rupert and Averil and their support crew did things absolutely properly and professionally. They knocked us all into shape and the upshot was a truly brilliant production, but then I would say that. It was rather strange playing the role of John Prescott. He came to see the rehearsals and the actual production, bringing with him his wife, the glamorous Pauline Prescott. The then Mr Prescott was a rather dapper chap and I don't think that he was particularly impressed at seeing me performing 'his' role (I'd had a few too many pies at that stage of my life and I was slightly larger than him), but he was funny, charming and very supportive. It was great having the opportunity to meet him, I was able to study his mannerisms and how he spoke etc at close quarters. It was a bit nerve-wracking playing the part of such a well known individual, particularly when one night he, the real article, was sat right behind me when I 'did' him. I was required to make a speech to the workers which entailed me going off on a political rant. I think that I got it fairly right as I wasn't the lucky recipient of one of his famous and lightning left hooks.

I must tell you the little story of how I helped to save 'God's' life - well, the chap who was playing the part of God in the play, 'Vital Spark.' God was, in real-life, an ex-trawler Captain who had seen off some 80 plus summers. We'd completed the first half of the play and thrashed off-stage at the interval to the dressing room to get changed for the second half. We didn't have a great deal of time for the interval because we had to get changed into different costumes and touch up the make-up, darling. 'Remould' had very kindly provided us with refreshments, small-eats etc. Now, you may or may not know this, but after being on-stage and under the hot lights, one is parched and a nice cool drink never goes amiss.

God, alas, decided that rather than have a drink, he would cram a rather large chunk of tasty looking quiche down his throat whilst he had the chance. Because his mouth was so dry, the quiche got lodged in his throat. I was across the other side of the dressing room, sat in just a pair of Gucci 'shreddies' (underpants) changing my trousers and thinking my lines through. There was a commotion and I saw a crowd of people around 'God' and noticed that he'd turned bright blue. He was choking. The dastardly quiche had got firmly stuck in his throat, cutting off his air supply, and no-one appeared to know what to do. Little old ladies fanned him with lavender scented handkerchiefs, saying "There, there, try and breathe luv" etc. My military training came to the fore and leaping up from my chair, I rushed forward and promptly went arse over tit in a tangle of trousers and braces. I recovered my dignity and ran over to God, who by now had gone an even deadlier shade of oxygen starved purple.

Grabbing hold of him I spun him around and performed the Heimlich Manoeuvre (or the Hamish Imlac manoeuvre as the troops refer to it), whereupon out shot the offending (huge) partially chewed piece of Quiche, followed by a full set of well-worn gnashers. God promptly drew in a huge breath of life-giving air and, the colour immediately flooded back into his face. He could breathe and I was thrilled to bits. All those years of Army first aid training had finally paid off. I was on cloud nine and busily congratulating myself.

Suddenly and without warning I received a stunningly fierce blow to the back of my head. At first I thought I'd had a stroke. "What on earth was all that about" I thought. Turning around I saw 'God's' wife, a feisty little Hull maiden also in her Eighties, swinging her huge handbag at my head and shouting – "You big silly bastard, squeezing my Mister's chest like that, you could have killed him, he's got Angina!" Someone gently steered her away from me whilst attempting to explain why I'd squeezed her man's chest. Slinking back to my chair, rubbing my bruised head I thought, 'Bloody ingrate, he would have died anyway." When I looked across the dressing room, 'God' had replaced his teeth and was having another crack at the Quiche, totally undaunted by his near miss. He looked across at me, smiled and gave me a cheery thumbs up. Ah, show-business. There was more drama in the dressing room than there would be on-stage during the second half.

I'll leave the city play there, suffice to say that it was a great success and an even greater experience. The things I learnt about sound, lighting, staging, publicity, presentation etc still hold good today. Needless to say, I always avoid consuming Quiche during any performance unless I've had a drink or two first.

'CURTAIN UP WITH THE CAST IRON THEATRE COMPANY/AGENCY!'

There is such a thing as 'happenstance.' In Hull there is a Café called 'Skeltons' now, unfortunately, no longer functioning as quite such a large establishment as it once was, having been demoted to more of a cake shop. In the corner of the café was a small wall-mounted display of theatrical memorabilia relating to 'Old Mother Riley and Kitty' (Arthur Lucan and Kitty McShane). The couple had started off as a music hall/variety act in the earlier part of the last century before hitting the big time on stage, radio and in films. Why, I'd pondered, was the display sited there in Skeltons Cafe?

**Arthur Lucan & Kitty McShane
as 'Old Mother Riley & her daughter Kitty'**

Skeltons Café was built on the site of the Tivoli Theatre, Hull when one tragic night, Monday the 17th of May 1954, Arthur Lucan collapsed and died in the wings of the theatre whilst waiting to go on stage in the show – *'OLD MOTHER RILEY IN PARIS.'* It was the end of a hugely successful career. I remembered seeing Arthur and Kitty's films when I was a kid and was therefore fascinated by those artefacts in the wall-mounted glass case in Skeltons when I spotted them whilst in there one day having tea and a sticky bun. Similarly, in a little compartment of my memory bank I remembered the grown-ups talking about Old Mother Riley dying, when I was a young child. Arthur Lucan is buried in Hull's Eastern Cemetery. Kitty McShane eventually disappeared off the radar and it isn't known what happened to her, although I believe that there are attempts being made to find out. I decided there and then that there was a story to be told and that I'd make it the subject of my first attempt at writing and put all of my efforts into presenting a 'proper' i.e. professional play.

I began with the long, arduous but enjoyable research of the subject and really the story nearly told itself. As with any good story, it needs a beginning, a middle and an end, which this one definitely had. At that time there was a Royal Military Police (RMP) Sergeant serving at Leconfield called Bill Jordan who, like me, was coming to the end of his time in the Forces and who also had an interest in writing and the theatre. We decided to get our heads together and come up with a script. Bill is a great bloke with a marvellous sense of humour and who is also a gifted writer and talented musician. We cracked on together and wrote the play. I ran the finished script, entitled 'Daughter Daughter' – (a Lucan catch-phrase), past Rupert Creed of Remould Theatre who, although up to his eye-balls in another production, very kindly took the time to read through the script and offer some constructive criticisms. Rupert is a cultured and talented man with a limitless well of patience and enthusiasm. I occasionally bump into Rupert and he has changed not a jot, whilst I continue inexorably to wither on the vine.

Eventually it was time to get the show on the road under the banner of the Hull based 'Cast Iron Theatre Company.' Naturally to begin with we had nothing, no reputation, no money, no scenery, no lights, no sound equipment, no cast or crew, no idea how to publicise the production and nowhere to rehearse. Mere bagatelles – and certainly none of that would stop us! Today Hull – tomorrow – Gilberdyke! We we're used to 'soldiering on' but it was grinding work and a steep learning curve.

Putting a 'professional' play on was certainly a leap into the unknown for me. Fortunately I'd bumped into Bryn Ellis (*from the Hull City Play*) who was at that time involved with running an outfit called 'The Cast Iron Theatre Company' based in the now defunct YPI Building in George Street, Hull. Bryn had been on the scene for many moons, (*he won't mind me saying that*) and had had a great deal of experience in Variety, Clubs, the Theatre, Films and Television – indeed, he had appeared in Coronation Street! A possessor of a fine singing voice, infinite patience and a wicked sense of humour. We had a lot of laughs – some of which I'll mention as we move along, some I have chosen not to, not wishing to be sued! With Bryn's expertise and ability to get his hands on start-up funding we eventually managed to raise a sufficient amount of loot in order to prepare, produce and present the play 'Daughter Daughter.' It was very challenging and exciting.

I just want to digress here and tell you a couple of things about the 'Cast Iron Theatre Company.' I had left the Army and was looking for something 'new' to do. Bumping into Bryn I'd been invited by him to join 'Cast Iron' and help him run the 'Cast Iron' office, which I gratefully accepted as I knew that the experience would be invaluable. As well as being a theatre company 'Cast Iron' was also well established as a local Hull based casting agency for Actors, Extras, Walk-on's and Variety performers in the Hull area who were seeking professional work. It was the usual thing, preparing tasty, eye-catching CV's with a nice photo and writing/telephoning Agents telling them that they really needed to have a look at the talent living in and around Hull who were available to guarantee a production's success at the box office. It was something of a precise art getting the artistes on Cast Iron's books noticed as one was always up against a lot of competition for roles and the need to whet the relevant agent's appetite. I even managed to get an audition for myself – for an advert. I remember being terribly excited, this was to be my first such audition and was the real thing. There was also the added bonus of cash to be had if you were successful.

I was called forward (*with great excitement*) to an audition in London. Once I'd gotten over the disappointment of having to pay my own bus fare (*no expenses, very rarely do they cough up expenses*) I took a leap into the then what to me was the unknown, arriving in London after a bum numbing ride on a National Coach (*it was that long ago that the coach had a 'Trolley Dolly' thrashing up and down the centre of the coach selling good healthy sandwiches and clacker scorching tea).* The 'Trolley Dolly' in her mid-twenties was straight out of a Beryl Cook painting, dressed as she was in her tight fitting air stewardess style cossie and looked brilliant.. She dared you not to smile. Aye, those were the days my friend, everything to play for and everything to pay for.

Anyway, after several changes of horses and pee stops, I eventually reached London a little early and found my way to the Casting Agency which was in rather grand premises just around the corner from Covent Garden in 'Theatre Land.' My excitement knew no bounds. If I could get this advert I'd be making money as a professional actor for the very first time. As I'd arrived in London a bit early, I wondered around aimlessly for about an hour until the time came for me to enter the Agency. Butterflies! Smile, look confident, flash the ivories (I still had most of my own teeth then). "Hi I'm Terry Cavender. I've been sent by Cast Iron, Hull." My name was ticked off from an alarmingly long list by a young lady manning the desk who didn't even bother to look up as she waved me towards a seat. There were some rather strange noises coming from the next room. I was eventually invited into the large room where there were two blokes, the Director, and his rather fey Assistant. They introduced themselves to me but the passage of time, thankfully, has allowed me to forget their names.

A few banalities passed between us then they hit me with the first searching question:

Director: What are you like with heights, love?

Me: No problem there. *(lying through my teeth).*

Assistant: Ever been on a trapeze, dear?

Me: *(Trying to be positive)* Er – not recently (*thinks – not chuffing ever*).

I saw them glancing upwards and was mortified to note that there was a trapeze type contraption suspended from the ceiling. Gulp City! (*This is true, I'm not making it up just to pad out a paragraph*). By this time my smile had become somewhat fixed and my top lip was sticking to my teeth like Humphrey Bogart's did when he said "Play it again Sham!" Here I was in a room in a place in central London, with two strange blokes and a trapeze suspended from the ceiling. Had I stumbled into something seedy? It really was onwards and upwards.

Director: Right then.

he said, grinning evilly as his assistant produced a long step-ladder:

Director: Nip up this ladder, suspend yourself from the trapeze, my assistant will give you a hand and then we'll give you a couple of lines to say whilst we tape it. Make yourself comfy once you're up there dear. OK?

"Well", I thought to myself, "I've come all this way, spent some money on a bus ticket, might as well go for it." I should add that at the time I was of moderately generous proportions i.e. there was no need to ask who had eaten all the pies – it was patently obvious – I had. I'd also consumed more egg sandwiches on the bus than was healthy for me. I nodded confidently and headed for the ladder. It wasn't going to be easy.

I heaved myself up the ladder, pausing at each rung and desperately trying to figure out just how I was going to cock a meaty hock over the trapeze bar and then haul the remainder of the Cavender carcase over the bar with the other leg, without doing myself a mischief and hurtling back to ground zero. With much undignified grunting, straining, belching and gentle farting (the egg sandwiches on the bus had a lot to answer for), I finally achieved the required state of suspension - hanging from that trapeze looking like a large piece of prime beef in Harrods food hall. Nevertheless I was rather proud of my achievement at having got that far. I was no longer a trapeze virgin.

I had a wispy fringe in those days, which because of the gravitational pull, made me look like an upside down threadbare mop. The blood had gone thrashing down through my body and every pint of it felt as if it had gone straight to my head. I knew that my face had turned puce, I could feel it! My eyes were bulging like organ stops and I was, in truth, feeling a little giddy. The two blokes were prancing around below, presumably trying not to giggle at my antics. Back to the Director:

Director: Right Trevor (*in case you've forgotten, dear reader, my name's Terry*) could you please say the line – "We won't keep you hanging around!"

Me: Er, yes OK."

Director: And – action!

Large breath, then I spouted, in stentorian tones –

Me: We won't keep you hanging around!

By this time having all of my very substantial weight hanging on to the bar of the trapeze, those two little ham strings behind the knee-caps had brought about a touch of excruciating cramp and given me a definite urge to whimper. Being British to the core, I continued hanging there as if I cared not one jot and pretending that nothing was remotely amiss and indeed, I was really enjoying myself. The Director and his Assistant continued chatting, discussing technical banalities, then:

Director: Trevor, could you say it again please, this time with a Scottish accent?

Me: Yes, of course, not a problem.

I replied, a rictus grin on my puce face:

Me: We'll no keep ye hanging around, pal!

(My time spent in several of the less salubrious of Glasgow hostelries had finally paid dividends).

Director: Hey that was really good Trev. Can you do an Irish accent?

Me: North or South?

I replied, trying to appear knowledgeable. The pain in my hocks was now excruciating.

Director: Either will do, dear. And - Action!

I gave it my best shot.

Director: O.K. That's fine. You can come down now, thanks Trev.

I thought, if he calls me Trevor again and I survive the dismount – I'll level him. So, I gave some thought as to how to achieve the dismount whilst retaining a modicum of dignity and my trousers, plus remaining in one piece. I was hanging there, my legs containing not a drop of blood, muscles knotted and with hardly the strength to pull myself upright onto the trapeze bar. I was too far from Mother Earth to do a flying leap onto the plush carpet. I couldn't stay up there for very much longer. Something had to be done.

Assistant: You OK up there Trevor, love? Really must ask you to move, we've got a couple more people to have a look at today!"

Me: No problem, just enjoying the view!

Assistant: Ha Ha – what a card you are, darling

I counted up to three and desperately heaved myself up onto the trapeze bar, knowing that I only had one chance at it, my sweating hands desperately clutching for the ropes. It was now or never. Pulling myself into an upright sitting position with great whoops of breath, I sighed with relief, tidied my few strands of hair, waited for a few seconds for the blood to flow back into its rightful places around my body and the feeling to return to my lower legs, before moving tentatively across to the ladder and hobbling down the steps towards 'Mother Earth.' I recall doing a passable imitation of Groucho Marx as I walked across the carpet on weakened legs towards the exit. The Director said to me, with the suspicion of a sneer:

Director: You OK Trev?

He was definitely cruising for a bruising. If my legs had been functioning properly I think I'd have gone for him. Because these people knew that you were seeking work and that they had the power to employ you, they could be thoughtless and quite dismissive.

Director: Nigel darling, could you be a petal and ask the next chap to pop in, please.

Me: Er, was that OK for you?

Director: We'll let you know Trev! Next!

As my legs had by now returned to normal, I was able to make a dignified exit to make my way back to Victoria Bus Station and the long haul home. I sat in the office and waited hopefully for the 'phone to ring for the next few days, but they never did get back to me, not even to say I hadn't got the advert. The thoughtless, unfeeling bastards – after all I'd put myself through for them. I'd even had to pay my own travel expenses. This was supposed to have been my big break into the world of TV advertising.

That was the first of many such demeaning auditions and if nothing else it taught me not to be quite so thin skinned. Auditions were never anything personal, it was simply a matter of if you fitted the bill for their specific requirements then you would more than likely get the work. Some of the work for adverts was quite lucrative so it was definitely worthwhile making the attempt. They could 'humanise' things a bit though. Glamorous it was not.

Trudging back to the cess-pit that is Victoria Bus Station, London I waited for the coach and four and off to Hull I went. The driver helped me onto the coach because my legs were still not quite functioning properly. As I hobbled and heaved myself on board the bus I said to the sympathetic driver, "I have to take my time, it's the shrapnel you know!" At least I had the Trolley Dolly and her glorious ham filled baps to look forward to. The whole thing had been a steep learning curve for me. Ah, cruel world. The feeling didn't fully return to my legs until well past the Doncaster inter-change. Still, at the very least I could add Trapeze Artist (failed) to my theatrical CV.

I had a great deal of fun whilst at the 'Cast Iron' Agency in Hull, working in the office alongside Bryn Ellis. Bryn, himself is an accomplished actor, singer, drummer and talented individual and knew a lot of the 'wheezes.'

Bryn was heading off for an audition early one day and told me that one of the Artistes on 'our' books would be in later on in the morning, just to see how things were going and check if there was any work in the offing for him. He warned me that once this particular guy usually got sat down with a cuppa (*we had a nice comfy 'casting couch' in the office, nothing seedy, just right for the odd kip*) the odds were that he'd be sat there for the rest of the day chatting aimlessly. Bryn advised me that on this occasion, as I'd not met the individual and Bryn would be absent on duty, the best thing to do was lock the office door and pretend that there was no-one in. Bryn departed and I continued with my office duties. Apparently the individual usually arrived at the office at about 10 o'clock, so just before 10 o'clock I got up and locked the office door as advised.

Shortly after 10 o'clock I heard the delicate footfall of the Artiste, (who shall remain nameless for reasons that will become evident later on), followed by a gentle tap on the office door. "Terry, are you there, love?" Tap tap. "Hello, Terry?" tap tap. You could see my desk through the key hole (*I'm not daft*) and I didn't know if he'd peep through and see me there so I quietly moved from behind my desk and tip-toed across to casting couch. Phew, much to my relief I heard his footsteps disappearing into the distance. Great, that's got rid him, or so I thought. He could come back the following day when Bryn would be there to deal with him.

Alas, it was not to be. I heard several rushed footsteps, followed by the sound of a metal ladder being extended, lifted up to and crashing against the small quarter light frame above the office door. "Oh My God" be sure your sins will find you out. "He'd got a ladder and is going to look through the window." What should I do? He'd know that I'd deliberately been hiding from him. All hell would break loose, followed by him taking his name off the Agency books. I was mortified. Bryn would undoubtedly be spitting feathers when he returned and found out about it, particularly as this individual was one of the few 'Cast Iron' earners on our books. These thoughts rushed through my brain. The only other main act on our books, incidentally, was a hand balancing act who had unfortunately gone arse over tit when tripping over a milk bottle, badly cutting his hand, so he was off the road for a while - thereby reducing our income by 50%.

Right, I thought, put your years of Army training to good use, lad – do something! So I laid out on the casting couch, put on some earphones and pretended to be listening to some music. Voice from the top of the ladder – "I can see him on the couch – I, I think he's had a heart attack! He's not moving" He was addressing the Building Manager, who'd come along to see what all the fuss was about. "Right," shouted the Manager, "I'll go and 'phone for an ambulance!" and ran off. Oh my God – out of the frying pan etc.

"What am I going to do now" I thought "a bloody ambulance! I'm doomed!" The situation had got terribly out of hand. The visiting Artist shouted, "I'll break the door in whilst we're waiting for the ambulance! He'll need mouth to mouth - he's not moving! I can save him!" OK I thought, time to bring this farce to a close. Sitting up, I removed the earphones and casually wandered, theatrically yawning and stretching, across the office, unlocked the door and smiled welcomingly at the man descending the ladder (who must remain nameless as he's still performing in the clubs). "Hello Smudge," (made that name up to protect the innocent). "What are you doing up a ladder?" He shrieked at the Building Manager, "Aaaaaagh! Cancel the bloody ambulance, he's OK!" Things eventually settled down a bit after I explained that I'd been listening to some music and yes, you've guessed it, like cheese and onion - he stayed with me for hours - drinking tea and boring me rigid with dated theatrical stories, none worth repeating here. Storm in a tea-cup or what! Bryn, needless to say, wet his pants laughing when I told him what had happened. Full of compassion he said, "I warned you not to let him in, son!"

Just as an aside, I accompanied that self-same artist to a night club on the far outskirts of Hull one evening as he wanted his act videoing. Bryn said that it was better that I saw his act so that it would help me when I was discussing his bookings with Agencies, (do you detect the stench of treachery here)? I videoed his act and at the end of a long and tiring evening, (he was performing on a late spot which finished after midnight), I drove the Artist home to Hull. As we drew to a halt outside his house he thanked me for accompanying him to the venue then glanced at me.

There was a long pause and I started to feel decidedly uncomfortable. "Was there something else?" I enquired. He glanced coyly at me, fluttered his eyelids and replied, "I suppose, Terry, a good night kiss is out of the question?" He was instructed to leave my vehicle at the earliest opportunity. I think I may have used a more fruitier military style phrase, ending in 'Off.' He was totally un-phased took the hint and departed into the night. Oh how Bryn Ellis laughed when I related the incident to him the following morning. I had a vague suspicion that Bryn may have known that something like that would be in the offing. You pay to learn.

Another 'Cast Iron "Agency' story (again, name changed to protect the innocent). One day Bryn and I were sat in the office when there was an authoritative knock on the door and a very glamorous middle-aged Indian lady entered. Bryn leapt up from his chair and offered the lady a seat on the casting couch. "Welcome to Cast Iron – and what can we do for you, dear lady" he said in his best Hull Shakespearean. "How may we help you?" "I want to become an Actress and would like some work on Coronation Street, Emmerdale Farm or East Enders," came the reply. "Right" replied Bryn as if this was the most natural request in the world. "Would you like to tell me a bit about yourself and what acting experience you've had?" "I haven't had any acting experience at all. I'm starting off here, today!" was her reply. "OK" said Bryn "We've all got to start somewhere. Let's write down some of your details on one of our standard Artiste forms."

The lady told Bryn her name, then said "But I don't want to use that particular name. I want to adopt a stage name. One that is as famous in India as your Winston Churchill is here!" "Ah," said Bryn, ever the wag, "You mean like er Mahatma Ghandi?" "No – I do not mean like Mahatma Ghandi. He was a man! I obviously am not." Bryn continued, "Well, yes, yes, I er appreciate that, but I don't know many other Indian names, only cricketers." This wasn't going particularly well I thought. I said, "May I get you a cup of tea?" She nodded regally and I legged it to the tea area whilst Bryn struggled valiantly on, digging himself into an even deeper hole.

"Right, Right, so what do you want to be known as?" said Bryn. Now, I'm going to make a name up again here. Let's call her – Amla Rewa (if there's anyone out there with that name – my apologies, but this isn't about you). "Amla Rewa" she said. "I'm sorry, what's your Christian, er, fore-name, er first name then love?" said Bryn, wrinkling his by now fevered brow "I've just said - I want to be known as Amla Rewa." "Right, Amelia" "No, No – it is Amla!" "Sorry, sorry Hemlia" "No, I said it's Amla! Are you perhaps a little deaf, sir?" Bryn - "Pardon?" "I said, are you a little deaf?"

"No, No, give us a chance, luv. I'm doing my best." By this time I am sniggering at Bryn's obvious discomfort, (payback time for the "Can I kiss you goodnight" thing). Bryn's face is now covered in sweat and he just wants the whole interview to be over and done with. "Well, er, Hemlock!" "Amla!" she shrieked. "Oh to hell with this damned stuff and nonsense!" said Amla, mightily affronted, leaping to her feet and sweeping out of the office hollering "I'll get a proper London Agent, not you, you bloody amateur – good day!" Office door slammed, followed by a lengthy silence, broken only by my sniggering. It was a truly magnificent exit.

Bryn was lathered and trembling. I had to make him a cup of tea whilst he recovered from his 'Amla' experience. He slowly sipped the beverage and said to me, "Can you do the next interview please, Terry? We've got a Polish juggling act coming in with a view to being booked by Pontins for the summer season" Little did Bryn know but I'd served with the Poles whilst in West Germany, so names like ' Wiszniewsky' and 'Sczupacki' held no fears for me …… "No problem Bryn, but what are we going to do about Hemlock?" We both dissolved into peals of laughter. "That's going nowhere," he said, smiling knowingly.

One evening, a few months later, Bryn was watching a very popular soap on TV, when whom did he spot sat in the bar of Coronation Street's Rovers Return but – 'Amla' – or was it Hemlock???? There she sat, apparently, knocking back a half and 'rhubarbing' for all her worth. Good for her, she deserved the break, particularly after surviving the 'Cast Iron' registration experience.

THE PLAY –
'DAUGHTER DAUGHTER'

Unless you are hugely successful, there's not a lot of money to be had in the theatre. To get things moving you have to use your initiative and a fair degree of animal cunning to achieve your aspirations I'd suggested to Bryn that we put a play together ourselves, I could write a script (so that we wouldn't have to buy one in) and we could use whatever bits of scenery 'Cast Iron' had tucked away and beg/borrow/steal costumes etc. We could then tour it about the local area, giving work to actors, technicians etc and in doing so perhaps make a few quid for 'Cast Iron' and ourselves for future productions. It would be an exciting challenge. We gave the sort of play we wanted to do a great deal of thought and finally decided the subject matter whilst having tea and toast in Skeltons Café and spotted the 'Old Mother Riley' link. So I began writing the script for 'Daughter Daughter,' eventually linking up with Bill Jordan and the fun began.

With the assistance of Bryn Ellis, we assembled a 'co-operative' cast and crew with which to tour 'Daughter Daughter.' The play was to be directed by the brilliant Martin Saxton, the title of the play being based on the catch-phrase used by Arthur Lucan, who used it when cross-talking to his daughter Kitty. It was all done on a very tight budget, but what fun we had doing it. We made a small profit – a percentage retained to be ploughed into our next production with the rest paid on an equal share basis to the co-operative members.

We had a great cast in the play and they worked extremely hard for very little reward to help make it the success that it was. I actually had a small part –

that of a whistling Vicar. Whilst writing the play I'd heard an ancient recording by the variety artiste 'Ronnie Ronalde' the professional whistler (known as a 'Siffleur'). I rather enjoyed performing the role and am proud to say that it got plenty of laughs along the way. By some miracle we managed to get a week at the Hull Truck Theatre in Spring Street, Hull. These days you stand more chance of winning the lottery then you do of staging something at Hull Truck. Anyway, we did very good business and the 'House Full' signs were up for most nights.

Something that was particularly nice and memorable for me about the play was that a coach party of my relatives managed to travel over from my home-town of Keighley to Hull and view my triumphant performance. I remember quite clearly the raucous laughter coming from the area where my Mother, Auntie Glenis and others of the Keighley contingent were sat – many of whom are, sadly, no longer with us. A nice personal memory. We did good business at Spring Street and then prepared to take the play on tour. That was the life for me, or so I thought.

Quite a few amusing incidents occurred whilst we were 'on tour' darling. As I said, we did very well at Spring Street and I thought to myself, as the 'House Full' boards went up, this show-business lark is a doddle. Knock up a quick play, take it out on tour, plenty of bums on seats, get a solid reputation and the money will soon come rolling in with which to fund future productions. It wasn't quite that simple.

Come along with me to the Civic Hall, Clitheroe, right in the centre of Clitheroe. It was a charming old theatre with, would you believe it, a nuclear bunker sited directly underneath the stage. The Manager, the late John Williamson, very kindly permitted some of our company to sleep overnight in the nuclear bunker on the premise that if the

Russians couldn't damage it, then it would be safe for a couple of strolling minstrels to kip up there for the night. His kind gesture would save our little theatre company quite a few quid. The Actresses (as they were called in those days), were despatched to a local hotel. The remainder of us 'underlings' nipped across to near-by Keighley in West Yorkshire, where my brother and his wife Nina very kindly provided us with a hearty repast and put us up for the night.

We returned to the theatre the following morning, a Sunday, to prepare for that day's show. On our arrival back at the nuclear bunker we noticed an obnoxious and ominous smell emanating from the bowels of the bunker. Something had obviously been burning. It became evident that one of our 'Cast Iron' thesps who had occupied a corner of the bunker had done something rather silly with an electric kettle, which was now a molten, smelly mess. Feeling a little peckish shortly after midnight, he'd decided to boil a couple of eggs in it. The eggs exploded, and the kettle went into melt-down at roughly the same time. The stench was appalling, burnt plastic with just a whiff of scorched eggs – a delightful combination and not to mention the mess caused by the foam from the extinguisher used to extinguish the flaming kettle.

The Manager of the theatre, John, was due back in a couple of hours and the kettle, (his kettle, incidentally) was beyond repair. It had to be replaced forthwith and the bunker had to be returned to a state of normality. We thrashed out to a local car boot and managed to find a very similar kettle and several containers of air freshener. Nipping back to the bunker we hid the remains of the burnt kettle and expelled the contents of the air fresheners. We cleaned up the fire extinguisher and replaced it back onto the wall, hiding the fact that it's contents had been used. A shameful admission I know, but needs must …… Shortly afterwards the

Manager arrived; taking me to one side he said "Terry, lad, you need to have a word with your Actors. I've never smelled feet quite like it. Knocked me back. Mucky buggers. Bloody awful!" I replied, "Yes, it's funny you should say that John. I've just warned them about it. Er, can I get you a cup of tea?"

The show went well at Clitheroe, although one particular incident I recall was when the erudite David Sandford, who was performing in the role of Sir Charles something or other, was stood backstage, dressed in white tie and tails waiting to go on stage. He was talking quietly to me and said something along the lines of "Do you know, I'm inordinately proud of the fact that in all the years I've been performing on stage, I've never missed a cue or been late for an entrance." I said to him, "Well you'd better get a shift on David because you've just miss your cue!"

Aghast, David went hurtling onto the stage via a door at the very centre of the scenery. Unfortunately there was a nail stuck out from rear of the door which snagged on the silk scarf that was carelessly slung around David's neck. He was moving at speed then suddenly jerked to a halt saying something along the lines of "I say chaps, there's been a...." Gulp, twang, his head jerked back and he was thrown backwards out of the door. The audience thinking that it was intentional and something along the lines of a Whitehall farce type move, burst into a spontaneous round of applause at this cleverly executed entrance/exit. David loosened the scarf and carried on as if nothing untoward had happened. A very professional actor and an extremely nice man.

In the same scene we had the rather tall and very funny actor Graham Elwell, (who now can be seen doing adverts on TV) amongst other things. His latest one is in an insurance advert where he can be seen vomiting over the side of a ship – ah the glamour of show-business. Graham's found fame doing commercials and was also fortunate enough to be a winner on 'Who wants to be a Millionaire' the prize money I think helped to pay his way through the Italia Conti Academy of Theatre Arts. Graham, a policeman in our play, had found a small hole in one of the pieces of scenery and was peeping through at the audience to see if there was any female talent waiting to be impressed by his impending performance. He was concentrating so much that he almost missed the cue for his entrance. Knowing that he'd cut things a bit too fine, he hurtled from one side of the stage to the other in order to enter stage left. Alas, as he sprinted across the stage in the gloom he went arse over tit over a cunningly placed, weighted French strut and hit the floor like a sack of spuds. The breath hurtled from his body. It must have stung, but he stood up, wheezing, dusted himself down and made his entrance as if nothing had happened – "Hello, Hello, Hello!" etc.

I was stood in the wings when I heard laughter from the audience (always gratefully received) but it was in a part of the play where it hadn't happened before. Picture the scene, a Burglar (played by our multi-talented Stage Manager, John Sims), had been caught robbing Old Mother Riley, so she places her metal wash bucket over his head and then bashes the bucket (technical term) with her scrubbing brush, making his ears ring. I heard the clanging as the bucket was struck and then the laughter spreading like wildfire in the audience. The cast on stage started to stumble over their lines, then sniggered and began to lose the thread. The inside of the bucket had been padded with lots of news paper so that the actor being thrashed on the head under the bucket wouldn't suffer any lasting injury. When Old Mother Riley had lifted the bucket off his head, the newspaper had formed itself into some sort of helmet and it looked like John was wearing a

Bishop's mitre. The 'Burglar' tried to maintain dignity as he was arrested and was dragged off-stage, his new head-dress wobbling furiously. Order was eventually restored on stage and the play continued.

Our lighting man, John Michael Adams, is also known on the 'circuit' for his activities as a Medium – and scaringly good he is too. My wife Maggie doesn't believe in that sort of thing, 'Stuff and Nonsense!" she says, but without doubt John is gifted. He has a long theatrical background (or that's what he tells all the girls) and for many years he was a lighting man at the London Palladium. The stories he tells about that period are just so brilliant. He met many of the legendary performers and stars during his time at the London Palladium and knows some very interesting tales. He should write a book about it. John told us that whilst we were performing our play on-stage at Clitheroe there was a shadowy figure of an old woman at the side of the stage, watching what was going on. No-one other than John had seen her and he didn't tell us about it until we were striking the set after the show because he thought that we'd be spooked. We were spooked and legged it out of the darkened theatre as fast as we could. Some of the cast thought that it was the ghost of Arthur Lucan, whose life-story we were portraying in the play. Not a particularly intellectual stretch, but who really knows?

Recently, and purely by chance a dear friend of mine, that fine character actor and expert photographer Roger Peace, (or 'Cod' as we call him), was passing through Clitheroe and to his abject horror saw that the wonderful little theatre in the centre of town where we'd had such memorable times was in the process of being demolished. Yet another outrageous act of thoughtless vandalism, ripping the artistic heart out of the community so that undoubtedly something important like a car park could take its place.

It eventually became apparent to me that I had trouble remembering lines, which obviously made things more than a little difficult and I'd decided that writing, not acting, was really my forté and the besides, there were lots of other things I could do like publicity etc. In essence I thought then that it would be better and less stressful for me to craft plays and hopefully entertain people that way. I enjoyed writing and discovered that if I worked at it I could make people laugh (and on occasions cry). Whether or not that was because of the quality of writing I'll leave that with you. But that's the path I chose. The whistling Vicar was no more.

AND THEN –
'THE ANLABY COMMUNITY CARE ASSOCIATION'

I applied for the post of Chief Officer of the Anlaby Community Care Association. I was short-listed, interviewed, offered and accepted the job as Chief Officer of the Anlaby Community Care Association, cunningly located at Anlaby, on the outskirts of Hull. The Association, a day care centre, did and still does an absolutely brilliant job, staffed mainly by unpaid volunteers, looking after senior citizens, providing them with essentials such as a hot meal, and more often than not the only 'companionship' that they've had for one week to the next. Needless to say, but I'll say it anyway, in this ridiculous society of ours, the Committee of the Association had to fight for every penny of funding in order to continue with their good works. This work was done by an entirely voluntary, unpaid committee who very cheerfully and tirelessly gave up their time and efforts to help with things like driving the all important mini-bus, going around the local shops getting food for the stunningly good hot meals and drinks that they provided for members on a daily basis – in fact everything that was required to keep the Association afloat. They were good and kind people. Britain at its best.

I can never really understand why it is that such key matters as looking after the elderly (of which I am now one myself) can only be done by organisations such as the Association by them continually having to scrounge for funds and relying upon the good will of unpaid volunteers. Although it is some time since I left their employ, happily their good work continues.

Anyway, I'd trotted along for a gruelling and lengthy interview with the Committee, receiving a thorough but fair interrogation to see if I was suitable for the job. "What is your name…." slap "What is your unit?" slap, "What is your mission?" slap etc. 'Stop hitting me when I'm asking you questions!" etc. They had to get it right, after all – their elderly members deserved nothing but the best. I'm not saying that I was the best, just indicating how thoroughly competent the Committee was. I got the job and gradually settled into my little office. To be perfectly honest, it was a bit of a flog. The salary wasn't particularly good and the job wasn't pensionable – but it was work that I thought had great value and I loved it.

I didn't have a 'proper' assistant when I started there but was assisted in the office by a magnificent old soldier named Harry Brown who was then in his eighties. Harry and I both being ex-military (Harry had also been in the Royal Army Service Corps so we had that in common), had many a good laugh together. Eventually though , after a bit of whining to the Committee, I was authorized to employ an assistant, a delightful lady called Kath Holland. Kath was an absolute ray of sunshine, with a heart of pure gold. Cool, calm, efficient under fire and who took no prisoners. The elderly (of which I am now one) can be quite cantankerous and demanding. So what – as far as I was concerned they'd earned the right! Kath was just right for the job. Harry Brown remained in the office helping as a volunteer. I nick-named him 'Hazardous' - he was a good, decent bloke. He is sadly no longer with us having gone on to his final posting to that 'Great Depot in the sky.' Harry was knocking on a bit and, unfortunately, as deaf as a post. I mention that in passing, it will become apparent why later on.

I was sat in the office at Anlaby one morning with a slight headache and mouth like the bottom of a budgie's cage, having been to a Regimental Dinner at the Officers' Mess, Leconfield the night before where we had been served with a particularly ferocious Gurkha style curry, washed down with copious amounts of the grape. I was paying the price, having a severe case of the 'Latin Two-steps.' Not only that, I was suffering from a wicked bout of crippling wind. Working in my little office with the afore-mentioned deaf Harry Brown, who was tucked away in a corner but not facing me, I was therefore able to break wind with carefree gusto, knowing that he wouldn't hear a thing. After one particularly elephantine bout of trumpeting from my nether regions, (which was, regrettably, accompanied by an appalling and undisguisable stench) Kath came bouncing into the office, stopped dead and rocked back on her heels. She glanced fiercely at Harry and whispered to me, "Oh My God! Don't old people smell! I don't know how you put up with it in such a confined space." I just nodded sagely and smiled, relieved that I wasn't getting the blame for polluting the atmosphere. She then dashed off to the lavatories to get some air freshener and then proceeded to sprayed both the office and Harry liberally with a lavender concoction.

Sorry for blaming you Harry, but the Chief Officer, an ex-officer and gentleman, could not be seen to be behaving badly. Needs must. "Where 'ere you be, let your wind blow free. In Church or Chapel let it rattle." During the course of the morning, Kath returned several times with the tin of air freshener, re-spraying the office and its two occupant liberally, but in the main, Harry. "Ooooh," said Kath, "You can smell him right down the back passage! It's eye watering. They're even complaining in the Dining Room." Another quick burst then she left the office. Harry sent me off into a bout of hysteria when he said, "Fookin' wimmin, they never stop bloody polishing things!" Thankfully, both my head and the air gradually cleared as the day wore on. Good old 'Hazardous.'

Anlaby Community Care Association was at that time the proud possessor of two vehicles, one being a tidy little mini-bus, used to transport our association members around and the other and an ancient Ford Truck, used for general transport duties such as removing garden waste etc. The Association provided gardeners to help those who couldn't, because of age and infirmity, manage their gardens. As an old 'transport' man it was evident to me that the truck was heading for the last roundup. So after chatting it through with the committee it was decided that the gardening vehicle had served its purpose and should be moved on to pastures new. It was advertised for sale.

One morning a somewhat boisterous and colourful character bounced into my office and said that he wanted to buy the truck. Let's call him Mr Smith. I recall that he was heavily tattooed and sported a gold ear-ring. A rough diamond. We negotiated a price for the clapped out vehicle, he coughed up the readies, a couple of hundred quid, and then departed with the vehicle, belching copious amounts of black smoke from the rear end, (the vehicle, not Mr Smith). Job done.

On my way home that very evening, (I lived on the outskirts of Hull in those days), as I drove past a housing estate I saw the truck parked up and there was Mr Smith doing some sort of work on it. I stopped and went over for a quick chat with him. "Hello Mr Smith, what are you up to then?" "Oh I'm just replacing some of the clapped out planking in the rear of t'truck. It'll be as good as new then," he replied. We chatted sociably for a while until suddenly a woman hove into view. Without being too unkind to the good lady, (picture the late Les Dawson in drag) she had on a green, patched leather raincoat, a colourful headscarf and on her feet wore a pair of sweat stained curly shoes somewhat reminiscent of well-crimped Cornish pasties. She was carrying several plastic shopping bags and looked, as they say oop here, 'lathered.'

The man said, "Oh. it's t'wife. Na then my love!" He pointed proudly at the truck and said, "What, ah sed, what about this then, luv? I've just bought it from this here gentleman." She looked singularly unimpressed. Without thinking of the possible consequences I decided to join in the general and at that stage light-hearted badinage, saying "Yes and it was a snip at a thousand quid," thinking that she'd join in the merriment and have a laugh. It was patently obvious that the vehicle was worth nothing like that amount. Mr Smith turned as white as the proverbial sheet and started gabbling like a turkey that's just seen a Christmas menu. Mrs Smith, lowering her bags to the floor, looked at him aghast and Mount Vesuvius like, she erupted:

Mrs Smith: A thousand pounds, a thou...... Well you useless, fat bastard! I'm out all day, every day scrubbing shit-houses and you spend my money, ah sed my money, on, on that heap of crap ...

As she pronounced each key syllable of her harangue she struck him with a shopping bag. He valiantly attempted to defend himself, hiding behind his arms. To give him his due, he didn't fight back.

Mr Smith: No, No, No love I didn't pay 'owt like that much. The Gentleman was only joking......

Mrs Smith wasn't in the receive mode. Vengeance was her primary aim. She'd had a bad day at the office.

Mrs Smith: Right (*thwack*), you useless (*thwack*), idle bastard (*thwack*)...

Mr Smith: No love, it weren't a grand I tell you, it were a snip!

Mrs Smith: That's summat your Father should have had! (*thwack*).

Without further ado she continued with a full frontal assault, chasing Mr Smith around the vehicle, knocking seven bells out of him. As the altercation continued and the air resounded with ripe badinage, a small but appreciative band of local residents gathered, cheering them both on. In the distance I heard the sound of police sirens. I smiled sympathetically and said, in a relatively quiet voice, "Well, I'd better be on my way then," tiptoed to my car and legged it as fast as common decency would permit. As I drove off I peered into my rear-view mirror and saw that Mrs Smith was still chasing her beleaguered husband around the truck, but was now wielding a shovel. A police car, with blue flashing lights, had arrived at the scene. Thankfully I have not seen either the Smiths or the vehicle since.

Christmas loomed and I decided that it would be a nice idea if I could lay on some sort of Christmas Party for the members of the Community Care Association. I had plenty of contacts from my 'Cast Iron' Theatre Company/Personal Management' days and did a bit of phoning around, calling in a few favours and eventually putting a little variety show together. It wouldn't be on a par with the London Palladium, but it was the thought that counted. The Pensioners could arrive to a welcoming glass of sherry, have their Christmas Dinner, be roundly entertained and then nip off home clutching a pressie and a piece of moist Christmas Cake, that sort of thing. The Committee scoured the local shops for donations of food and best buys so that a truly splendid and traditional repast could be prepared. The Community Centre was 'tinselled' up and everything looked very 'Christmassy.'

The 'gig' went swimmingly well. As the Pensioners arrived they were handed a generous schooner of sherry just to help get them fired up, prior to them being served a traditional Christmas Dinner that had been lovingly prepared for them. Crackers were pulled and paper hats adorned their highly coiffuered silver hair and much jollity was in evidence as even more sherry was consumed. After the meal, the dining chairs were turned around and the dining room converted into a little theatre. Several of the volunteer acts performed successfully, one was an excellent 'Old Mother Riley' look-alike (Ashley K Howard) who sang and did a little comedy sketch. A member of the audience was heard to say "Bloody hell, they don't know when to pack it in," believing Ashley to be the original article. "I used to watch him when I was a lad!" (the Music Hall Artist, the late great Arthur Lucan, had actually died in 1954). It was in fact a compliment to Ashley's professionalism.

Then - enter the Magician. Let's call him 'The Great Magico,' just for the sake of propriety. 'Magico' was technically beyond criticism, but his act went on for a bit too long (possibly by about twenty minutes). The majority of the audience, aided by the warmth of the dining room and generous amounts of sherry, had by then settled back in their seats, many of them having drifted off into the land of nod. As 'Magico' ploughed through his act, a great deal of high-pitched whistling and clacking could be heard in the background, which I was later informed was courtesy of either loosely fitting NHS dentures and/or badly tuned, pink, NHS hearing aids.

As 'Magico' valiantly continued with his admittedly rather clever act he performed one of his tricks with a large elongated balloon, a cardboard tube and a knitting needle. It went spectacularly wrong as the needle pierced the balloon which burst loudly when it quite obviously shouldn't have done. One old lady, snoozing gently in the front row woke up with a start and said in a loud voice, "Fookin hell fire, is that useless bugger still on!" "Aye," joined in several others, "Gerrim-off!" I'm sure that they thought they were watching television. The Magician took the hint and quickly wound up his act, exiting stage left, virtually to the sound of his own footsteps. There was a slight smattering of begrudged applause from arthritic hands, showing token appreciation. Enter then the pianist, who knocked seven bells out of the ivories in the style of Russ Conway and a rattling good sing-song began, livening things up immeasurably. After that, the brandy soaked Christmas cake and little pressies were distributed by a cunningly disguised Santa, along with a final drop of sherry.

The Pensioners eventually departed into the late afternoon, singing some rather dodgy war-time songs as they clambered into their transport. It was a happy and memorable day for all of us. The Pensioners had really enjoyed themselves and the spirit of Christmas abounded. Job done. I had, however, by that stage decided to hand in my notice. There wasn't a lot of money floating around at the Association and quite understandably they didn't have sufficient funds to pay me a full time salary. The job was becoming all-consuming and I was working well beyond my hours without the commensurate amount of recompense that I thought I deserved. Regrettably, it was time to move on.

BACK IN 'MILITARY' HARNESS

In reality, despite being surrounded by lovely people, I wasn't particularly happy working at Anlaby. I was missing the Army and my old mates. I'd seen a Retired Officer's (RO) post advertised at the Army School of Mechanical Transport (ASMT), Leconfield. I'd been away from the place for two years, but still in a funny sort of way regretted not being involved there. The incumbent of the advertised post had reached the end of the perch and was ready to retire. I liked what I'd read about the job and after a lengthy chat with the incumbent decided to apply for it. If I got the job it would mean that I would be back working with the sort of people I knew and really enjoyed being around. Firstly though, I had to produce a spiffing and relevant CV that would pluck me from obscurity and get me as far as an interview. I carefully prepared my CV and managed to get an interview on the strength of its contents. That vital first step.

The job interview, I knew, would be a long, gruelling and searching one. There'd be no quarter given, they wanted only the best. There's a common misconception within the ranks of the Civil Service that these sorts of Retired Officer jobs, (RO), were 'Jobs for the Boys' and somewhere to tuck ex-officers away until their final retirement. Let me honestly assure you that that wasn't the case, certainly not at Leconfield anyway. Once jumping various hurdles and being employed, maximum effort and a full pound of flesh was expected and inevitable given by RO's who were old school and knew what was required.

The day of my job interview came around and I discovered that there were six officers applying for that particular post. One had even travelled over from Cyprus. Candidates sat in a little waiting room at Headquarters the Army School of Mechanical Transport, Leconfield making polite conversation. I was the fourth on the list to be interviewed. My nerves were twanging with the anticipation of it all. My wife had warned me on pain of death to give it my best shot! Even then I wasn't 100% sure that I really wanted to be back in MOD harness. Those who had been interviewed before me legged it from of the Headquarters, making a point of saying absolutely nothing to those waiting to go in. No clues, you had to fight your own corner.

I was eventually summoned into the Interview Room and sat there facing three severe looking individuals, two serving Lieutenant Colonels and a retired crusty full Colonel, the Chairman. A retired Major was also sat at the back of the room taking notes and ensuring that the correct procedures were adhered to at all times. It was like a court martial scene from 'Mutiny on the Bounty.' All that was missing was the sword on the table. The full Colonel looked as if he was sucking a lemon and I just knew that he was going to be particularly difficult. I answered the board's searching questions to the best of my ability and thought that I was doing reasonably well. I eventually got asked the old chestnut – "And why do you want this job?" I did my best with that one, then started to answer a lengthy and complex question that had been fired at me by the Colonel. He rather rudely, I thought, stopped me mid-answer, saying:

Colonel: *(Haughtily)* Major, I didn't ask you that! You're not answering my specific question! Get to the point will you!

I remember thinking, "Who is this arrogant toe-rag!" The two Lieutenant Colonels gazed studiously at their immaculate fingernails. I remember thinking to myself that I'd spent all of my military life kow-towing before people like this bloody Colonel and that really I'd had quite enough of it. I fixed him with my best steely glance and went off on one, (not the best thing to do in the middle of a job interview). I managed not to swear though and said, through gritted teeth, something along the lines of:

Me: Colonel, if you'd give me the opportunity to formulate my response and let me present it to you properly and logically, you might get to hear what you want to hear! Do you wish me to continue?

Wow, I thought, where did that come from? I was quite impressed with my little self. The Colonel was gob-smacked at my impertinence and I have to say, his cheeks went a little pinker as he nodded grumpily and indicated with a regal wave of his hand for me to continue. I saw that the Lieutenant Colonels had sly little grins on their faces and thought, "Well, that's it! I've bollocksed it up big style. Kiss the job goodbye." I was obviously destined to remain at Anlaby as their Chief Officer. The MOD would have to manage without me.

The retired Major taking notes at the back of the room was shaking his head and making sucking noises with his teeth. It was rather obvious, to me anyway, that I would very shortly be sent on my way. The interrogation continued, however, the Colonel even more frosty faced. We battled on to the end of the interview, the two Lieutenant Colonels throwing in various 'snarlies.' Much to my relief I then got the polite "Thank you for attending, Major Cavender, we'll let you know" etc. I left thinking that I'd given it my best shot, but that my little 'spatette' with the Colonel had holed me beneath the water line. Before leaving the Headquarters building I popped into the waiting room and told the few remaining candidates to "Watch out for the Chairman, chaps – he's a nasty little bastard!" They paled visibly. I then trudged off into the distance.

Much to my surprise – and pleasure, I received a telephone call a few days later telling me that I'd got the job. Apparently it had been a deliberate ploy to try and put candidates under pressure by a senior officer (the Chairman in this instance) firing hard-line questions at them. The old 'Good cop, Bad cop' routine. The interview panel wanted to see, amongst other things, what the reaction of candidates would be to a difficult situation, particularly as a key part of the job would be dealing with very senior officers, top level civil servants, government ministers, general staff officers and their ADC's and palace staff dealing with royal visits etc. They didn't want someone in post who was a 'Yes man' who would wilt before authority. My reply when questioned somewhat acerbically by the Colonel, apparently was just what they wanted to hear. The job was mine. It was not simply a matter of 'Jobs for the Boys' which is oft quoted. My interview was lengthy, thorough and very properly conducted.

I'd obviously had a great deal of experience working behind a desk and was well used to what is called 'Staff Speak.' Having been out of the system for a while, though, I had to get used to all that again. Ah, the delights of being a staff officer, learning to write and use 'staff speak' with the ability to use it imaginatively and to devastating effect. Some examples of 'Staff Speak':

- Ending an e-mail with "Thanks" as a warning that you're perilously close to losing your temper."

- "Perfect." – <u>Translation</u> – Well that's well and truly bollocksed that up then.

- "It's fine." – <u>Translation</u> – "It really couldn't possibly get any worse, but no doubt it will do."

- "A bit of a pickle." – <u>Translation</u> – "A catastrophically bad situation with potentially fatal consequences."

- "Not to worry." – <u>Translation</u> – "I will never forget this!"

- "That's certainly one way of looking at it." – <u>Translation</u> – "That's certainly the wrong way of looking at it."

- "If you say so." – <u>Translation</u> – "I'm afraid what you're saying is the height of idiocy."

- "Just do it when you get a minute." <u>Translation</u> – "Now!"

- "No harm done." – <u>Translation</u> – "You have caused complete an utter chaos."

- "With all due respect." – <u>Translation</u> - "You have absolutely no idea what you're talking about."

Incorporated into my new job at Leconfield was the role of Unit Press Officer for the School. That was the sort of thing I really enjoyed doing, particularly with my background. It was a very busy number and oft times I met myself coming back. I loved it though and was fortunate enough to work alongside and meet some extremely nice and dedicated people. Civil Servants in the Ministry of Defence, for some reason, do not get a very good press, which is rather unfair. They work long hours under immense pressure, uncomplainingly. The public don't get to see much of that, imagining Civil Servants ligging in comfy chairs behind their desks, reading newspapers and drinking gallons tea. Nothing could be further from the truth.

One testing part of my job was to field complaints from the general public who were usually seething because they had been driving behind a military vehicle which had maintained a specific speed (as per the law of the land), and that they – the military – were responsible for the complainant being late for an appointment. That sort of thing. The general public can be very rude and belligerent when they want to be. I picked up quite a few new swear words and often had to terminate rude and abusive calls. I always tried to be respectful and pacify complainants when dealing with their issues but I had to bite my tongue on many occasions. Only recently there was uproar from some of the locals in this area when a military helicopter flew over a village. They thought that it was flying too low (as it came in to land). What are the Armed Forces supposed to do – just where and when are they supposed to train? Give 'em a break. They'll be there when you need them.

I once got a telephone call from 'Irate of Hull' about our training vehicles, saying that "It was fookin' ridiculous, all these military trucks driving around all day with nothing on the back of them. Why couldn't they deliver fruit to the areas local supermarkets?" Suggestion noted. Dealing with the general public was one particular aspect of my job that I didn't miss once I'd finally retired. They could be extremely rude and ungracious. Having said that, I fully agree that they have every right to complain, after all they're paying for everything. They just needed to remember though that it's another human being at the other end of a telephone.

A particular little delight and responsibility I had inherited at Leconfield was to organize a Christmas Party for the children on the base. I'd attended a party organized by my predecessor to see how things were done. The party consisted of the usual sort of thing – filling the kiddies faces with jelly and custard, games etc and then a show performed by a professional magician before Santa arrived to dish out presents. Naturally by the time the show was staged i.e. at the end of a troughing session, all of the children were having sugar rushes and were hyper-active. The very professional Magician, who I won't name because he deserves to be protected, called one young man (about six or seven years old) onto the stage to assist with a magic trick. The child, ginger haired and totally obnoxious, was a nightmare and behaved badly, culminating with – just as a rabbit was pulled out of a top hat, thwacking the poor Magician straight in the knackers. There was a whooshed expelling of air not only from the Magician but from the male adults also in the audience. It must have been agonizing for him.

How the Magician continued performing I'll never know, it was a tribute to his bravery and professionalism, albeit he sounded like Joe Pasquale's for the rest of his act. After his grand finale, he exited the stage, totally ignored by the disinterested children, who by this time were bored out of their little skulls and flinging food around. He told me that he would never perform at Leconfield again – and I didn't blame him. He wasn't being paid enough to have to tolerate that sort of behaviour from children whose parents just stood there and let them run wild. To my amazement, a lot of the parents just dropped their children off at the venue, then went shopping in Beverley, returning to collect their, in the main, badly behaved offspring (I'm not talking about natural Zebedee type exuberance, which one expects from kids) at the end of the party. We were, in reality, acting as a baby-sitting service for a couple of hours. That wouldn't do and I made copious notes for future reference.

I recalled that when I was a stripling, the local British Legion Club used to book coaches and send club member's children off to the lovely Bradford Alhambra each year to see the pantomime. We were given an apple or an orange and sixpence to buy an ice-cream. The whole thing was very orderly and as far as I could recall, apart from screaming at the baddies, we behaved impeccably. I decided that it would be better the following year to have a children's pantomime on the base. I'd had quite a lot of experience staging unit pantomime's and knew what fun they could be. Santa could still arrive at the performance, so the Christmas spirit wouldn't be lost.

I did some research and found a marvellous touring company that would arrive at your location, stage a full traditional style pantomime and then depart afterwards without any fuss or bother. This was an excellent solution and just the job at Christmas as a build up to the more traditional festivities. It had the added bonus, for me anyway, of getting children interested in 'live' theatre at an early stage. Funnily enough when the pantomimes were eventually staged it became patently obvious that many of the children hadn't experienced live theatre before and didn't know how to behave. It was as if they were watching TV! talking and misbehaving throughout the various performances.

Sheffield based 'Stage Door Productions' run by Sean Glenn, did the biz for us. Sean organized (and appeared in) pantomime productions that unfailingly provided superb touring shows with glittering costumes, hilarious traditional scripts, backed up by excellent sound and lighting. Value for money! It was just the ticket and kept the children enthralled. We'd learnt the lesson about making the children hyper and so dispensed with the jelly and custard routine. The children were handed a small packet of sweets and a soft drink when they arrived at the camp's Goodwood Theatre and then the professional performers did the rest. We also invited children in from the local villages, who also enjoyed the experience, although it was a bit of a security nightmare getting everyone in and out of the base. Well worth the effort though to see them enjoying traditional, clean and safe entertainment.

In one of many memorable panto productions, ('Little Red Riding Hood'), Sean Glenn played the part of the Big Bad Wolf. He was so fiercely realistic with his 'Big Bad Wolf' performance that several of the children in the audience ran screaming into the lavatories, cowering and refusing point blank to come out until the Wolf had gone! I can tie one particular pantomime performance down to a specific date – Sunday the 13th of December 2003. I was sat in the theatre manager's office having a sly cup of tea and watching football on the telly. The pantomime was heading for its grand finale, children screaming 'Behind You' etc like banshees, when a newsflash came on TV. The dictator/tyrant, a proper villain, Saddam Hussein had been captured by the Americans and taken into custody. There was a great deal of triumphalism at his being captured and we all celebrated wildly. Another baddie bit the dust. Little did we realise at the time the ongoing chaos and uproar that deposing Saddam would bring about.

As they say in pantomime – "I've bounced off at a tangerine!" The pantomimes continued until I departed Leconfield. I think that pantomimes are just the ticket for children – and many times I saw the accompanying parents getting into the swing of things shouting "Oh no he isn't" etc with great gusto. I hope that children attending the Leconfield pantomimes will retain fond memories of doing so. I know that I do. The Camp Commandant (that's an appointment – not a predilection) also continued to invite children from the local area in to see the pantomimes, which I thought was very generous of him – particularly as entrance was free and they also got some of the 'goodies.' We're all children at heart. I just wish that I could remember some of the names of those Artistes who performed in the pantomime's at the Bradford Alhambra way back when as I have a great love for theatre from that period. The pre-panto excitement when we were getting onto a 'single-decker' bus and heading for the Bradford Alhambra Theatre was beyond exciting. I recall reading much later on in life that one of the most memorable things for those performing on-stage at pantomimes was the smell of pee and orange peel from the auditorium! Well they shouldn't have got us so excited!

'SHOWS FOR THE TROOPS'

There was an organization set up in 1939 specifically to organize entertainment for the troops, called ENSA – the Entertainments National Service Association. Many very talented entertainers, including film stars, worked for ENSA. Because the Armed Forces were spread throughout the world, ENSA was necessarily 'spread thinly' over the vast areas it had to cover. Unfortunately many of the entertainers and shows were substandard. Their acronym was ENSA - *"Every Night Something Awful."* What a gem. Anyway, ENSA provided variety shows, plays and that sort of thing, anywhere in the world where our armed forces were doing their duty. A lot of people will be familiar with the superbly written and performed TV comedy series – 'It Aint Half Hot Mum' based on the antics of an army concert party in India, which gave us an idea of the type of entertainment available to the forces at the time. Along with the not quite so well known, many of the stars at that time did their bit, such as: Gracie Fields, George Formby, Wilfrid Brambell (later of Steptoe & Son), Joyce Grenfell, Vera Lynn, Laurence Olivier etc. These days an organization called Combined Services Entertainment (CSE), operating as part of the heftily titled 'Services Sound and Vision Corporation' has taken on the

ENSA role, providing entertainment in such distant outposts as the Falkland Islands, Afghanistan, Belize etc. They did and continue to do a wonderful and much appreciated job for our Armed Services.

When I was a mere stripling of some 18 summers, I was serving at Aldershot whilst waiting for a posting to the Far East (Singapore, as it turned out). Someone asked me if I was going to see the 'CSE' show that was being staged at a gymnasium on Queen's Avenue that very night. I didn't know what CSE meant or what sort of show it would be, but natural curiosity took over and off I toddled. Someone had also mentioned the magic word 'Free!' I can't remember a great deal about the show other than that I enjoyed it. What I do remember though, is the appearance of Harry Secombe (later Sir Harry), which as a lifelong 'Goon Show' fan was a great delight to me.

Supporting him in the show was Hull's very own top comedian Norman Collier. He was doing his 'chicken' act even back then – and wowed the troops. In one of life's little coincidences I was later to appear alongside Norman Collier at a Hull New Theatre Show and had the privilege of being able to spend some time with him in his dressing room. He spoke enthrallingly about his show-biz experiences, where he'd worked and with whom, for a good hour or so. It was a rare privilege to have been there listening to him.

I remember saying to him "You should write a book Mr Collier. Those stories shouldn't be lost." He later wrote a very funny autobiography, 'Just a Job.' I'm not so sure it was because of what I'd suggested, although I like to think that I'd encouraged him a little bit. He told me a very funny story about a magician in a variety show at Leeds City of Varieties who performed his act then went off the stage on the wrong side (apparently you can only exit from one side of the stage there) and then sneaked back across the stage to the proper exit whilst the act following him was performing, causing mayhem and hilarity. Mr Collier made it sound much funnier than I can write it.

A few years later I went to see another great comedian, Jimmy Tarbuck, performing a 'One-Man' Show at the Leeds City of Varieties and he told exactly the same story as if it had happened whilst he was performing there. It was virtually word for word. I wasn't bothered because it was just as funny the second time around. I'd heard stories about 'waves of love' washing across a stage from an adoring audience and had thought 'what a load of old cobblers' but it's true. When I was on-stage at Hull New Theatre and Norman Collyer was introduced the audience went wild with enthusiasm and you could feel that something very special had happened. They loved him and it showed. I often saw him with his family, walking around Hull, dressed immaculately and taking the time to stop and talk to his legion of fans. A magical, very special man, now, sadly, no longer with us.

In my own little way, I also got involved in producing shows for the troops in an out of the way post – at Leconfield in East Yorkshire. I was in my office there one day, sometime in 2006, when the Commandant popped in to see me. I made the relevant arse kissing noises and invited him to take a seat. He sat down, demanded a coffee then a conversation, something along the following lines took place:

Commandant: You may stop genuflecting now, Major Cavender. *(I made that bit up)*

Commandant: Terry, you're into this theatre thing. There's been a bit too much indiscipline and Trainees getting into trouble on camp for my liking.

I'd like you to organize a 'CSE' style show to keep them entertained. I'll provide some money from the welfare fund etc – can you do it?

Me: Does a chicken have lips, your Eminence?

Commandant: What?

Me: Yes, of course I can, sir.

Commandant: Good. Crack on then. I'll leave it with you. Keep me in touch with what's going on.

He swept out of the office, taking my brush with him, and a light went out in my world. The next few weeks were taken over by a flurry of telephone calls, setting up a committee to help me and in general sorting things out. Because Normandy Barracks at Leconfield used to be RAF Leconfield until the Army invaded, there were several large hangars in use. One such hangar was used as a gymnasium and it was decided that that was where the show would take place. We had a huge mobile stage (in reality an extended boxing ring) and millions of yards of black hessian (normally used as camouflage material) so the basics were there. A Hull based company was hired to provide professional sound and lighting. I got on to the Quartermaster's Department, who got on to the Army Chair Unit and ordered a thousand wooden folding chairs for the troops and civilian instructors (there would easily be an audience of a thousand plus). Select Officers and others of perceived importance, naturally, would be provided with padded chairs, as befitted their status.

There were, in fact, only several padded chairs, or 'Chairs Arm Easy Resting,' as they are referred to in military parlance, at the front centre of the auditorium (Hangar), reserved for the Commandant, the Chief of Staff, the Padre and the Regimental Sergeant Major etc. This seating arrangement also helped the Artistes who would then know where the VIP's were sat and precisely whom they could then 'victimize' throughout the show. The remainder of the seats were on a 'first come first served' basis, which I thought was much fairer than seating being allocated by rank and status as used to be the case in the 'olden days.' I suddenly became everyone's best friend when the jostling for seat positioning became more and more important as show-time drew near. As it was the troop's welfare money that would be paying for the show it was only right and proper that they should get a fair crack of the whip and I ignored all requests to sneak a front seat.

With the money I had to hand, I managed to obtain the services of that brilliantly funny comedian 'Mick Miller' to both headline and compere the show. Unfortunately I'm unable to remember the names of the supporting cast, Dancers, Singers, a Magician and a Ventriloquist, but I know that we had a cracking evening. It was a good, old fashioned but well-rounded variety show. The troops loved Mick and he went down an absolute storm. Chatting with him before the show, he asked me what the parameters were and I said something along the lines of, "Well, anything goes really Mick, but I would ask you not to use the 'C' word at any time during the show as there were ladies attending (this is going back a few years). He was more than happy with that minor requirement (and kept his word). The troops loved him to bits as did the rest of the audience, ladies included. A very entertaining man. I went to see Chubby Brown in Scarborough a few months later and his language would have made Satan's hair curl. Mick Miller was charming by comparison.

Mick was safely ensconsed in his dressing room, Everyone was seated and there was a definite air of pre-show excitement as we waited for the Commandant to arrive, then the show could begin. To my horror, the Commandant appeared with his wife in tow. I hadn't expected that and we had to rapidly rearrange the 'posh' seats. As you can imagine, the troops were pretty raucous and already enjoying themselves, (courtesy of the controlled NAAFI bar). There was the usual amount of polite booing and raspberry blowing as the VIPs were shown to their seats. Pre-show drinks were allowed, but none to be taken into the auditorium. Notwithstanding, an air of mischief abounded, which was a good thing, after all we wanted the troops to relax, enjoy themselves, let off a bit of steam and forget their worries - if only for one night.

We were very lucky in that we were able to build a huge stage in one of the old RAF Hangars that was in use as a gymnasium. It looked spectacular. So, house lights down and the show began with thrashing music, flashing and colourful disco style lights, dazzlingly sexy dancers - cheered to the rafters by the troops (male and female). I was lucky to be helped on that occasion by the erudite enthusiast, Captain Terry O'Hagan, who is now a senior officer in the Australian army. Enter Mick Miller. Things were going swimmingly well. Mick started off with his warm-up jokes and patter, only to be interrupted by a gobby squaddy in the audience – whom Mick silenced with a witty bit of polished repartee – "Fuck off - dick splash!" Tastefully done, I thought. The Commandant's wife was sat near to me, stony faced, as was the Commandant. I felt myself breaking into a muck-sweat and sinking lower into my seat. This would be the end of a beautiful career – mine.

As the show rolled along to the interval, I noticed the Commandant's wife leaving the venue. I remember thinking that I would definitely be getting my feet sharpened by the glorious leader. However, he explained to me after the show, much to my relief, that he was sorry that he'd brought his wife to see the show and should have known that it might put a bit of a dampener on things having her there, which was very fair of him. I did, in fact get a 'good boy' chit on my annual report for my efforts.

Everyone enjoyed themselves and had a riotous evening (I like to think so anyway). I was asked to organize several shows after that, so it couldn't have been that bad. Incidentally, if you ever get the chance to go and see Mick Miller perform you should make the effort an go. It'll do you the world of good.

T C with comedian Mick Miller after a show

One particularly memorable show, based on similar lines, was headlined by a famous Comedian, let's call him Mr X, who had hit the big time and had recently appeared on the prime-time Des O'Connor Chat Show. I won't name him, why will become apparent later on. The show was roughly based on what was now to me normal procedure, stage, lights, sound, lots of flashy, noisy entertainment culminating with a top act to finish the night off. On this occasion it was going to be Mr X. I'd also booked a particularly racy set of female dancers called something like 'Sexy Devils' or something along those lines, to help build an air of excitement. There were six Dancers, all of them stunningly gorgeous. The troops went wild with ecstasy as the dancers appeared to open the show and tastefully gyrated to appropriate disco style music. I was getting a little concerned as halfway through the show the headliner, Mr X, still hadn't arrived. I smiled and pretended that I was enjoying myself and cared not a jot. Thankfully, the Provost

Sergeant came over to me and whispered in my ear that the main man had arrived and was waiting back-stage to meet me.

I nipped around to the dressing rooms to introduce myself and say hello to him. I recall that he was immaculately dressed and looked the part of someone who was very successful at what he did. I said something along the lines of "Good evening Mr X, nice to meet you." It was then that I noticed that he was as white as a sheet. He blurted out "Major Cavender, I'm afraid that I can't go on!" I laughed at what I thought was his little jest until I realised that he was being deadly serious. I asked him what the problem was, as disaster loomed. He said, "Have you heard them out there, they're like wild animals baying for blood!" I said, "Look old chap they're only a bunch of squaddies enjoying the evening. If anything you'll get a brilliant reception. We've been building you up all night!" "No," he replied "I can't do it. I can't face them. They'll eat me alive!" As if on cue, the troops began howling like the 'Hounds of the Baskerville's.' Gloom.

I turned a little shirty, saying, "It's a bit late in the day to be telling me that – after all, you knew full well that it was a Services gig! There's plenty of security laid on to stop any silliness and you must have done these sort of shows before?" "Well I have," he said, nearly in tears, "I've done the working men's clubs and all that sort of thing, but this one's different." "In what way?" said I. "I can't explain it really," said he, "But I'm shitting myself!" "Well," I told him, "I'm sorry to hear that, but if you don't go on – you don't get paid. It's as simple as that! I'll fill your spot with the girl dancers." He pondered for a split second, thinking of the readies (a substantial amount) then agreed that he would perform.

At the peak of the show, he stood in the wings, trembling, waiting to be introduced. I couldn't believe it really. Surely a man of his vast experience (and he was genuinely funny) had performed before this sort of audience before? He must know how to handle all sorts of audiences. The show must go on!

"Ladies and Gentlemen, please put your hands together for our headline act, the fabulous, the fantastically funny - Mr X." There was a huge cheer as Mr X walked gingerly onto the stage. He was booked to do a thirty minute spot but spoke so quickly that he sounded as if he was on laughing gas. He gabbled through his entire thirty or so minute act in fifteen minutes then legged it off-stage, trembling and still as white as a sheet. The troops were disappointed as they were looking forward to seeing him. I hadn't expected that little drama. Notwithstanding, as he rushed off I brought the girl dancers back on to finish the show. Both the performers and troops loved it. Everyone, apart from Mr X, had a spiffing evening's entertainment. Mr 'X' jumped into his Range Rover and headed for the hills. I was physically and emotionally drained.

In closing this segment, I must tell you about one particular show that caused me to lose most of what hair I had left. Once again, a standard variety format, Dancers, Singers, a Magician, Headliner etc. This time though, the fun and games was with the dancers who were called 'Red Hot' – something or other. As delightful a bunch of maidens as ever you would wish to see, very easy on the eye and certainly very popular with the troops, who cheered them to the rafters, ecstatic at their every appearance. As the show progressed I was summoned back stage to the dressing rooms. The lady in charge of the dancers, a dancer and group member herself, had asked to see me. I entered the dressing room, which was full of very nubile, bronzed, naked young ladies. I didn't know where to look. The boss of the dancers sidled across to me.

She also wasn't wearing a stitch, so that made things doubly difficult for me. I couldn't concentrate. The conversation went something along the following lines:

Head Dancer: Hi there hunk! (*I made that bit up*).

Me: What's up?

Head Dancer: When we open the second half, I'd like the girls to come on topless. They're quite happy to do that. We do a disco style thing with fire torches and it's all very magical. Apparently only you can give it the nod, boss?

Me: What! Absolutely not, not under any circumstances. No topless stuff!

Head Dancer: The girls don't mind getting their baps out, sir – do you girls!

"Neh" was their disinterested reply.

Me: Well I do mind. I've had explicit instructions that there is to be no nudity and that was made clear to your management when you were booked. Any of that sort of thing and I'll be in big trouble. I'd probably get the sack.

Head Dancer: I can't see what the problem is, we've played at lots of other bases. Come on – be a sport! We've flashed our tits on telly and all over the world.

Me: Well you're not flashing your Bristol's at Leconfield. Stick to what was agreed.

The 'Tits – No Tits' discussion continued for quite a while between us. It finally ended when I got a bit butch and told her that I would have the Provost Sergeant pull the plug on the lighting if so much as one uncovered bap appeared on-stage. The dancers would be removed from the base and not only that, they would be in breach of contract so wouldn't get paid. Political Correctness had started creeping into the Forces and any unit getting involved with something negative that might hit the Media could prove to be life changing (for me anyway). One could just imagine the headlines in The Sun newspaper – 'Show Debauchery at Leconfield' 'Sex Mad Squaddies on the Rampage' etc. Our leaders all had Field Marshal's batons in their rucksacks and didn't want any unnecessary drama's on 'their watch.' It sort of took the fun of doing something a bit daring out of life I suppose. The threat of removing the dancing girls payment had the desired effect and clinched the argument in my favour. It was a shame really because they only wanted to spice things up a bit, it's not as if they were going to turn Leconfield into 'A Night at the Casbah.' They thought that if they, the performers, didn't mind a bit of nudity, then neither would the audience.

A sullen mutinous silence had descended in the dressing room, and I thought, will they or won't they ignore me? In reality I wouldn't have pulled the plug, had I done so, the troops would probably have rioted. I would just have to take my chances with the girls and if things went 'tits up' on stage then I would just have to take the flack.

The VIP Guests, Commandant etc, had been fed and watered at the Interval and then returned to their seats for the second half of the show. I nodded to the Stage Manager, the houselights went down then with blue light bathing the stage - church style organ music started to play from the speakers. Where was all this going? Six or so 'Nuns' meandered reverentially onto the stage whilst the solemn organ music continued to soar throughout the auditorium (hangar actually). I began to feel a little uncomfortable as I didn't really know what to expect.

The Nuns came to the very front of the stage, looking like something from 'The Sound of Music' - then suddenly whipped off their Nuns costumes to huge cheer from the troops. As the Nuns revealed their very shapely and finely dance honed bodies, extremely scantily clad (but fortunately no Bristol's on display), the troops went wild with ecstasy. These were not the sort of Nuns we were used to seeing, boys and girls. Sister Concepta was never like this (or was she)? The troops were loving it, the odd one or two even attempting to run out of the audience and join the dancers onstage, inevitably to be gently but firmly ejected from the venue by the Provost Staff, (their feet slightly off the ground and arms up back) and warned not to return on pain of death. A number of burly members of the Provost Staff had been stood by to maintain law and order in the event of such misbehaviour. I needn't have worried on that score because 'Miss Behaviour' was performing onstage!

The dancers were nearly naked, apart from wearing some sort of red plastic sort of Sam Browne belt affair, with a large red heart at the end of the tail covering their prosecutable areas. Their outfits were finished off with long spiky heeled red shoes and they were all carrying bull-whips. Where was this going? "Don't panic Captain Mainwaring!" The vision is forever burned in my memory. It was similar to something that I'd last seen in Berlin's Charlottenburg. The dancers then proceeded to do the raciest dance I think I've ever seen, bordering on the lewd, nay, beyond lewd, but just this side of legal action, all the time cracking their whips and making suggestive gestures with the phallic shaped whip handles. I started to perspire and took a sneaky sideways glance at the Commandant. His mouth was agape and his eyes were glued to the stage.

I was mortified and relieved that neither my wife or daughter were present, thinking "Here we go again! I'm in the khazi now!" The Padre, who was sat a few chairs down from me would surely be hot under his clerical collar, and seething, but no, he too was gazing raptly at the Mother Superior and her cohorts. I couldn't really tell if he was offended or not until he saw me looking at him and gave me the old thumbs up, mouthing "Cracking show T.C!" What a nice man! The Regimental Sergeant Major looked a little uncomfortable, but that was the least of my worries. If the 'nobs' were happy, I might just get away with it again. As it turned out, another great show much enjoyed by attendees – and I got a very nice thank you from the Commandant and other senior officers in attendance, but more importantly the troops had lapped it up. I listened to their comments after the show as they departed for the fleshpots of Beverley/Hull post-show and heard not one criticism. That was one of the last shows I organized before retiring from the scene of battle, I do miss that particular challenge though. It was fun.

'AN UNEXPECTED VISITOR'

Part of my job was getting involved in the organisation of Beverley Armed Forces Day (BAFD) and t'was the Friday night before one such event. I'd been heavily into the planning processes into what was turning out to be quite a large event (eventually some 10,000 visitors passed through the hallowed portals of Beverley). After dinner that Friday evening I was sat with the Memsahib having a nice glass of chilled white wine and unwinding. I got what I thought was a bout of indigestion (Oh Oh!). It refused to go away and I knew that things were a little more serious when I started having trouble breathing. My right lung was having difficulty inflating. I eventually rang the NHS

Help-line and whilst I was on the telephone explaining my symptoms to a very helpful lady. Whilst we were speaking, a Paramedic arrived at our front door and began to examine me..

Regrettably his equipment wasn't charged up properly and he was unable to continue making an assessment. Fortunately an ambulance arrived a few moments later and I was taken into the very capable hands of two young ladies. I was blue lighted off the Hull Royal Infirmary with my poor beloved wife in tow, thrashing along behind the ambulance in her turbo-charged 'Smart' car. It was the last thing she needed after having had her own very busy week at work. Anyway, to cut a long story short, I was held in the Acute Assessment Ward until seeing a Specialist early the following morning. Lots of X-Rays and popping in and out of tubes for scans. A triple pulmonary embolism was diagnosed. Not single – it had to be a triple, no half measure for me folks. Apparently if I'd ignored the symptoms and gone to bed it would probably have been curtains for me. To cut a long story short there followed lots of medication and a relatively quick course on how to self-inject Warfarin, after which I was able to be released from the hospital and allowed to return home.

It was such a relief to be able to leave the Acute Assessment Ward. I stepped out of the main entrance of Hull Royal, passing through a fairly large group of patients who were stood there in pyjamas etc smoking and coughing, out into the sunshine and into a lovely crisp day. Plan A - I could have waited for an hour or so for my beloved to come and collect me or – Plan B – I could make my own way home. As it was such I nice day I decided to take a very gentle saunter to the railway station and get a train to Beverley. I felt absolutely OK and thought that the fresh air might do me a bit of good. It did, it helped to clear my head and get me away from the confines of the hospital.

As I made my way to Hull's Paragon Station I couldn't help but notice that people were glancing at me and then hurriedly proceeding along their way. I checked my zip to see that nothing was untoward, everything was OK there and then I noticed to my horror that the shirt sleeve on my left arm was thoroughly blood-soaked. The site where I'd had various needles and instruments of torture inserted throughout the course of the night was gently but determinedly bleeding. The medication I had received meant that my blood was now very much thinner and consequently took ages to clot. Plan C – I rolled up my sleeve to hide the blood. As I tottered through Hull's Paragon Station I looked like what is described by the Scottish as a 'Jakey' i.e. someone who has consumed copious amounts of 'Buckies' and who ought not to be approached under any circumstances.

Fortunately there was a train about to leave for Beverley, so I hopped on board. I was starting to wind down now like a broken old toy. Knackered. Indignity heaped upon indignity. A rather generously proportioned lady came and plonked her heavily perspiring frame next to me, crushing me against the side of the carriage. I couldn't have cared less by this time. When the Conductor came along the train I was unable to provide the full amount of ticket money required, I was a few pence short. I gave him a brief overview of what had happened to me over the past few hours and that I had unexpectedly been discharged from Hull Royal Hospital. He was most understanding and very kindly permitted me to finish the journey to Beverley without any further dramas.

As the train drew into Beverley Station I made to leave, but the rather large rotund lady stuffed into the seat next to me, for some reason, didn't appear to want to move and let me get off the train. I explained to her that I needed to get off the train there, (I had visions of finishing up in Bridlington – and how would I explain that to she who must be obeyed)? For some reason the lady studiously ignored me (she probably thought I was some old piss-head). This called for a bit of delicate negotiation, so falling back on my military training I bellowed "Madam, please remove your lardy arse from that seat, I have to get off here, Now!" That worked a treat and I left the train seconds before it moved off. Staggering across to a platform seat I lowered myself gently onto it. The dragon lady was glaring at me through the train window as it left Beverley Station. As a farewell gesture, with two trembling fingers I flashed her a venomous 'V' (a reverse Churchill). As I sat regrouping, I heard a little voice bouncing around my head i.e. the Memsahib, whom I knew was going to flay me alive for not waiting for her at the hospital. Not a wise decision, but I wasn't thinking straight. Time to move on before fellow travellers started depositing money on the side of the seat, such was my advanced state of decrepitude.

I managed to totter across to my Mother-in-Law's residence, a short walk away from Beverley Railway Station and there await the arrival of my Mistress. After a good strong cup of Yorkshire tea I immediately revived and was fit for, well fit for a good kip really. 1 x Wife duly arrived and administered the expected severe bollocking before I was transported home in close arrest. As we passed through Beverley we paused momentarily outside the lovely St Mary's Church. I wanted to see the Spitfire aircraft that I had booked to fly over the town to highlight the Beverley Armed Forces Celebrations that day. Regrettably it didn't appear when it should have because apparently there was too much wind and it couldn't be risked, (story of my life), so I went off home to nurse my wounds.
One upshot of having had a 'triple' pulmonary embolism was that I am now required to wear those tight, elongated travel socks at all times. Women

who wear tights every day of their lives have my every sympathy. At the end of each day my legs resemble two little pink egg-timers. The Memsahib and I were due to go on a recuperative cruise which meant flying to Dubai to pick up the ship. When I asked my Doctor if I was safe to fly to Dubai, he said, "Terry old chap, you're safer than the pilot. At least you know that your blood is thin enough to travel without any problems!"

'BEVERLEY TOWN ARMED FORCES DAY'

I received an unexpected request from Councillor David Elvidge of the East Riding of Yorkshire Council and Organiser of the Beverley Armed Forces Day, to do a poetry reading at the event in Beverley on Sunday 1st July 2012. Other such readers would be Graham Stuart MP, Conservative Member for Beverley & Holderness and Councillor Brian Pearson - local luminary and also a member of the East Riding of Yorkshire Council. Esteemed company. I gave the matter a little thought and decided that I would accept the invitation. I also decided that perhaps I should do a slightly different reading to the norm. It might be considered contentious to a degree, but for the boots on the ground, not a lot had changed over the years and I wanted to read something reflecting that. This is what I chose to read:

Preamble:

"Fairly recently, a British Soldier fighting in Afghanistan rewrote a famous poem, written originally by Rudyard Kipling, about the hellish conditions faced by troops in that country. The Serviceman based his words on Kipling's 1895 poem 'The Young British Soldier.' It graphically described the tough conditions British Forces faced when in Afghanistan in the 19th century. The British soldier who 'amended' the verses I'm about to read, chose to be 'anonymous' so I am unable to give him or her a name-check.

This poem highlights the harsh conditions of soldiers having to make do with poor pay, equipment and a fierce enemy – and implies that not much has changed for the members of our valiant Armed Forces more than a hundred years later on."

*** AFGHANISTAN ***

WHEN YOU'RE LYING ALONE IN YOUR AFHGAN BIVVY,
AND YOUR LIFE DEPENDS ON SOME M.O.D. CIVVIE,
WHEN YOUR BODY ARMOUR'S SHARED - ONE SET BETWEEN THREE,
AND THE FIRE-FIGHT'S NOT QUITE LIKE IT IS ON TV,
THEN YOU'LL LOOK TO YOUR OPPO, YOUR GUN AND YOUR GOD,
AS YOU FOLLOW THE PATH THAT ALL TOMMIES HAVE TROD.

--*--

WHEN YOUR WEAPON HAS JAMMED AND YOU'RE DOWN TO ONE ROUND,
AND THE FAITH THAT YOU'D LOST IS SUDDENLY FOUND,
WHEN THE TALIBAN HORDE IS CLOSE UP TO THE FORT,
AND YOU PRAY THE ARTILLERY DON'T DROP A ROUND SHORT.

--**--

STICK TO YOUR SERGEANT LIKE A GOOD SQUADDIE SHOULD,

AND FIGHT THEM LIKE SATAN OR ONE OF HIS BROOD,
YOUR PAY WON'T COVER YOUR NEEDS OR YOUR WANTS,
SO JUST STAND THERE AND TAKE ALL THE TALIBAN'S TAUNTS,
NO GENERAL'S OR CIVVY CAN DO 'OWT TO AMEND IT,
BUT KEEP YOU IN A PLACE -
WHERE YOU JUST CAN'T SPEND IT,
A FEW QUID AN HOUR IN YOUR AFGHANI CAGE,
ABOUT JUST THE SAME AS THE MINIMUM WAGE.

--***--

YOUR MISSUS AT HOME IN A FOUL MARRIED QUARTER,
WITH DAMP ON THE WALLS AND A ROOF LEAKING WATER,
YOUR KIDS MISS THEIR MATE, THEIR HERO, THEIR DAD,
THEY'RE MISSING THE CHILDHOOD THAT THEY SHOULD HAVE HAD,
ONE DAY IT WILL BE DIFFERENT, ONE DAY BY AND BY,
AS YOU STAND THERE AND WATCH, TO SEE THE PIGS FLY.

--****--

JUST LIKE YOUR FOREBEARS IN MUD, DUST AND DITCH,
YOU'LL MARCH AND YOU'LL FIGHT AND YOU'LL DRINK AND YOU'LL BITCH,
WHETHER FROGGY OR ZULU, OR JERRY, OR BOER,
THE BRITS ALWAYS FIGHT ON 'TIL THE BATTLE IS OVER.

--*****--

YOU MAY TREAT THEM LIKE DIRT,

BUT NOTHING UNNERVES THEM,

AND I WONDER SOMETIMES,

IF OUR COUNTRY DESERVES THEM.

'FORGET ME NOT'

In 2014 I was honoured to be asked by local Councillor David Elvidge to write a play specifically for performing at Beverley Armed Forces Day, emphasising the involvement and sacrifices of soldiers from Beverley both during and after World War 1. I wrote the play 'Forget Me Not' which was performed on Sunday the 13th of June 2014 at the beautiful and historical St Mary's Church in North Bar Within, Beverley, by members of the newly formed ERT (East Riding Theatre) 'Other Lives Production Group.'

The performance was well attended, well received, beautifully and sensitively performed by ERT and I was extremely proud to have been involved with it. We must never forget those who gave their all.

'FLOOD HEROES'

'It was a dark and stormy night, the rain came down in torrents.' The great floods of 2007 were upon us.

On the day the drama began, I was working with my old mate Major Peter Todd, in the Headquarters of the Defence School of Transport at Leconfield. Little did we realize that we would be remaining in the Headquarters for a number of days and would be required to set up and man an Operations Room, linked to the local authorities, to assist with flood relief. It was excruciatingly busy but at least we weren't out there with the soldiers who were valiantly filling manky sacks with sand and building flood barriers out in the cold, lashing rain. Everyone just sort of got on with it and there was a definite Churchillian spirit abounding.

The only really sad moment was when we heard that a young chap had been trapped in a drain and unfortunately the rescue service, despite their valiant efforts, were unable to rescue him and that he had died. Eventually the rain stopped, the flooding was dealt with as best as everyone could and slowly over the next few days life returned to normal, for us at least. Just a few 'factoids' about what the military provided for the local populace (as well as whilst working in horrendous conditions). They filled 9,000 sand bags, delivering them to local authorities at all times of the day and night in constant pouring rain and also ground-loaded many more. They also loaded 600 or so sandbags onto vehicles as stand-by, ready to be delivered when called upon to do so at short notice.

A few days after the floods had abated and things calmed down a bit, to our great surprise, both myself and Peter Todd were nominated as being 'Flood Heroes' along with another mate of ours,

Captain Bob Mather RE (now Major Bob Mather MBE RE – no finer man sat on a pan). We three were invited down to Lancaster House in London to be presented with a certificate by the then Prime Minister, The Rt. Hon. Gordon Brown MP. I should tell you before we go any further, that just prior to the London visit, Peter Todd and his wife Linda had returned from a holiday in Sri Lanka where, on their very last day they had attended a beach barbecue and unfortunately, for Peter, he had eaten copious amounts of locally caught lobster. Peter said later that there was something not quite right about the smell of the lobster but that his appetite took precedence. On the journey back home to the UK, Peter was attacked by a severe bouts of wind and tummy rumbling. T'was the Sri Lankan lobster getting its own back. This made it necessary for the Officer Todd to visit all available toilet facilities on very frequent occasions in order for him to 'open the bomb doors.' It was a problem that was destined to torment him – and us - for quite a few days afterwards.

Notwithstanding, having received a Prime Ministerial invitation, we boarded a train in Hull, Peter and I accompanied by our wives, and proceeded on our way to London, having met up with the officer Bob Mather at Beverley Railway Station. I remember the date well because it was my 60th birthday, the 3rd of December 2007.

Things were going swimmingly as we boarded the extremely efficient and reliable Hull Trains and head for the capital city. I couldn't understand why the bold Major Todd kept disappearing every five minutes or so and then returned to the carriage with a look of sweet relief on his features as he gingerly lowered himself onto his seat. There was great excitement in our carriage as we realized that the TV legend that is Peter Levy, the main news anchor for BBC Yorkshire & Lincolnshire, was also travelling to Lancaster House, also as it turned out in his capacity as a 'Flood Hero.' The day had a lovely feeling about it, particularly as we merrily quaffed a couple of bottles of fine wine along the way to London. We reached Kings Cross and went to our hotel to change into our posh gear for the Lancaster House gig. Unable to take our wives to the formal function, we agreed to meet them in the Ritz hotel just around the corner from Lancaster House, after the certificate presentation.

The 'Three Musketeers,' Todd, Mather and Cavender, arrived at Lancaster House and were directed into a truly splendid hall where we were knee deep in waiters, dispensing copious amounts of government funded chilled white wine. Not wishing to offend our host, the Prime Minister, we felt that it was our bounden duty to drink as much of the wine as we could in the time available to us. The wine tasted perfectly delightful and was certainly an improvement on that which we had imbibed on the train coming down, (a cheeky little number picked from the South side of the NAAFI Services Shop). After about half an hour everyone was in a very merry mood and the level of conversation had risen from being merely loud to a raucous hubbub. Totally ignored in the background was a Quintet doing their best to entertain with tasteful music. Word spread that Gordon Brown had arrived and was about to make a speech. He had one of his Ministers with him, the diminutive Hazel Blears, who had to stand on a box at the side of the PM in order to be seen. They looked like the Krankies.

I was extremely impressed by the PM who is much handsomer than he appears on TV. He was also a very erudite speaker, exuding passion, humour and confidence. Why the hell didn't those qualities come across on TV, we asked ourselves. Mr Brown gave an excellent and humorous speech then went around the assembled gathering pressing the flesh and talking to as many people as he could. He eventually left us alone to finish off what was left of the official wine stocks. We, now official 'Flood Heroes' thought that we'd better be making tracks for the Ritz as the free wine was running out and girls would be getting impatient. Not only that, there were ominous rumblings emanating from Peter Todd's nether garments, so yet again he had to nip off rather sharpish to the Lancaster House 'heads.' He returned, walking like Max Wall and grinning sheepishly - warning us that if we needed to pay a visit ourselves it might be better to wait until we got to the Ritz as the heads in Lancaster House would probably be declared unsafe for human use for a wee while. so we hot-footed it out of Lancaster House whilst we were still ahead of the game. Oh, on our way out we bumped into the erudite and debonair Peter Levy on the main staircase of Lancaster House where Toddy demanded a photograph of himself alongside Mr Levy, whilst telling him how much he really, really loved him to bits, although he did apologize profusely for occasionally watching the opposition's ITV News.

We Three Musketeers 'linked up' bade our fond farewells to the Lancaster House security staff and then tottered around the corner past St James's Palace, shushing our way past Clarence House, stifling our raucous giggles in case we disturbed any slumbering member of the Royal Family, then on to the Ritz. We caused a frisson of confusion by thrashing loudly into the wrong entrance of the Ritz, finishing up in the Casino, where we were pursued by a rather glamorous but panic stricken blond who said that the Casino was for members only and were we members? The officer Todd gazed at the fair maiden, with rheumy eyes, (his not hers) and told her to bugger off and mind her own pigging business, we were 'Flood Heroes' and were there to meet our wives. That went down like a fart in a space-suit and it was quite apparent to the young lady that it was more than likely that we weren't regular members of the Ritz Casino's exclusive clientele.

We were all politely but firmly ejected from the premises by a couple of respectful but very muscular gentlemen, only for us to nip around the corner to the main entrance of the Ritz and meet up with our waiting spouses. We shared a swift nightcap with them in the bar, (the payment for which was the equivalent of a mortgage 'Oooop North'), then it was into a taxi and off to our own hotel where we had booked a celebratory Supper. Major Todd was outraged at the prices in the Ritz and wasn't particularly enamored to discover that the crisps in little crystal bowls on the table were in fact pot pourri. Peter still consumed a couple of bowls, which actually sweetened his breath, although the pieces of cinnamon bark, jasmine and fennel seeds stuck in the spaces between the gaps in his teeth did nothing for his avuncular smile. The understanding doormen at the Ritz very kindly poured us into our chariot and we vanished into the night, Peter continuing to break ferocious wind and shouting "I'll leave that one with you," before laughing uproariously to himself.

We encouraged Todd to sit in the far corner of the vehicle as there were still strange bubbling noises and occasional exotic whiffs emanating from his nether regions. We eventually arrived back at our hotel after a thrilling ride and had a nice spot of Supper. Bob shouted, "Champagne for the Birthday Boy!" pointing at me and we wellied a bottle of something nice and fizzy. I am not going to impart what happened later to disrupt the festivities of the evening, that will remain classified forever, but it transpired that I finished up at the table all by myself, 'Billy No-mates,' and polished off the bottle of champagne. I also had to pay for it! The outrage – me the birthday boy - left with the bill! We returned to Hull the following morning, slightly delicate but triumphantly clutching our 'Flood Hero' certificates, signed by the PM. The Officer Todd had entered the recovery stage but nevertheless continued to make full use of the train's toilet facilities all the way back home. The Toddmeister is, thankfully, now fully recovered. Later on that year we went on a cruise with our wives that skirted Sri Lanka and I'm sure Toddy's face paled and his floral shorts billowed in sympathy when our cruise liner steamed past the Sri Lankan coast.

'ROYALTY AND LESSER BEINGS'

Various members of the Royal Family have had the good fortune to cross my path in the course of my time both with the Military and the Civil Service. Along with the Memsahib, I'd been invited to attend a Garden Party at Buckingham Palace. I've been accused of being a social climber and a name dropper, but as I was saying to the Queen only the other day ……..

Being at the Garden Party was, for us, tremendously exciting, particularly as HM provides such marvellous sticky buns in the Lyons Tea Tent. Needless to say, whilst at the Garden Party there was a happening. Prior to the arrival of the Royal family, the 'Gentlemen of Honour,' immaculately turned out in top hats and tails all of them looking to a man like Fred Astaire, sashay around the crowds looking for interesting people to be introduced to the royals and judged as being relatively safe for a quick and interesting chatette. The crowds were gently eased, like compliant sheep, into manageable squares by the Gentlemen of Honour and the attendant Beefeaters, threateningly clutching their erect halberds. A military band struck up the national anthem as a palace French window magically opened and the Royals were beamed down onto the patio before respectfully being guided to the front of their allocated pen of awe-stricken subjects, nodding regally and being presented to the pre-selected few.

As we were looking particularly well-scrubbed that day, we had been selected for a chat and were eagerly awaiting the arrival of Prince Charles, who had been allocated our square. It may have been something to do with me wearing an RCT regimental tie or Maggie wearing an RCT brooch. The Armed Forces were inevitably safe territory. HRH arrived in front us and was about to strike up a conversation when he happened to glance at the porcine little 'Mr Grimsdale' style figure stood at our side. The man was wearing a very old style suit, in parts very shiny, with the waist-band of his trousers tightly gathered, courtesy of a scarred leather belt, just underneath his pendulous breasts. In the button-hole of his suit jacket was a proudly displayed union badge. I have always worked on the premise 'Don't judge a man until you've walked a mile in his shoes' etc but it was quite apparent to us all that this individual had made no effort whatsoever to dress smartly for the occasion. He may not have had the money to do so, not everyone has, but a bit of shoe polish wouldn't have gone amiss.

The following conversation then took place between these two ends of the social spectrum, HRH Prince Charles, who is touched by grace, and the lower decks, who aren't :

HRH: (*Pointing with a well manicured pinkie at the man's union medal*) Aaaah, now there's a medal that I don't recognize.

Man: (*Puffing his pigeon chest out and bawling out in a Lancashire accent*) Aye, well you wouldn't, would you!

HRH: (*HRH grimacing and confused at the man's negative response*) Er, er, I beg your pardon?

Man: Ah sed, you wouldn't would you! Recognise me medal!

HRH: (*Still puzzled*) Well I er, I er …. Wouldn't what?

Like him or not, Prince Charles is inevitably controlled and gracious and was so on this occasion.

Man: (*Tapping his medal with a gnarled, nicotine stained finger*) I had to work bloody hard to get this.

HRH: (*Fighting to be pleasant*) Well I'm sure you did. I, er ...

Man: *(Rudely interrupting)* I had to earn this, I wasn't just given it by my Mother!

Now, we were standing extremely close to HRH (so close in fact that I could see that his man had missed a small area just underneath sir's nose when shaving him that morning). HRH had, by this time, turned a deep shade of furious puce at the implied insult, but commendably stayed his temper. He spoke politely but icily to the man:

HRH: Good for you, sir. I sincerely hope that you continue to wear your medal with pride and in good health. (*By now really seething, and just holding himself in check (should that be Prince Charles check*)?

Poor Prince Charles, so many years of schmoozing pillocks, but still exhibiting an air of innate politeness. Notwithstanding, he executed a grass grinding right turn and stomped off, heading for the Royal Tea Tent for a cup of undoubtedly calming tea, his day obviously having gone downhill at a rapid rate of knots. We were very disappointed at not being able to have had a meaningful chat with our future Monarch. I had so many things that I wanted to chat with him about, like how does Teflon stick to frying pans etc, on this never to be repeated opportunity

After the premature departure of HRH there followed a momentary shocked silence amongst our gathering, the rather self-important little man standing there looking like an angry 'Pilsbury

Dough' doll. He announced grandly, to no-one in particular:

Man: Aye well, that bloody told him straight, eh! *(He at the rest of us for approbation that was not forthcoming)*

We were mortified, angry and embarrassed for HRH. Those surrounding 'Pilsbury' turned on him, saying things like:

"You ungrateful wretch – how dare you speak to Prince Charles like that!   You know that he can't answer you back!"

A Miss Marples look-alike prodded the little fellow with her umbrella and said:

Miss Marples: You sir are a bloody disgrace! You are an invited guest of Her Majesty here at the Palace and you have behaved intolerably. If you don't like the Royals then why are you here, eh! Why don't you just feck orft!"

Man: Well there's no need for that sort of language, Madam …

Cries of: "She's right, you know! Go on – clear off you rude little swine!"

Man: I've got every right to say what I think! It's still a democracy!

Miss Marples: Well bugger off and say it somewhere else!

By this time the crowd was turning a little ugly (the Miss Marples look-alike, if I recall, was turning extremely ugly). There were comments from various other members of the assembled guests – like:

"You rude little swine!"   "Nasty little Bugger!"
"Northern Oik!"

We were all appalled at the man's rudeness to our Heir Apparent and there was, without question, a distinct air of looming violence. Fortunately at that moment a 'Gentleman of Honour' who had obviously been tipped the wink that there was something amiss occurring in Pen Three, hove swiftly into view and politely but firmly escorted the little chap far from the madding crowd and out of harm's way. The remainder of us repaired to the tea tent for the cup that refreshes and some delightful sticky buns, thoughtfully provided by Her Majesty.

That was our first Royal Garden Party experience. The second one, a few years later, was equally as memorable but for different reasons. We, the Memsahib and Missen, were stood idling in the crowd in the lavish gardens to the rear of Buck House. When hearing a familiar voice I turned around and found that we were stood close to the odious Jimmy Savile (this is long before his proper colours were nailed to the mast and we know what we know now of his activities).

Jimmy Savile

Savile was surrounded by a coterie of innocent young admirers, both male and female. The following conversation took place:

Young Lady: *(Shyly)* Hi Mr Savile, could I have your autograph please?

Savile: *(Impatiently)* Oh, come on then!

The young lady was taken aback, a look of surprise on her face. She clearly hadn't expected 'attitude' from her hero Meanwhile I noticed that Savile was constantly looking over his shoulder. He obviously considered that the young girl was a nuisance and getting in his way prior to the arrival of the Royal family.

Savile: *(Whey-faced and eyes bulging malignantly)* Well, come on then, give me a piece of paper and summat to sign it with! I don't wander around with a pocket full of pens and bits of paper you know!

He was extremely overbearing and there was a definite undercurrent of unpleasantness and nastiness about him. The young girl was thrown into a state of confusion; this wasn't the attitude that she'd expected. She managed to find a pen and a piece of paper and Savile rather ungraciously and begrudgingly scribbled out an autograph for her and then for some of the others stood there. She disappeared back into the crowd, her little day ruined. A few other brave souls asked him for an autograph whilst he stood there, exhibiting an arrogant indifference. Just then the military band struck up with the National Anthem and the Royals arrived.

It was as if someone had waved a magic wand over Savile. He immediately morphed into his TV persona, smiling and making those strange little noises that he was known for and repeating his mantra of "Now then, now then!" type of thing. I thought then that he was, in reality, a nasty little man. I was very disappointed because, like everyone else, I'd seen and admired all of the good work that he'd done raising money for Stoke Mandeville and other such worthy projects. As we all now know, things ultimately caught up with him as his true activities were revealed, fortunately for him after his death, and I'm sure that he's now 'down there' where he deserves to be, shoveling coal in Hell's furnaces.

Shortly after that little incident, the familiar and stately figure of the ex-Prime Minister, The Right Honourable Sir Edward Heath KG MBE ploughed his way through the crowds, cutting a majestic swathe as he headed for the Royal Tea Tent. Nothing as vulgar as the Lyon's Tea Tent for Sir Teddy.

The Right Honourable Sir Edward Heath KG MBE

It had been his birthday the previous day and there were many well-meaning, jocular and hearty cries of "Happy Birthday, Sir!" "Well done, Sir!" (*as if he'd done something really special to survive and reach his advanced years*) and lots of smiles with polite smatterings of applause. With a face like a slapped arse and obviously inhabiting a parallel universe, Sir Ted studiously ignored everyone and trudged, head down, through the crowds and into the Royal Tea Tent. How bloody ungracious, I thought, not even a nod or a smile to his fans, just a sour, miserable face. When those sort of people reach the pinnacle of their careers and no longer need to impress those that helped put them there, their true colours are nailed to the mast. Well, "Merry wind to his arse," as my late Mother was oft wont to quote, a nautical term of which Sir Ted would no doubt have approved.

We Brits are very strange. At the drop of a hat a very old person will gaze at you through rheumy eyes and through clacking false teeth will proudly proclaim – "I'm eighty seven you know!" as if they've done something particularly special to survive. They always seem to put their longevity down to something like "two ripened banana's and a glass of sherry a day does it for me!" In reality it's all down to genes and luck, boys and girls.

As a serving officer, I attended a Supper at the Station Officers' Mess, Hamm, West Germany some time ago where one memorable evening the, by then ex-MP, Enoch Powell, had been invited and as the guest speaker, was required to 'Sing For his Supper.' There was much excitement in the ranks at having this particular luminary as our Chief Guest.

The Right Honourable Enoch Powell MBE

T'was, forsooth, a night full of Latin quotations/political prose and 'heavy classical English' that thrashed straight over the majority of our collective heads. I do recall, though, that Mr Powell had the most mesmerizing and hypnotic blue eyes and that when he was speaking you felt that he was addressing you personally. It was something of an intellectual stretch to absorb the essence of what he was saying (for me anyway). Having said that, his pronunciation was perfect and his speech was delivered with such passion and intensity that you could have heard a pin drop. If the infamous 'Rivers of Blood' speech hadn't finished him off, goodness knows what else he could have achieved, prescient as his sentiments seem to have become. It was quite apparent that like

Sir Edward Heath, Enoch was a different breed to us lesser beings - Patricians both and quite obviously occupying a higher intellectual plane than the rest of us mere mortals. I blame state education.

One story has it that Mr Powell went to get his hair cut and had the following brief 'chatette' with the Hairdresser who was well known for boring the arse off his customers, talking at great length on any given subject:

Hairdresser: Good morning, sir – and how would we like our hair cut today?

Enoch: In silence!

Funny people, Hairdressers. There was a marvellous Hairdressing Salon in the town centre of Aldershot that had several Barbers busily cropping mainly military bonces throughout the day. There were signs prominently displayed on the mirrors in front of each of the Barber's chairs stating:

'Sport' 'Politics'
'General Matters' 'Silence'

and you chose to have your hair cut and discuss a particular subject with the Barber by leaping into whatever subject matter chair suited you. The 'Silence' chair was, rather unnervingly, just "What would Sir like ?" "Er, just a trim and tidy up please," and that was that. Sometimes when the place was busy you just had to cop whichever chair was available. I remember one day when the door of the salon burst open and a gentleman (most certainly a Squaddie) entered, smelling like a brewery, eyes glazed and obviously pissed as a rat, gazing with rheumy eyes around the salon. The Head Barber (Geddit?) said to him, snootily:

Head Barber: And do we have an appointment, sir?

The man glared at him with bleary, red eyes and mumbled,

Man: I want a fookin' haircut, norra fookin' filling! Oh, get stuffed!

and then, much to everyone's relief, staggered out of the place, tottering off down Aldershot High Street. I think I know which chair Enoch Powell would have preferred. I did, however get to meet and spend a few minutes with the great man himself and must admit to being more than a little mesmerized in his presence. He had some sort of aura about him. It's easy to understand how so many people were swayed by him and his thoughts, and those like him who are blessed with the gift of the gab.

Back to the Garden Party and the beautiful and well-kept gardens at the rear of Buckingham Palace. Things definitely progressed to a different level of excitement when HM Queen Elizabeth the Queen Mother hove into view. Seeing this most delightful lady, all thoughts of lesser beings such as Jimmy Savile, Sir Edward Heath et al, faded into the background. They could not hold a candle to HRH, who was much loved and a national treasure.

HM Queen Elizabeth The Queen Mother

HM was a little later than the other Royals, as was her wont, and was surrounded by Corgis (*that's dogs, not Gas Fitters*). She was trotting along the garden path, smiling and waving regally to everyone with the special little wave of hers that bordered on a rude gesture, and heading for the Royal marquee for tea and stickies. A little ray of sunshine is what she was. As she went past us we were rewarded with our very own regal and personal smile with a jolly "Hair Lair" thrown in.

Ma'am (*as in Jam*) was wearing a diaphanous lavender creation and around her shoulders she wore a matching lavender feather boa. As she floated past me about a foot of the ground, (which she seemed to do), a feather fluttered from off the boa and I caught it. I now have it framed and keep it as a little memento of a very gracious and truly regal lady, sadly no longer with us.

I'd heard a story from a friend who'd been invited to lunch as a guest of the Queen Mother. Prior to lunch and the little 'chatettes' that she had, Ma'am would invite particular guests to sit beside her on a banquette. HM apparently, always kept some toffees in her handbag, one of which she would hand to the person to whom she was chatting. HM would then sit back and fire questions at the guest who would try to answer whilst chewing the toffee. Mischievous, but all done in the best possible taste!

Incidentally, there are different types of tea-tent in situ at Royal Garden Parties; a really posh one for the Royals and their guests, one for the Diplomats and slightly lesser beings and, last but not least, one for the lower decks (such as missen and the Memsahib) and anyone else, presumably, from North of the Watford Gap. It was quite amusing to see that the tent poles on top of the Royal Marquee had golden crowns fixed on them. One wouldn't want to wander into the wrong tent, would one! Whilst in London recently, the Memsahib and I called in for afternoon tea at the Buckingham Palace Hotel (vulgar not to, whilst in 'Town'), which is just across the road from Buck House itself. We could see teams of workmen moving the tentage into the rear of the palace, in preparation for that year's round of Garden Parties. Seeing them brought back some happy memories as we sat there sipping tea and munching sticky buns.

Continuing with the 'Royal' theme, one of my jobs at the Defence School of Transport at Leconfield was to organize Royal visits. Organizing these visits was a necessarily long and complex process and of course everything had to be absolutely spot on. I was informed by the Lord Lieutenant's Office that HRH Prince Andrew would be visiting the area in December 1996 to open the odd school etc and would we like him to visit the base? Once my superiors had decided that the visit was a goer, the necessary arrangements were then made with Buckingham Palace. Amongst a thousand other things, I had to arrange for the Prince's personal standard to be sent to the Headquarters as it had to be flown whilst he was in situ, similarly we had to arrange for the pennant for his staff car as that had to be fitted and flown whilst he was travelling in the vehicle. Little things mean a lot. There was also a complex and interesting (for him) visit programme to be compiled, with every second to be accounted for. Eventually all of the preparations were made and we awaited the arrival of our Royal hero.

(HRH The Duke of York)
(Photo courtesy of the Northern Ireland Office)

On arrival, HRH bounded into the Headquarters, making a bee-line for the Orderly Room where he had spotted several fair clerical maidens who were soon swooning in his handsome presence. One particularly responsibility I had that day was that as HRH had to change into a pair of brand new (highly 'Pledged') - Boots Wellington, Pairs 1, (as he was being taken onto the muddy driver training area) I was placed in sole charge, (see what I did there), of his shoes. I can't tell you just how thrilled I was about that. All my years of training both as a soldier, warrant officer and commissioned officer now came to the fore. This was a very important task because if I got it wrong and misplaced a Royal dap, HRH would have been hobbling around Driffield opening schools wearing one MOD Wellie and one princely Turnbull and Asser shoe.

A room had to be set aside at the Officer's Mess for HRH to change out of the Boots Wellington Pairs 1, once his training area experience had been concluded. There were quite explicit instructions about what had to be in the room i.e. a decanter of 'quality' whisky and a couple of bottles of Canadian Dry Ginger, also a couple of that day's Newspapers (no Red Tops) and a TV switched on and tuned to the BBC.

As 'Shoe Equerry,' I escorted the Royal shoes over to the Officer's Mess and took them to HRH's Room, now renamed 'The Duke of York' Suite. He was going to be some time, so I decided that as it had been a long day I would share a glass of Whisky and Canadian Dry Ginger with HRH, although he wouldn't be there whilst I did. I settled down in 'his' chair with a substantial glass of Whisky and read the newspapers etc. Seeing the fleet of staff cars approaching the Officers' Mess in the distance, I quickly polished the drink off, cleaned the glass and then made sure that everything was replaced in ship-shape fashion. HRH arrived, changed back into his shoes, then repaired to the Officers' Mess No1 Ante-room where a tasty lunch had been lovingly prepared for him.

There was a special table set to one side in the Number One Ante-room, for his and his Equerry's use, with crisp linen, silver cutlery and sparkling crystal etc. To be fair, he would have none of it, he just grabbed a plate, went over to where the food was laid out on the hot-plate and helped himself. He had a chat with all of the Chefs then moved around the ante-room, making use of every second to meet everyone whilst having his Lunch. For some strange reason I recall that his teeth were sparkling white and that he had more than his fair share of them. The visit went well and the Prince eventually vanished into the ether with lots of "Jolly well done, chaps!" ringing in our ears from our glorious leaders.

A member of the Royal Navy who was attending a driving course at Leconfield, if that makes sense, had previously served on the same ship as Prince Andrew, HMS Edinburgh, and although obviously not bosom buddies, the Sailor claimed that they knew each of other. The Prince had a very busy visit programme whilst with us but it was agreed with his staff beforehand that the Sailor could stand at the side of the main runway where the Prince would pass en route to another location. The Prince's staff car would then pause briefly, thus giving them both an opportunity to say a quick hello before HRH went about his official duties.

The Sailor, who was thrilled at the opportunity to renew his acquaintance with HRH, stood at the side of the road as the Royal limousine bore down on him. Jolly Jack Tar sprang to attention and threw up a snappy salute. This was his big moment. Inside the limousine the Prince was informed that his old shipmate was at the side of the road waiting to say a quick hello. The Prince, apparently, glanced at his watch and instructed the driver to drive on. The Royal vehicle swept past the Sailor, who was, quite naturally, extremely disappointed, gazing forlornly at the back of the Prince's head as he was driven off into the distance. Not so much as a glance, how crushingly disappointing that must have been for the lad. It would only have taken a few seconds.

I remember seeing the Royal limousine and fleet of escort cars sweeping out of the base with HRH, on his way to his next engagement and in doing so passing the NAAFI. The troops were queuing up for their NAAFI break, belching, farting, scratching their arses and being their usual brilliant selves and, as is their wont, treated the gleaming vehicles and their important passengers with studied indifference, pretending that they hadn't seen them. They'd got their priorities right.

Here's a little jape that you can try on those with whom you would like to have a titter, say for example - Prince Andrew. Slide up to him and say, "Excuse me, Sir, but you've got something on your shoe." When he lifts up his heel to examine his footwear, that's your cue to shout (*mincingly*) "Hello Sailor" and laugh uproariously. Go on, try it, it's well worth the effort and I'm sure that HRH would be highly amused.

HM the Queen and HRH Prince Phillip graced us with their presence at Leconfield a couple of times. One occasion, in July 2002, was when they were travelling around the country celebrating the Queen's Golden Jubilee. The Queen and the Duke of Edinburgh do such a brilliant job and in essence are the glue that holds the fabric of our society together. It seems to me they've always been there (certainly in my lifetime), smiling and waving and looking as if they were enjoying themselves, but then you can never be sure. Apparently when something particularly gormless is said to or asked of HM that does not please, she smiles gracefully and says "How quaint," or "Oh really," before moving on down the line. Also if the Royal handbag changes hands, that is a sign that HM wishes to move on – so – you've been warned!

Anne, Princess Royal KG KT GCVO G C St J QSO GCL - HRH Princess Anne, the Princess Royal. I have a great deal of admiration for this no nonsense Royal. She visited Leconfield recently on a really cold and miserable November's day to see what we were up to. It was just starting to snow. HRH took the time to stop and speak to every single soldier who'd been stood out in the wilds waiting to show her what they did for a living. She was extremely patient and pleasant, laughing merrily throughout the visit. I do recall that her Lady-in-Waiting used many salty and impressive phrases, making us all laugh out loud at some of her saucier comments. The Princess Royal is a much admired Royal (certainly with the troops).

When Princess Anne arrived at Leconfield she was wearing a very fetching fox fur hat. On being compliment by the Commandant about her hat, HRH said that she'd bumped into the Queen just prior to leaving London and that the Queen had asked her where she was going. Princess Anne had replied "DST Leconfield," whereupon the Queen replied "Oh, Leconfield – wear the fox hat!"

HRH with Commandant DST Colonel Paul Ash and RSM John Ford

With the increased demand for operational driving courses, DST saw a dramatic uptake in the numbers of students passing through the School, which led to an increase in vehicles and instructors to support that demand. At that time Student numbers were at about 1600 on the base during any one day, supported by a permanent staff of military numbering some 300 and in turn supported by some 800 civilian instructors. It was very busy and hectic.

The Medical Centre at Leconfield, built as part of the original Air Force Base, was never designed to meet with such numbers and was struggling to cope. Although the Army Primary Health Care received more funding for staff, they didn't have the infrastructure to accommodate them and for a while struggled with the limited space and facilities. That's the joy of the military – they just get on with things and make the best of what there is available at the time.

Anyway, eventually funds were made available for the provision of a total rebuild providing a 12 bed Medical Reception Station (MRS) with seven purpose built Treatment Rooms, a 2 bed Physiotherapy Department and a Pharmacy. Nothing but the best for the chaps and chapesses. Work commenced in 2009 and some six months later the new facilities, named 'The Nesbitt Medical Centre,' became available.

The opening of such a facility couldn't be allowed to pass without some sort of ceremony and we were informed that Vice Admiral Sir Timothy Laurence, KCVO, CB, ADC(P) who was coincidentally visiting DST Leconfield, had kindly agreed to do the honours. The 'tom-toms' told us that Sir Tim was very approachable but that we would have to be our toes because he was always superbly well briefed and ready to pose relevant, incisive questions at the drop of a hat. Not only that, he had important connections, he was married to the Princess Royal and we therefore had to tread carefully.

When Sir Tim arrived he did the ceremonial opening honours, proved to be an extremely approachable fellow and an absolute pleasure to deal with. Bright as a button and absolutely no edge to him whatsoever. As you would expect from such a well versed member of the Royal Navy, the visit went swimmingly well.

That was, thank God, just about my last involvement with Royal visits at Leconfield, or anywhere else for that matter and I'm glad to say that it was something of a relief. Most of the in-depth planning and preparation is done well before each visit and can be a right balls ache, but it must be spot on. The chance of dropping a huge clanger was always lurking in the background and could easily prove to be a definite career stopper. In addition, the news of any cock-up would spread like wildfire.

One particular joy at DST Leconfield was the day I got to meet a true hero and was lucky to be able to capture the moment on camera. The then Corporal Johnson Beharry VC had unexpectedly called into Leconfield to meet up with his brother who was attending a driving course there. The Guardroom staff rang me to say that he'd arrived and I informed the Commandant that we had a holder of the Victoria Cross on the base.

The Commandant invited Corporal Beharry across to the Officers' Mess for coffee and a chat with the Officers where they'd assembled for a meeting. Needless to say, Johnson Beharry was a thoroughly nice and totally unaffected bloke and it was an honour to be in this very brave man's presence. A few years earlier I'd also met ex-Welsh Guardsman Simon Weston OBE of Falklands War fame, also a brave and very special man.

Such was life at Leconfield, one day just a run of the mill Vice Admiral, the next – meeting up with proper heroes!

T C meets the then Corporal Johnson Beharry VC

'THE RAF LECONFIELD MEMORIAL'

The RAF Search and Rescue (SAR) Flight, E Flight 202 Squadron RAF (an organisation for whom my admiration knew no bounds), was based at RAF Leconfield, although it has since been disbanded. It was co-located with the Defence School of Transport at Normandy Barracks. Fiercely protecting their independence the RAF retained the title RAF Leconfield for their own operating area. E Flight moved into newly built premises inside the base, remaining on site at Leconfield. The Flight was relocated to the far side of what is termed historically as 'the airfield' although the airfield is now operationally decommissioned and used only for driver training purposes by the Defence School of Transport. E Flight's original Headquarters in Hangar 5 was eventually demolished. The demolition took some doing as the Hangar had originally been built to withstand enemy attack!

Hangar 5 was duly demolished and a portion of a bomb proof door was retained. A team of enthusiasts on the base decided that it would be a worthy project to have a memorial site built where E Flight had been located and that the memorial would, in the main, be constructed using the metal from the bomb proof hangar door, right on that very spot. The memorial was imaginatively constructed and eventually a dedication ceremony was held, the finished memorial being dedicated by Air Marshal SGG Dalton CB BSc FRAeS MCMI RAF. It is well worth a visit and has a lovely, respectful feel about it. The Hangar 5 doors had once been machine gunned, courtesy of the Luftwaffe, during World War 2 and a portion of the metal from the reinforced door - with bullet holes (which can still be seen) was used to make the memorial, which included the metal door segments being shaped as aircraft that had been in use on the base during its history.

A key member of the RAF Memorial Planning Team was Alan Bakewell, a civil servant on the base. Alan loves all things historical and, after doing a great deal of research, put together an extremely comprehensive background of the events that had taken place at RAF Leconfield during World War 2, also what had happened there after the war, leading up to when the RAF handed the majority of the base over to the Army. One such event was the visit of HM Queen Elizabeth the Queen Mother, who visited Leconfield in 1961, an interesting event in itself. Alan managed to obtain some old film footage of the visit. During the course of the visit, Her Majesty had visited a married quarter and there is quite a delightful segment of the film showing HM meeting a typical RAF Family. Stood with the family on the doorstep is a cute little girl with head respectfully bowed as she met the Queen Mother. That little girl was the Actress/Comedienne/Writer – Miss Dawn French, whose father was an RAF Flight Sergeant serving on the base. Chatting with Alan Bakewell, he and I decided that it would be a nice idea for us to send a copy of the short film, and some stills taken from it, to Miss French in the event that she didn't have them. It proved a little difficult to find a contact address for her, but her then husband, top comedian/actor Lenny Henry (now Sir Lenny), was undertaking a theatre tour so I wrote to him and asked him to pass a copy of the film (now transferred onto CD) on to Dawn.

I heard nothing for quite a few weeks and forgot all about it but was then pleasantly surprised when I received a hand-written letter from Dawn thanking me for sending her the film. It was a very touching and personal letter (and that's why I won't repeat any of it here) but she was very grateful to receive the film and funnily enough it was the first time that she'd seen it. There's a copy of still from the film in her recent autobiography 'Dear Fatty.'

Little Miss Dawn French, her brother and parents meet HM Queen Elizabeth the Queen Mother

Just an aside regarding one of the 'elder' Royals who had visited RAF Leconfield in its hey-day. I remember when I was with 8 Regiment RCT at Portsmouth Barracks in Munster, West Germany. We were visited by Princess Alice, Duchess of Gloucester. The visit was made more memorable because we were ordered to return home from work and remove the dustbins from outside our married quarters. The bins were due to be collected by the German dustbinmen that very morning. Those in authority did not wish the Royal visitor's eyes to be offended by the sight of dustbins and dustbinmen.

Princess Alice was taken to have a cup of tea at a 'normal' married quarter which, it goes without saying, had been totally redecorated, refurnished and re-carpeted. She stayed in there for about two minutes, floating in and out, whilst we'd all been kept waiting for hours. I wondered if HRH had dustbins at her residence, Barnwell Manor?

HRH Princess Alice, Duchess of Gloucester GCB GCVO GBE CI

Princess Alice was married to Prince Henry, the Duke of Gloucester. When I was a young soldier working at the RCT Training Centre in Buller Barracks, in the mid to late 1960's I heard my boss saying that the Duke was visiting Buller Officers' Mess and that a young officer had to be nominated to remain at his side throughout his visit and firmly steer him away from the bar at all times. Apparently he had a great fondness for Gin and would get falling down drunk at the drop of a hat! I didn't really know who the Duke was and certainly I'd never tasted Gin. Royals inhabit a totally different world to the rest of us.

HRH Prince Henry, Duke of Gloucester KG KT KP GCB GCMG GCVO

Another little story, although not Royal, that might be of interest to you and one that crept into the RAF Leconfield Memorial Project equation. Apparently one very murky night during World War 2 a flight of American Bombers had landed unexpectedly at the base as it was unsafe for them to proceed any further until the inclement weather had cleared. The American bombers were allegedly commanded by the very famous actor James Stewart, who was a Lieutenant Colonel Pilot with the American Air Force at that time.

Those sort of stories grow in the telling and are greatly enhanced by the passage of time. I don't believe there is any factual evidence for this tale, but who really knows, it could have happened.

James Stewart

What do you mean –'Who was James Stewart?' The fabulously successful American actor James Stewart (*The Philadelphia Story, The Spirit of St Lois, Vertigo, Flight of the Phoenix*) to name but a few of his successes, that's who. He entered the United States Army Air Force as a Private and worked his way up to Colonel. He served as a bomber pilot, leading more than 20 missions over Germany, and taking part in many air strikes. Stewart earned the U.S. Air Medal, the UK's Distinguished Flying Cross, France's Croix de Guerre, and 7 Battle Stars.

In peace time, Stewart continued as an active reservist and reached the rank of Brigadier General before retiring in the late 1950s. At Leconfield, during the course of the demolition of E Flight's Hangar 5 and the construction of the Memorial, some American coins from that era were found buried in the ground! A tenuous but titillating little link. And who knows, maybe James or someone from his Flight just might have dropped the coins….

At the conclusion of the Memorial Dedication Ceremony, we all repaired to the Officers' Mess for a swift sippers, then tottered off to get changed etc in time for Dinner, which was to be served in a specially erected marquee. Later on that evening we were sat at various tables inside the marquee each table with some twenty diners or so enjoying themselves after a bit of a complex day. I had the immense privilege of being seated at the same table as the pilots who had carried out the fly-past during the course of the afternoon. At the time I was writing a play about 'Jack the Ripper' (the 'original' Ripper, not the 'Yorkshire' one). Seated next to me was the Group Captain in charge of the aircraft who had, coincidentally, visited the Metropolitan Police's 'Black Museum (can you still say that?) a couple of weeks previously and seen some of the actual artifacts from the period. He asked me if I thought I knew who 'Jack the Ripper' really was and I told him that yes I thought that did – having spent many hours researching the play. When I told him (reluctantly) who I thought the Ripper was he nodded sagely and told me quite confidently that I was wrong. He went on to say having seen the evidence, that he knew who 'Jack the Ripper' really was (as did the Police) and told me the name. It was ..... sorry someone's at the door.... so I'll leave that one with you. The thot plickens.' Sat at our table was a group of vibrant young RAF pilots, one of whom looked rather familiar. A tall, handsome chap, with a hearty laugh. Could it be him? No, surely I was mistaken, or was I?

We knew that a well known member of the Royal Family was undergoing pilot training at RAF Leeming, near Catterick. There'd been no whispers that 'He' might be one of the Pilots. We usually heard something on what is rather impolitely termed – the 'Shit-house Tom Toms.' As is the norm in such situations i.e. a private social occasion, the Royal, if indeed that's who he was, was politely 'ignored' and left to enjoy himself. Surrounded by his fellow pilots he was relaxed and obviously enjoying himself, without being larded with deference and greased up to by some self-seeking feather-bedder. I often recount the tale that I have dined privately with our future Monarch. Before glazing over, victims always listen to me politely but obviously take the story with a pinch of salt. Being retired and writing this story, I had the time and decided to find out if indeed it had been Prince William, so I wrote to Kensington Palace to seek clarification of HRH's presence at the said Dinner. They were very gentle with me and eventually I received a nice reply. It was couched in polite 'staff speak' but I took it as clarification that HRH had indeed been present at the Dinner. It wasn't an outright denial - but as it suits my purposes, I would say that wouldn't I?

Normandy Barracks, (RAF Leconfield as was), is a lovely old place, the skeleton of which has changed little over the years since it was built (although very recently a great deal of major construction work has been carried out). Inside the base there's what looks like an elongated Nissen Hut which is used as a Briefing Room/Unit Cinema (now named The Phoenix Cinema) – not quite a listed building but recorded as a building of historical interest. It was used as a Briefing Room for the very brave Pilots and their Crews during World War 2.

Incidentally, the very first bombing raid that took place on Germany was from RAF Leconfield, when they flew over to Germany and dropped leaflets. Such was the impact of these leaflets that the Germans surrendered unconditionally a couple of years later. Anyway, in my capacity as the tantalizingly named SO2 Co-ord/Visits, we'd received a written request from a young lady whose Father had been a pilot at RAF Leconfield during the war but now lived in retirement in New Zealand.

The young lady was over in the UK on a visit and as she was in Yorkshire wanted to see where her Dad had worked as a pilot all those years ago. Her Dad was getting on in years and wasn't in the best of health, so she wanted to take a few photo's of the base to take back home with her and perhaps bring back some happy memories for him. She was accompanied by a gentleman who was an airline pilot and who naturally also had an interest in the base. I took them both all around the base on what I called the 'Ten Bob Tour' and showed them things like the Garrison Church, which was a parachute packing shed during World War 2, the Aircraft Tower (now Headquarters the Driver Training Wing), the old red GPO telephone boxes opposite Headquarters DST, one of which still had the fittings on the door to secure it prior to aircraft taking off on operations – for security reasons, 'Walls Have Ears,' (seems quite strange now what with the preponderance of mobile 'phones), but that's how they did it back then.

We had a look inside what is now the Phoenix Cinema but which had originally been a Briefing Room for Air Crews during World War 2, and rather amazingly the young lady produced a CD which had a recording on it of an actual World War 2 pre-flight briefing that had taken place in the cinema, and at which her Father had actually been present. The voices are very clipped and BBC style. We sat and listened to the full recording in the darkened cinema, which in a way was a bit spooky. Just for that little moment we had stepped back in time to the 1940's. All that from one tidgy visit.

The years flew by and as the lunacy and cost-cutting increased, I decided that the time had come for me to retire from the Civil Service. I was more than a bit drained and thought it only fair to quit whilst I was ahead of things. I prepared to retire and divest myself of my job and its many responsibilities and in due course handed everything over. As is tradition, there were several TTFN (Ta Ta For Now) parties held and I was also 'Dined Out' from the Officers' Mess.

I thought that if I reproduced my farewell speech from that 'Farewell Dinner' it just might give a flavour of the bitter, sweet occasion, and of my many experiences whilst at ASMT/DST Leconfield. It encapsulates most things of note that happened to me during my time there:

'EXTRACTS FROM THE RETIREMENT SPEECH FOR MY 'DINING OUT' AT THE OFFICERS' MESS, DEFENCE SCHOOL OF TRANSPORT ON SATURDAY 17TH OF MARCH 2012'

"Colonel, Honoured Guests, Ladies and Gentlemen, Peter Todd,

Not for the first time today do I rise from a warm seat clutching a piece of paper.

I joined the Royal Army Service Corps in 1963. I served for 30 years in the Army and have completed 18 years in the Civil Service here at Leconfield. I remember when I joined up at the Bradford Recruiting Office they said to me – "Would you like a commission?" I replied, "No – just a straight salary will do!"

Regrettably little bursts of ill-health (*more of that later*) have stopped me supporting this venerable place as well as I have done in the past. The indignities of old age and decrepitude, I'm afraid.

Well, yet again here at the Defence School of Transport you've all got your toes curled around the edge of the furnace. I can't recall a single year of the time that I've been here, which includes my time as Officer Commanding Licence Division, when we weren't strapped to a desk waiting for the gleaming Ministry of Defence swinging blade to descend and eviscerate us. Each year different inspection teams descended on the School, hungrily looking to take our jobs and thereby make a name for themselves with their masters with proffered swingeing cuts.

An example of just one year when we were visited by 'privatisation' hopefuls:

> THE MENTOR BID TEAM
> THE METRIX BID TEAM
> THE HOLDFAST BID TEAM
> THE RAYTHON BID TEAM
> THE SERCO BID TEAM
> THE WESTLAND BID TEAM
> THE 'EL PASSO' DRIVING SCHOOL BID TEAM

Not one of these applicants succeeded with their bids because they couldn't possibly achieve the highest standards that we consistently achieved and make a profit. This time though, I don't believe that it's going to be a case of new labels on old bottles, this is the big one. We were unable to resist the forces of change and were required to be and flexible when faced with the inevitable swingeing cuts.

Despite the slings and arrows of outrageous interference emanating from our vast chain of laughingly named 'superior' Headquarters, there's still a great quality of life to be had here at Leconfield – there are so many excellent people here, people who take great pride in what they do and what they achieve. We should all be justifiably proud of what we do for the Nation. When I first started working here I think that we had some eight or nine thousand students passing through the system annually but now it's well over nineteen thousand plus.

As you all know, I organise, or should I say organised, the visits here, and I'd like to tell you briefly about one that went spectacularly wrong. The Head of the Indian Army Transport Corps, General Bhatnagar, decided to come and pay us a visit. Our Commandant then was a Brigadier who shall remain nameless. On the day in question, the Brigadier started to get changed from out of his working dress into his military finery some 30 minutes before the General was due to arrive. To his abject horror, the Brigadier realised that his wife had failed to put his uniform trousers on the hanger, alongside his bemedalled Service Dress jacket. Alas, he was 'Sans Pantalons' as they say in Hangar One.

The first I heard of it, as the then SO3 Co-ord Visits, Lavatories Carpets et al, was the commotion when the Brigadier came thundering down the main passage of the Headquarters, long spindly legs a blur, bawling for his driver to "Go and get my bloody trousers – and tell my wife she's a .... "*Expletive Deleted*." Verily a miracle was speedily performed and one pair of nicely pressed pantaloons appeared, not a moment too soon – indeed, just as General Bhatnagar rolled up to the entrance of the Headquarters in his finely tuned 'Tuk Tuk' (that's RCT terminology for staff car).

Meanwhile, in the lavatory, located immediately above the Officer's toilets on the ground floor of the Headquarters, a doddery Retired Officer (RO) had decided to relieve the appalling strain on his gin-soaked and well abused bladder, as things were bordering on the critical. The old chap duly eased springs then went to wash his trembling, ink stained hands. For some reason, and it was never really explained at the subsequent regimental inquiry, he had left the sink tap running with the plug firmly jammed in the plug-hole, causing it to eventually overflow, with tragic consequences. He, the RO, cared not a jot, having left the lavatory to return to his office and continue causing mayhem.

At the same time, downstairs, the Brigadier had been schmoozing the General, fully briefed him and supplied him with copious quantities of biscuits and Yorkshire tea. He then invited the General to avail himself of the downstairs facilities prior to him setting off for a grand tour around the base. "Jally fine idea, my boy," said the General – trying his utmost to make us all feel at home with a cod Yorkshire accent.

A key part of my job was showing VIP Visitors to the facilities – it's the little things that count. So, I escorted the General to the 'Officer's Only' Lavatory. As he entered the hallowed portals, the General broke thunderous, and if I may say so – very impressive wind. On a recent visit to Mumbai with my venerable friend Major Peter Todd and our Ladies, we sailed into Mumbai Harbour – and the stench of ancient rotting vegetation wafting across the deck of our luxury liner reminded me of that Bhatnagar moment. Anyway, back to General Bhatnagar. I gently closed the lavatory door and took up a defensive stance in front of it to prevent unwanted intruders.

After a minute or two, a furious cry of four star outrage emanated from within the bowels of the lavatory. Something along the lines of: "Aaaargh! What the bleddy dickens is going on here!" "Bugger it!" thought I, "No toilet paper!" I tapped gently on the door and entered the facility. There stood the General with what can only be described as a huge, unedifying Poppadum swathed across his shoulders. He pointed a trembling but well-manicured finger at the ceiling, which was now spraying water not unlike the Trevi Fountain, and said – "Look Major, something's leaking. I think it's time you got a plumber chappie in!"

The water leaking from the upstairs sink had brought the ceiling down in one complete piece and there was a cloak of old distemper swathed about the General's person. I respectfully eased this 'Poppadum' off the General's shoulders and gently brushed him down. He was very understanding about the whole thing and gave me a valuable career tip: "Get those bloody pipes fixed, old boy, or you're finished!"

A lot of fences, and pipes, had to be mended that day, although to give the General his due, he saw the funny side. Our Brigadier, of course, didn't. He was mortified and I was summoned to his presence at the conclusion of the visit to have both my feet sharpened and held to the fire. The Retired Officer actually responsible for the outrage, in the time honoured fashion, denied all knowledge, blamed someone else and minced off to the golf course for a couple of rounds. "Bugger all to do with me, old boy."

There were many more such visit 'happenings.' I did a rough calculation recently and found that during my time at Leconfield I've been involved with over a thousand visits. I don't like to name drop, but as I said to Princess Anne, or was it Prince Andrew ….. "sometimes things do go wrong."

A few examples of those Nationals who have visited the School during my time here:

AFRICA, ARMENIA, AUSTRALIA, AZERBAIJAN, BELARUS, CANADA, CHINA, CZECHOSLOVAKIA, FRANCE, GEORGIA, GERMANY, INDIA, ISRAEL, JAPAN, KAZAKHSTAN, NEW ZEALAND, PAKISTAN, POLAND, RUSSIA, TADZIKHSTAN, TURKEY, TURKMENISTAN, UNITED STATES OF AMERICA and UZBEKISTAN.

That's enough – but you get my drift. Leconfield was and continues to be a very important, colourful and vibrant place.

I can see that you're a religious bunch – because you're praying for me to finish, so in closing I'd like to say thanks to every single one of you. You've all helped me out at one time or another, but this time I won't be coming back. None of it would have been possible without your humour, understanding and occasional co-operation. Tonight has been a very pleasant way to round off a most rewarding career and I'm grateful not only to those who have organized everything but to those of you who came along to share this very special evening.

A special mention to our dear friends Major Andy Cornet and his wife Maureen who have travelled here all the way from Scotland in the hope and expectation of a 'Full English' tomorrow morning. Chaps, always remember that – "The best things in life are free," as the Scotsman said when he stood over a Baker's grating wearing his kilt.

A special message also for my workmate Donna Murphy, who is 'taking over' from me:

"DON'T PANIC AND EAT PLENTY OF CAKE!"

My final thanks go to me long-suffering and beloved wife Maggie, without whose tender support, sage advice, enthusiasm, love and occasional severe beatings – without her by my side I would have achieved nothing at all.

Only last week she said to me, "Would you like to buy me a new dress for the Dinner Night. Something to match my eyes?" I said "Do they do them in bloodshot?" She hit me with the frying pan, but it's OK because it's non-stick. I must tell you about when we met all those years ago. I sidled up to her and said "Hello gorgeous, where have you been all my life?" She said, "Hiding from you!" We met at a dance, she was the prettiest girl on the floor, I can still see her lying there…"

Anyway, enough is enough. I'd like to finish with an old Italian saying, taught to me by my old mate (and very brave bomb disposal man) Major Graham Robinson:

'ARRIVEDERCI PENIS'

Which freely translated means:

"`Ta Ta Cock!"

The speech was well received and I sat down to thunderous applause, lathered, a little emotional, but my duty finally done.

'HOLD THE FRONT PAGE'

The retirement festivities were not quite finally over. I discussed purchasing a farewell present for DST, as was the tradition, with my beloved wife Maggie and we decided that a suitable gift should be something that was lasting and one that would be appreciated in the years ahead. We decided that, based upon the activities of the senior staff at the Ministry of Defence, a 'Monkey Puzzle Tree' or 'Araucaria Araucana' as we staff officers would say, would be rather appropriate. So off to the local garden centre we toddled and ordered a Monkey Puzzle Tree. I arranged with my old sparring partner, Major Peter Todd, for a suitable hole to be dug at an appropriate site in readiness for the tree to be planted.

In due course I collected the tree and delivered it to Leconfield where a site had been reserved in the central reservation of the roundabout outside the main Headquarters, quite appropriate really, as that's where I had spent my working life as a civil (and occasionally not quite so civil) servant (that's the Headquarters not the roundabout). The Monkey Puzzle Tree was duly planted, in readiness for the more 'formal' ceremony later on that morning. I went home to get cleaned up and change into my 'demob' suit. Then it was back to Leconfield for my very final farewell – and to hand in my identity card plus sign the Official Secrets Act.

My final day at work at DST Leconfield,
planting my farewell present to them – a Monkey Puzzle Tree ((planted directly opposite the Headquarters – make of that what you will)

The tree was duly planted in the presence of my work colleagues and, much to my surprise, the Memsahib had sneaked into camp and was in hiding in the back of a Mastiff (that's a military vehicle, not a dog) which was lurking in the background. After the planting ceremony we both went for a little meander around the base in the Mastiff which was driven by WO2 'Huggy' Hugill – know on base as 'Mr Mastiff.' Huggy is my honorary cousin. My Grandfather was called Hugill and emanated from the same geographical area as Huggy – so logic suggests that we might be related, no matter how tenuous the lineage link is. Anyway, I liked 'Huggy,' so it didn't matter!

After our little drive around the largest residential driver training school in Europe, which took us about 20 minutes, we were returned to the Headquarters, shaken but not stirred. On stepping out of the vehicle there was one more surprise waiting for me. I'd had the Headquarters roundabout named after me and was asked to unveil the new name plate. Wasn't that a lovely thought, boys and girls!

My very own Roundabout!

I felt both humbled and slightly regal as I uncovered the roundabout sign. Imagine, my very own roundabout – and not only that – right in the middle of it – my 'Araucaria Araucana.' What more could a chap ask for. The Commandant of the School, Colonel Paul Ash, gave me a most charming valedictory speech, a key phrase of which was "He's had more farewells than Frank Sinatra!" and we all disappeared into the Headquarters for a final glass of champagne and a curly sandwich. This was all very nice stuff, particularly when one's wife was at one's side to witness how truly wonderful her partner really was.

I received a 'phone call from TV's Jeremy Kyle and ITV's Director of Aftercare, the genius that is Graham Stanier, on that last day, talking about retirement and instructing me that I wasn't to spend my retirement sat staring at walls etc. There was no way I'd be sat staring at walls, there was too much other 'stuff' for me to be getting on with.

When sufficient quantities of champers had been imbibed, missen and t'wife were transported out of the main gate never to return (not strictly true, but I thought a nice dramatic conclusion would look good on paper). Talking of paper, I'd received rather a generous write-up in the Hull Daily Mail, an august organ, which I have had permission to repeat below.

'Marking the road to retirement.'

(Byline: Kevin Shoesmith)

'In short Major Terry Cavender had an unusual retirement present - a roundabout named after him at Defence School of Transport, Leconfield. It's a roundabout way of marking a popular officer's retirement. Major Terry Cavender's last day at Leconfield's Defence School of Transport (DST) was marked with the unveiling of a roundabout named after him at the base. The Cavender Roundabout, as it is known, is outside the headquarters building at the world's biggest driver training base. Terry, who lives in Beverley, said: "The roundabout was a lovely surprise and I was

absolutely thrilled that everyone had taken the time to make my last day so memorable.

"I have worked with so many nice people and I shall miss them all." Terry joined the Royal Army Service Corps - now part of the Royal Logistic Corps (RLC) - in January 1963. He retired from the Royal Corps of Transport, also now part of the RLC, some 30 years later having served in the Far East, West Germany and Northern Ireland. Terry returned to military life in 1995, joining the Civil Service at the Army School of Mechanical Transport (ASMT), now DST, as a Retired Officer dealing with co-ord and protocol. During this time he was also press officer for the base, which brought him into contact with visiting celebrities, including TV presenter Jeremy Kyle, who filmed a series of programmes there.

Although Terry is retiring, he will continue writing. Terry's pantomimes are performed by local amateur theatre groups. He also writes, produces, directs and performs in the annual Christmas pantomime for Kingstown Hospital Radio. He is secretary of the local charity Leaps (Local Entertainers and Performers Society). Terry is also a member of the BBC Radio Humberside Charity Fundraisers Committee Candle Appeal, raising money for St Andrew's Children's Hospice in Grimsby. Terry, who planted a Monkey Puzzle Tree in the centre of the roundabout, said: "I was 14 and three-quarters when I signed up for 22 years in the Army. "They asked if I wanted a commission and I said a straight salary would do."

DST provides driver and transport management training to military personnel from all the Armed Forces. In addition to training the military, DST provides specialist training to the police and fire service and overseas training to Defence Attaches. It provides 140 courses for about 19,000 trainees a year. I have worked with so many nice people and I shall miss them all said Major Terry Cavender.'

It was a nice little article and kind of Kevin Shoesmith to take the time to write it.

'THE MIGHTY ANTAR'

There were a few things left to tidy up, one of which was that during my last few months I had been appointed Project Officer (normally know as being 'spammed') for the restoration of a Mark 3 Thorneycroft Antar Tank Transporter. This had been decided based upon the age old premise, operated by our Chief of Staff, Lieutenant Colonel Sean Glynn RLC – i.e "Anyone here handy with a piano, chaps?" Volunteer puts hand up – "Me Sir!" "Good, pop over to the Officers' Mess will you, one wants moving."

As I'd been both an Administrative Officer and a Quartermaster with 617 Tank Transporter Squadron RCT in Hamm, West Germany, in a previous existence, the task of overseeing the restoration and re-siting of the ancient vehicle somewhere within the barracks came my way. I was, seriously, quite delighted to be given the task and thought it somehow fitting to be involved with it at the end of my working life.

So, the world of Tank Transporting came back to haunt me when I was invited to get involved in the restoration of the vehicle and its eventual siting outside HQ DST. After a great deal of paperwork and fiddle-farting about, the vehicle was readied, restored, a site was found and then the Antar was officially dedicated by Hereditary Peer, Earl Attlee (President of the Thorneycroft Register), who has an interest in these matters.

I was asked to help write a Press Release on behalf of the major Sponsors of the Antar, which explained things more fully. We had obtained funding from a Sponsor in order that the public purse would not be drained by the project. It was highly likely that without the generous financial support of Hull based 'Rapid Solicitors,' the project would not have reached fruition. The Press Release relating to the Antar is repeated below, purely as a matter of historical interest.

Press Release:
(based on a Question and Answer format)

'Terry, tell me a bit about you and the DST?'
I'm employed as the SO2 Protocol at the Defence School of Transport (DST), Normandy Barracks, Leconfield, which is a staff officer post. DST is the largest residential driver training school in the world. The full scope of training here is very impressive. I've been here for some 17 years. DST performs a vital function training personnel from all three Services in a vast range of transport and vehicle operating roles, all of which are crucial to front line activities in such places as Afghanistan. DST is one of the largest employers in the East Riding of Yorkshire and pumps some £55 million into the local economy annually.

'How did DST get involved with Rapid Solicitors?'
Rapid Solicitors very kindly sponsored a recent ITV documentary about the DST and that's how we became 'known' to each other. We invited some of Rapid Solicitor's key members up to the base to see what goes on here. Purely by coincidence we're in the process of restoring a Thorneycroft Mark 3 ('The Mighty Antar') which when finished will become what we call a 'Gate Guardian.' We'd managed to obtain an Antar which required restoration, but it was in need of a full cosmetic restoration. We were in the process of finding

Sponsors to help us and Rapid Solicitors very kindly stepped up to the plate. Times are very tight and we were extremely fortunate to receive an offer of support. Without it, it is highly unlikely that the project would have gone ahead.

'The Mighty Antar'

Once the vehicle has been restored to its formal splendour, we're hoping to have a formal dedication ceremony in February 2012. We've managed to get a VIP to agree to come along and dedicate the vehicle, but we're keeping his name under our hats for now. OK, it was Earl Attlee

And finally

What do you feel about the 'Antar' Restoration Project?

I'm thrilled to bits with it and jumped at the chance to become the Project Officer for this. In a previous life I served for 5 years in what was then West Germany with 617 Tank Transporter Squadron RCT who used these vehicles to great effect, so it's really nice for me to become involved. I think that it's our duty show people some excellent examples of various workhorses that have served the great British nation throughout the years (that's why I've sent you a photo of myself). The Antar will be seen on a daily basis and will serve as a constant reminder that we shouldn't lose touch with our past and it's great that Rapid Solicitors has seen fit to give us their vital support.

I then departed the Defence School of Transport and the Ministry of Defence for a life of seclusion and penury at a Monastery in the outer Hebrides. Actually I went home for a cup of refreshing Yorkshire tea and a few digestive biscuits to help me recover from the emotion of no longer being a useful member of society and worse than that - no longer receiving a regular wage packet.

'TELEVISION'

I have been involved with Television in various capacities, now and again, so I'll mention a bit about that.

'THE BBC'

The BBC has/had a series of committees which they invited various members of the general public to sit upon and advise. One has to be interviewed by local BBC luminaries to filter out the inevitable loons and if successful you are then invited onto local committees. I was invited to join the BBC Radio Humberside Listeners Advisory Council (LAC). It was very interesting seeing the inner workings of the BBC and a bonus was that I made some nice new friends amongst the other committee members. I got right into it – if a job's worth doing etc.

Eventually I moved up the ranks and was 'promoted' into some of the other council appointments (all voluntary unpaid, I hasten to add) within the colossus that is the BBC. It was also a great opportunity to sit and discuss the BBC's current and projected activities and see just how they were developing. There was an element of 'them and us' with our committees considered to be a 'necessary evil' but in essence all that we wanted to do was contribute positively towards a greatly admired and much loved organisation. I found that inevitably those people employed by the BBC were hardworking, creative and really nice. I met the occasional nob, but that was indicative more of society than the BBC as an organisation. If I'd thought that 'Management Speak' was highly evident in the Ministry of Defence, it was as nothing compared with the BBC. It was a steep learning curve. Lots of "At the end of the day," "Glad to have you on board," "I have to say," that sort of cack.

Eventually I was appointed Chairman of the Listeners Advisory Committee (LAC), Chairman of the Regional Advisory Committee (RAC) for BBC Yorkshire and Lincolnshire and a member of the English National Forum (ENF). Just thought I'd drop that into the conversation. It's not only the MOD that goes wild with abbreviations! It meant doing a great deal of reading and obviously one was required to listen to and watch much of the BBC's output, as well as watching and listening to other radio/TV stations. I did that sort of thing anyway, so it was no great hardship as far as I was concerned. If you get an opportunity to have a go at it, you should give it a try, it's all very interesting, but be warned, it's time consuming. One of the little perks as a thank you for all of the long hours of committee work, I was invited as a guest of the BBC to the Royal Albert Hall to one of their annual 'Proms' presentations.

On arrival at the Royal Albert Hall, the upper echelons of the BBC and their invited guests assembled in a posh side room for a glass of sparkling white wine and some delightful canapés. We then proceed into the 'Hall' proper to settle down and ready ourselves for listening to the concert. Much to my delight, we were seated in a very nice box, with yours truly to the fore. Comfortable seats, an excellent view and in addition to all that, we were able to take our drinks into the box with us. The concert began and it was some sort of weird, modern style concoction that I'm sure that not many of us either understood or appreciated (I certainly didn't). People made lots of appreciative noises and pretended that they were enjoying it, but I thought that it wasn't much cop, but then what do I know. For me, the atmosphere perceived shortcomings.

As the torturous style music continued, I sipped a glass or two of very reasonable Chateauneufe du Pape and my mind wandered back to the year 1959 when as a young lad I'd travelled down by ancient omnibus from Keighley in West Yorkshire, with the remainder of 1st Keighley Company The Boys Brigade (the BB), to their annual festival at the Royal Albert Hall. On that occasion we had been seated in the very highest part of the Royal Albert Hall, near the ceiling. Any higher and we would have needed oxygen masks. Across the road from the Albert Hall, prior to the 'gig,' we'd had our photo's taken standing rigidly to attention in front of the Albert Memorial (one of the more affluent members of the BB having possession of a Brownie 127 camera).

It was a magical experience for a lad from a Northern mill town to visit the capital city where the streets were supposed to be paved with gold and the Royal family lived just up t'road from the Albert Hall. I really enjoyed missen. The one big disappointment was that the miserable scrote of a coach driver wouldn't take us past Buckingham Palace on the way home – that would be rectified in years to come when I managed to wheedle my way inside the Palace for tea and stickies.

I thought how times had changed, as there I lounged in a rather posh box, elbows resting indolently on the plush velvet padding, clutching a glass of hooch, suited and booted. I gazed up to the top of the Albert Hall and my mind whizzed back in time as I pictured a rotund, grinning, bespectacled face (me) in BB uniform, looking down at the auditorium. Life's funny, innit!

The exalted BBC personage sat next to me in the box said at the conclusion of the first half of the musical programme – "Terry, did you understand any of that music?" "Not a bloody note!" sez I, ever the Philistine. "Hmmmm," replied the BBC big-wig, "That's good because I thought that it was a load of old bollocks." More wine was taken.

Fortunately the second half of the programme was much better, in my humble opinion, as we were by then on familiar musical ground ('Peter and the Wolf' or something like that). By that time we cared not a jot as the wine had helped to ease the assault on t'lug-holes. It was, though, a very pleasant and memorable evening with a definite touch of nostalgia thrown in.

Whilst carrying out my BBC Committee 'duties' I travelled over to Sheffield University one afternoon/evening, where we were to be introduced to the latest technological advances in both television and radio. It was very interesting to see how things were to develop and have a look at the new equipment, but the most interesting part of the evening was, for me, meeting up with Doctor Trevor Bayliss OBE, inventor of (amongst many other brilliant devices) the wind-up radio. What a charmer he was.

Doctor Trevor Bayliss OBE CBE

Doctor Bayliss was a very interesting man to talk to, completely down to earth – and, in the nicest possible way, a bit scatty. During the course of our delightful conversation one of the subjects we spoke about was our time in the Army. It transpired that Doctor Bayliss had led a very colourful and interesting life, at one stage being a muscle-bender in the Army Physical Training Corps (APTC) and another working in a circus in Berlin – part of his duties was being fired out of a cannon and hoping to land in the net at the other side of the circus ring)! His autobiography is a brilliant read and I recommend that you nip out and buy a copy -('My Secret Life'). A genuinely nice man and a genius to boot. He's the sort of bloke that should be covered with honours, not some transient pop star who gets a knighthood for record sales.

I also got the opportunity to attend several meetings at BBC Birmingham's 'The Mailbox.' That was very interesting. One day, after ploughing through tons of documents and discussing various riveting organisational matters, as a bit of light relief we were taken around the large studio where 'The Archers' was recorded. My particular triumph that day was buying an Archers tea-cosy for my Mother-in-law (that got me a gold star). Other highlights were shaking hands with a Dalek, getting inside Doctor Who's Tardis (which was very small and with a definite whiff of urine in there) and meeting Michael Grade. One of my ambitions, unachieved, was to visit the old BBC building in central London to see if Arthur Askey and Dickie Murdoch were still up there on top of the roof, but I never managed it. Those of a certain age will know what I'm waffling on about. Maybe someday, who knows. Regrettably, ill-health crept up on me and I had to reduce my commitments, so my days as a BBC Committee member drew to a close. It was a very worthwhile time and I met some lovely, committed people. The BBC is priceless and we should all be very proud of what it does.

T C at BBC Birmingham (The Mailbox)

'BLAZERED, BOOTED AND BLADDERED'

One of my tasks whilst employed at the Defence School of Transport was to organize the annual 'Beating Retreat Ceremony and Cocktail Party.' The function was organized as a way of saying thank you to the great and good who had given their support to DST throughout out the preceding year. A major headache for me each year was finding a Guest of Honour to take the salute at the actual Beating Retreat Ceremony. I could usually obtain the services of a local General, the Lord Lieutenant or visiting Admiral etc but I tried to make things a little more interesting by inviting those who were in the public eye and could give the occasion something of an 'Ooooh' factor. One could only invite the Lord Lieutenant so many times before familiarity bred contempt.

Speaking of contempt. One particular Lord Lieutenant had notified us that he would be arriving a little late due to attending another ceremony prior to ours. I said that I would forgo my cocktails and wait at the entrance to the Officers' Mess and escort the Lord Lieutenant to the VIP Group once he arrived. I waited at the front door of the Officers' Mess and in due course a shiny car arrived, disgorging the Lord Lieutenant. I should mention at this stage that it had been raining and he was carrying a raincoat.

As he entered the Mess I held out my hand to shake his and welcome him. He threw the wet raincoat over my arm saying, rather demeaningly, "See to that will you!" I dutifully smiled and said "Certainly sir" before introducing myself as Major Cavender, the event organizer and added, icily, "I'll hand your raincoat to the Mess Manager if I may, he usually deals with that sort of thing," before mincing off in high dudgeon, going around the corner and hurtling the said raincoat across the cloakroom. What a cheeky bastard he was, didn't he realize that I was important in the scheme of things. I certainly wasn't a 'bag-carrier.' I was even wearing a name badge, to give him a clue."Huh, see to that" indeed. It still rankles after all these years. Know thy place, Cavender.

We invited the local BBC TV Personality Peter Levy one year. He was thrilled to have been asked, but as he would be presenting his news programme 'Look North' on the evening of the Cocktail Party/Beating Retreat, timings would be a bit tight. He would have to come straight up to Leconfield from the studios at Queen's Gardens, Hull as soon as he was 'Off Air.'. We got all that sorted and a staff car was waiting for him when he came out of the TV Studio's at Queen's Gardens in central Hull. He arrived at Leconfield to sound of women guests dutifully swooning. One of the crustier older chaps pointed at him and said, sotto voce, "Good Lord, the bounder's wearing make-up!" Peter had come straight off air, and then thrashed up to Leconfield in order to participate in our Beating Retreat Ceremony. The poor bloke couldn't win. He looked rather dashing and we were grateful that he'd made the effort to join us.

Peter Levy - BBC TV & Radio Presenter

The one and only Dickie Bird OBE MBE very kindly agreed to be the Chief Guest at our annual Beating Retreat Ceremony, held at DST Leconfield on Thursday evening 18 June 2009. We were honoured that he made time in his very busy schedule to be there. Dickie, a favourite among the public, is also greatly admired and respected by players. He diffused many situations on the cricket pitch with common sense and good humour. All of the 'names' in cricket rated him highly: Sobers, Richards, Lillee and Botham. Arguably the most famous Umpire in the history of the game of cricket, he is a great advocate of the family unit and knows first hand the tremendous support and enormous sacrifices his parents made to ensure he was able to follow his destiny.

Dickie Bird went on to play Cricket for both Yorkshire and Leicestershire between 1956 and 1964, scoring over 3000 first class runs, before turning his attention to Umpiring. He Umpired his first Test Match in 1973, finally calling it a day at Lords Cricket Ground in June 1996. Dickie Umpired 68 Test Matches, 92 One Day International Matches, 4 World Cup Finals, the Queen's Silver Jubilee Test at Trent Bridge between England and Australia in 1977 and the Centenary Test Match between England and Australia in 1980.

Yorkshire Personality of the Year, Yorkshire Man of the Year in the People of the Year Awards in 1996, Honorary Doctorates at Hallam and Leeds Universities, Freeman of the Borough of Barnsley, Dickie also has life membership of: The MCC, Yorkshire and Leicestershire Cricket Clubs, Barnsley Football Club and Cambridge University Cricket Club. Since his 'retirement' Dickie Bird has become a best-selling author, writing 6 books between 1968 and 2002 and is also a chat-show guest and after dinner speaker. He received his MBE from the Queen in June 1986 (and has since been awarded the OBE). So, we were very lucky and privileged to obtain his services for the evening. Dickie thoroughly enjoyed the experience, his first ever Beating Retreat and was greatly honoured to have been asked. He was particularly touched that the Light Cavalry Band performing for us that evening had included a selection of 'Yorkshire' tunes in their programme of music.

***WO1 Ian Collins- Bandmaster of the Light Cavalry Band
requests the permission of Dickie Bird MBE OBE
to march the Band off parade***

I'd obtained Dickie's telephone number (an initiative test in itself) and had given him a call to see if he was willing and available to accept our invitation to be Chief Guest at the ancient ceremony and do us the honour of taking the salute. He said that he would be thrilled to do so. All we had to do was collect him from his home near Barnsley and return him there the following morning after he'd had a 'Full English' breakfast.

The miserable, quill-dribbling, penny-pinching misers at the MOD had directed that we were not permitted to send a staff car to collect him, so my old mate Major Peter Todd (a huge cricket fan) went to collect Dickie and bring him to Leconfield. I volunteered to return Dickie home the following morning after breakfast, all at our own expense. Dickie was a very pleasant man and, after consuming the odd cocktail or two, greatly enjoyed taking the salute at the Beating Retreat Ceremony. He spent a great deal of time chatting to the other official luminaries, Lord Mayors, Mayors, Miscellaneous Lurkers, other lesser Civic Dignitaries and anyone else wanting a moment of his time.

Purely by coincidence the military band performing at the ceremony played a hymn that was one of

Dickie's favorites' from his school days, bringing a nostalgic tear to his eye. He was quite emotional and it was rather touching to see. After the Beating Retreat Ceremony, when the civic dignitaries had departed, (having recognised that there were no further freebies to be had), the remainder of us repaired to the bar in the Officers' Mess to have an elongated 'chatette' and further drinkies late into the night.

The next morning we all joined Dickie at the Officers' Mess for a traditional 'Regimental Breakfast,' (that's a hearty full English washed down by the finest champagne). I then spent a most enjoyable couple of hours chatting with Dickie as I drove him back to Barnsley (and before you ask, I hadn't had any of the champagne). He was in fine fettle and waxed lyrical, telling me some very interesting and amusing stories, one such being that he had been invited to lunch at Buckingham Palace several times by HM the Queen. Naturally I was very nosey and asked him about HM the Queen and other members of the Royal Family in attendance at the lunches and what they'd spoken about. Yes, it was all very nice and interesting, with the odd juicy tale to savour. I gave my word that the stories would not be repeated and they haven't been. I eventually dropped Dickie off at his home and bade him a fond farewell, sorry to see him go but felt privileged to have spent some time in his company. I felt that the whole thing had been a bit special.

A couple of months later, my amigo Major Peter Todd and I were invited by the then Mayor of Scarborough to watch a day's cricket at their home ground. This was a singular honour and we accepted the invitation within seconds. We booked a days leave and then 'Suited and Booted' travelled from Beverley to Scarborough by train, knowing that alcohol would be consumed throughout the day. On arrival at the cricket ground we rather grandly waved our official invitation card and informed the gateman at the entrance to the cricket ground that we were personal guests of the Mayor.

The gateman, who couldn't have given a flying fart who we were, directed us to a white tent sited at the other side of the cricket ground. We meandered across to the tent and entered. It was beautifully laid out, carpets, 'posh' seating and – joy of joys – at the far corner was a well-stocked bar dispensing alcoholic beverages. We elbowed our way through the assembled gentry, reached the bar and ordered two glasses of lager, which was duly delivered. Cool and refreshing. Things were looking up. For once in his life, Todd volunteered to pay. To his absolute delight, the barman informed him that there was no charge for the drinks as they were being provided by the Sponsors. Our joy at this unexpected bonus knew no bounds. We looked at each other and grinned, like two naughty schoolboys. This could be the start of something big.

Firmly clutching our 'free' lagers, we went outside, claimed our deck-chairs and commenced watching the cricket from a sun-kissed prime spot, taking it in turns to go and recharge our glasses. Splendid! The weather was scorching, so the lager slid down our parched throats nicely. It was Peter's turn to go and collect two further pints of lager from Aladdin's cave, so off he cheerfully staggered. Just after he'd gone, the Mayor's Secretary, the fragrant Irene Webster, hove into view and we had pleasant chat, during the course of which I asked her to pass on our thanks on to His Worship the Mayor for his very kind invitation for us to come and watch the Cricket then take tea with him later on in the afternoon.

Irene kindly agreed to do so and then, to my horror, pointed towards a different tent to the one that we'd been using, telling me that it was the Mayor's Tent and that that was there the Tea and Sandwiches would be dispensed later on (can you see where I'm going with this)? She then went on to tell me that sited immediately adjacent to the Mayor's Tent was one of the Match Sponsor's Tent, (provided by 'Boyes' Stores) and commented that it was quite disgraceful how every year, without fail, uninvited guests would slide into the 'Boyes' tent and filch some of the complimentary drinks that were freely available there. The penny dropped rather rapidly; things were not quite as liberal as Toddy and missen had thought, and I remember nodding sagely at Irene and mumbling something to her along the lines of, "Mmmm, that's quite disgraceful behaviour," and "Outrageous! What's the world coming to!" etc.

At that precise moment, Major Todd tottered back into view, sweating like a welders foot in a clog, but triumphantly clutching not two but four ice cold pints of lager, spilling not a drop as he lurched over to us. I remember thinking, "Oh my God, not now Peter!" He smiled that very special alcohol fuelled vacant smile of his, known and recognised by his close friends everywhere, and said - "Hey up Terence, here's another couple of buckshee pints, lad. Bloody brill day this, innit!" I smiled at Irene and said something banal to her along the lines of "Er, I er, Irene, this is Major Peter Todd. We'll no doubt bump into you later in the Mayor's tent?" Irene 'harrumphed' and swept off like a stately galleon in full sail without, thankfully, any further comment - although the distasteful look on her face said it all. She was, quite understandably sucking a metaphoric lemon. Toddy, sensing that something untoward had occurred but not quite sure what, said – "Have I done summat wrong?" passing me a chilled lager.

We were totally innocent in all of this, having been misdirected in the first instance by the Gateman (well that's our excuse M'Lud). Believe me when I tell you that it was an honest, (albeit pleasant) mistake. I would, however, like to take this opportunity to say a belated thank you to 'Mr Boyes' who, although not intending to do so, had ensured that both Major's Todd and Cavender had a most refreshing, memorable, inexpensive and pleasant day. Later on in the afternoon we tottered into the Mayor's tent, upright, but well and truly 'refreshed' for the promised tea and stickies, chatting with various other guests, although by that time it would have been difficult for them to understand us as we were both talking in Klingon.

At lunchtime, during a break in play, we'd decided to freshen up, get a bit of sea air and have a little wander around the Scarborough sea-front. To our delight, as we left the ground who should we bump into but the inimitable Dickie Bird. Our faces lit up and we went to say a quick hello to him. To our great disappointment he dropped his head down, totally ignored us and marched off into the distance. Both Peter and I had very recently spent many hours in his company so he couldn't have failed to have recognised us. We had been well and truly 'kicked to the curb' - another illusion shattered. It wasn't as if we were going to ask him for a loan or anything! In retrospect and having given the matter a bit of thought, I recall that as he wasn't wearing spectacles he might not have recognised us. We gave him the benefit of the doubt, but it was so disappointing.

Peter Todd, Dickie Bird MBE OBE and T C after scoffing a 'Regimental Breakfast'!

Toddy and I eventually returned to the cricket ground after a most pleasant lunchtime interlude at a local pub. At the conclusion of the cricket match, most of which I regrettably missed as I had drifted off (metaphorically speaking) in a deck chair, my venereal friend Toddy and I then tottered back up a never ending Scarborough Hill to the railway station, our spirits high but our wind definitely broken. Fortunately there wasn't a train to Beverley for another hour or so, so we were obliged to imbibe further at an adjacent hostelry. It was quite outrageous – we had to pay for it. I recall that once on the train we slept most of the way back, having asked those cricket fans (fellow revellers and Klingon speakers) in our carriage to give us a nudge as we neared the Beverley Railway Station, which they failed to do. We woke up a lot further down the line in Hull's Paragon Railway Station and had to take a further train back to Beverley. We were collected from Beverley Railway Station by 'Todd's Taxi's' and in a dishevelled condition returned to our respective residences to be met by our thin-lipped wives. It was a day to remember with great fondness apart from the 'Dickie' disappointment.

There are other occasions when I get myself into some really embarrassing situations, usually when I'm trying to help others. For instance, the Memsahib and Missen had gone on a visit to Scotland, to see our daughter Sara and son-in-law Ian. After the visit we were wending our way back to Yorkshire and decided to stop for a 'Kipper Tie and Sandwich' at one of those truly dreadful Motorway Café's. Prior to recommencing our journey we decided to make use of the facilities. After 'easing springs' and on my way out of Gentlemen's lavatories I bumped into an obviously confused lady of a certain age, sporting Scottish plaid trousers, a rather butch but smart tweed jacket, 'Hush Puppy' suede footwear and with blue-tinged highly coiffuered hair. Ah, thought I, the poor dear's lost. I'll point her in the right direction, knowing full well what it's like when the water tablets kick in!

Me: (*Helpfully*) Excuse me Madam, the Ladies facilities are around the other side of the building.

The elderly person looked at me with what the Scots would term a 'glaikit' expression. (If someone is described as being glaikit, it means that you think them to be bordering on dense. Similarly, even the brightest of people can be considered as being glaikit if they are having a bad brain day or if their brain is not in gear). This little, shrivelled old person appeared to me to be bordering on glaikit. Failing to respond to my helpful advice, I thought, ah, the poor dear must also be a bit 'mutt and jeff.' Deciding to be terribly British, I tried once again.

Me: (*Slightly louder voice and speaking slowly*) Er Madam, excuse me. These are the Men's facilities, the Ladies facilities are around the other side of the building.

I was rewarded with another chillingly vacant stare. Thrashing on regardless, I decided to give it one last go. I raised my voice by a few decibels (casual passers-by paused to view the performance, sensing that there was sport to be had):

Me: (*Smilingly sweetly, forcefully gripping her arm and shoving her towards the Ladies*) You need to be over there, my dear! This side is for Men only! We're not France you know! Hah Hah!

The elderly person glared at me, snorted then drew 'themself' up to their full height of 5 Feet 3 inches, by now trembling and puce with indignation, then said, (rather too loudly in my humble opinion):

Elderly Person: I.... am.... a... man, you bloody English half wit!

Whoops. I'd struck again. I was aghast and felt myself blushing from what had been the roots of my hair, then burbled something vacuous to the poor chap, made my excuses and hurtled out of the building.

When I got back to our vehicle, my wife took one look at me and said – *"Terence! What have you been up to now?"* She knew, as wives unfathomably do, that some form of mischief had been afoot and that I'd involved myself in yet another 'happening.' We thrashed out of the car park at a great rate of knots as I'd seen the 'Elderly Person' heading our way, with a face like a slapped arse. I didn't want eye contact with him again if I could help it. If he ever reads this, my apologies sir, – I was only trying to help – but you do need to do something about that over-coiffuered hair - blue-rinse is so yesterday.

Whilst relating the story to a friend of mine he said that he'd had a similar unfortunate experience on a crowded London bus when he'd attempted to give up his seat for what he'd thought was a heavily pregnant American lady – (who apparently, as it turned out had not been impregnated but had been heavily into Burgers and Fries). My friend, accompanied by his wife and two young sons – and wishing to give them an example of impeccable British grace and good manners, had stood up and gesticulated towards his vacant seat, saying something along the lines of – "Madam, I can see that you are pregnant, would you care for a seat?"

He was rewarded with a venal glance and then a few tortuous words were delivered by the 'lady' (one suggestion she gave was anatomically impossible but she suggested that he try it anyway). There was a pregnant (!) pause then my friend was informed in no uncertain terms that (a) she wasn't with child – and (b) he'd better return to his seat and mind his own fucking business. My mortified friend sat down, head shrinking into his collar having learnt a salutary lesson. It doesn't do to give up one's seat any more or show even a modicum of good manners. Those days, sadly, seem to have gone. His wife and children pretended that they weren't with him.

I enjoy a laugh as much as the next person, so a few years ago I bought an electronically operated 'Fart Machine' from Dinsdale's Magic Shop in Hull. At a fairly important and well attended conference in HQ DST, Leconfield, one gloomy Monday morning, I decided to liven things up a bit by cellotaping the fart machine under the chair of a rather self-important officer who usually prattled on for hours, driving everyone off to the Land of Nod. The fart machine was operated by an unseen remote switch firing out an electronic signal, cunningly hidden in my trouser pocket. The conference began and occasionally I fired off the machine, causing a series of different sounding farts, ranging from little feminine squeaky noises to great elephantine trumpeting, Krakatoan farts. As the conference progressed, the 'victim' got redder and redder until the Chairman, halted the proceedings and said to him "Rupert, old chap" (*name changed to protect the innocent*) - "Perhaps you'd care to leave us for a couple of minutes and, er, sort yourself out?!" The victim, by now puce with embarrassment, left the room, protesting his innocence and looking puzzled.

At the end of the conference when everyone else had left, I removed the fart machine from its hiding place and tottered off happily to my office, having had a good morning's sport. I did though, eventually confess to the unfortunate officer and got called a rather rude name. He had the good grace to smile and borrowed the fart machine for a couple of days so that he could have a bit of fun himself. Boys will be boys – anyway, a day without a titter is, in my humble opinion, a day wasted!

Whilst on the subject of breaking wind, everyone does it, even in the best of circles. One day I'd gone shopping with my wife Maggie. She legged it into the Supermarket whilst I locked the car etc. As I bent over and inserted the key, I glanced around, surreptitiously before expending a blast of none too pleasant hot air from my nether regions, thinking smugly that I'd got off lightly because my beloved wasn't there. All clear. So, working on the principle, "Where 'ere you be, let your wind blow free. In Church or Chapel, let it rattle," that is precisely what I did.

To my horror I heard a delicate, though theatrical, cough and glanced around to see from whence it came. Unfortunately, sat in the passenger seat of a car parked right at the business end of my posterior was a well coiffuered middle-aged lady, who was in the process of quickly winding her car window closed. She rewarded me with a withering glance and said, icily, "You men are such foul beasts!" I mouthed, "Sorry," and legged it into the Supermarket. When I met up with Maggie at the fruit and veg aisle, she took one look at my face and said, "What have you been up to now!?" How do wives know these things?

One of the few perks I received as a BBC Committee Member was that I was fortunate enough to be invited to the premier showing of what was then the new BBC TV series 'Robin Hood' at Lincoln University. Guest of Honour at the showing was the actor, the late Richard Todd, whom many of you will surely remember from his appearances in such epic films as 'The Dam Busters' and 'The Bridge at Remagen.' I was permitted to take a guest along and as my wife Maggie wasn't available, I took the star-struck Major Peter Todd with me. Peter had hinted darkly that it was possible that he was a long lost relative of Richard Todd (which proved not to be the case.

We thought, mistakenly, that the largesse (!) of the BBC would extend to them providing copious amounts of wine etc, particularly on such an auspicious occasion. In actual fact all we got was a curly sandwich or two, with the odd glass of manky wine.

We spent a very pleasant evening viewing the very first episode of 'Robin Hood' then discussed it afterwards in open forum with those present. After the formal chinwaggery, we circulated around the gathering in cocktail party fashion, and eventually got to meet the great man, Richard Todd, who although by then well into his nineties, was ramrod straight, bright as a button, smart as a carrot and very sparky. In truth, however, I don't think that he really wanted to be there.

During the Second World War, Richard Todd joined the British Army, receiving a commission in 1941. Initially, he served in the King's Own Yorkshire Light Infantry before joining the Parachute Regiment. and being assigned to the 7th (Light Infantry) Parachute Battalion as part of the British 6th Airborne Division. On 6 June 1944, as a Captain, he participated in the British Airborne 'OPERATION TONGA' during the D-Day landings and was among the first British officers to land in Normandy as part of 'OPERATION OVERLORD.' His Battalion were reinforcements that parachuted in after glider forces had landed and completed the main assault against Pegasus Bridge near Caen. He later met up with Major John Howard on Pegasus Bridge and helped repel several German counterattacks. Not just a film star but a brave and courageous man.

I introduced Peter Todd to Richard Todd and we joked about how Peter might be his long lost son. This comment fell on decidedly stony ground and wasn't greeted with the expected hoots of laughter from Richard Todd. The atmosphere turned a tad icy, so we made a little more polite conversation and returned to the merry throng. What neither of us knew at the time was that two of Richard Todd's sons had committed suicide, which explained why the jocular comment about Peter Todd being his long lost son wasn't particularly well received. We meant no offence and it was a great pleasure to have met him.

Richard Todd, T C, Major Peter Todd

During the 'Question and Answer' session at the latter end of the evening, Richard Todd had been asked what he thought of the new TV series and although impeccably polite about it, it was quite apparent that he was overcome with indifference. He was, after all, a Golden Globe 'film' man and didn't really rate TV – and that was that. At the end of the evening he departed and I read only recently that regrettably he is no longer with us. I consider myself very fortunate to have met him and only the other day I was watching him performing heroically in 'The Dam Busters' film. He had definite star quality about him.

I was also given the opportunity to attend a recording of the BBC's Antiques Roadshow' which at that time was hosted by Michael Aspel. This particular episode was being recorded at the Lincolnshire Aviation Heritage Centre at East Kirby, between Boston and Lincoln, on the 11th of November 2007. I was required to act as a Steward for the event as my part of the deal for being there which wasn't a problem as it was so interesting seeing all of the 'goings-on.' There was a massive queue waiting to get into the grounds to have their antiques examined by the experts. I was on ticket patrol and was having a chat with a lady in the queue. She said that she was supposed to have attended with a friend but that the friend (who was suffering from cancer) was too ill to make the journey and accordingly was very disappointed. The lady in the queue then asked me if I knew Michael Aspel (which of course I didn't) and would it be possible to get a signed photo from him for her friend. I said that I would see what I could do.

Off I tottered and headed for Michael's dressing room where he was getting ready to present the show. He was extremely approachable and nice and I explained about wanting a signed photo. Although about to start the recording, he asked me to take him over to the queue and point the lady out, which I did. He then spent some time chatting to her, asking several questions about her friend and sent her his best wishes before handing over a signed photograph. I was very touched by his generosity of spirit, he didn't have to make that extra effort and could easily have just signed a photo and handed it to me to deliver.

Michael Aspel OBE

During my lifetime I've had occasion to meet quite a few 'personalities.' They're normally very nice and patient with the many demands that are constantly placed upon them, but as that's one of the prices of fame it shouldn't prove too difficult for them. There's been the odd exception who proved to be a bit aware of themselves, but not many. After all - no public – no fame and fortune. I remember being at the BBC TV Centre in London, pre-show, preparing for a recording of 'Blankety Bank' sat in the studio chatting with such luminaries as Beryl Reed, Keith Harris and Orville (both of whom were very nice), Windsor Davies, Barbara Windsor, Yootha Joyce, Alfred Marks and a couple more whose names escape me. There was a 'hot' Radio 1 DJ there whom it was patently obvious didn't want to speak to anyone not 'in the business' and bathed in fame, as was he. He was protected throughout by his Manager who surrounded the DJ with a force-field that couldn't be breeched. A couple of the show's contestants just wanted a quick chat with him and a photo to record the occasion, but they couldn't get past his feisty Manager. The DJ just sat there with a bored, vacuous look on his face waiting for someone to peel a grape for him. I saw him fairly recently at a BBC Radio Awards do in Birmingham. Very little had changed apart from his very obvious wig and his entourage, which was somewhat larger then when I last saw him.

'ITV'

When I was at Buller Barracks in Aldershot I was nominated to act as co-ord for a visit by the 'Game for a Laugh' television people, with host Jeremy Beadle. He turned out to be a very nice chap and it was a pleasure to spend most of the day with him. Last year whilst I was researching another book, I was tottering around Highgate Cemetery in London when purely by chance I came across his gravestone. It was a bit spooky really. He was taken away from us far too early.

Now for another Jeremy.

'JEREMY KYLE'

Me and my oppo, Donna Murphy (both Media Ops with DST Leconfield) were summoned to a meeting at which we were told that ITV wanted to come to DST and shoot a something like six episode documentary which would eventually be aired at prime time and would also be going out world-wide on the Satellite channel – National Geographic. We were very excited by this because although it would mean a great deal of hard work it also meant that we would be able to spread the 'good word' about DST and its activities to a huge audience. The Commandant, who was chairing the meeting, went on to tell us that TV presenter Jeremy Kyle would be fronting the production. The announcement was met with a stunned silence. 'Jeremy Kyle' wasn't he the chap that did the morning programme on ITV that all of our students are glued to TV screens watching? "Yes, that's the chap." Now I hadn't really had the opportunity to watch JK because it went out whilst I was at work. I had seen the occasional show, so I made a judgement on JK without knowing the facts, deciding without any real knowledge, that I didn't really like him.

I must be honest, we ducked and dived and tried to see if we could get another presenter, but it wasn't to be. We were told by the MoD to just get on with it and stop whining, which is precisely what we did. We did mountains of preparation and outlined a series of activities that we would show to JK once he arrived and hoped that it would meet up with his what we were certain were going to be demanding requirements. There was a lot of unseemly sniffing from the 'Officer Corps' and various Civil Servants when it was announced that JK and an ITV Crew would be with us for several weeks to get all of the material they required in the can for the documentary. I was also called into the Commandant's Office before everything commenced and told in no uncertain terms that if this project went 'tits up' then it would be my 'balls that would be in a sling,' (am I mixing metaphor's here)? So, no pressure there then. We were also required to travel down to the Ministry of Defence in London several times to attend various meetings to discuss the planning and preparation for the documentary. We had to get everything spot on.

The accompanying paperwork was horrendous, such niggles as getting insurance cover for those civilians who would be travelling in DST's military vehicles whilst with us. The authorising documents had to be signed off by a two star General would you believe. Generals must have much better things to do with their time. The endless amounts of crap that had to be written seeking authority for an activity that emanated from the Ministry of Defence in the first instance was breathtaking. The MOD had authorised the project in the first instance yet we still had to seek all sorts of authorities to get the job done. Go figure.

Donna Murphy and TC lurking and shirking at the MOD whilst not a few yards away the Prime Minister, Gordon Brown, was resigning his commission!

The day came when Jeremy arrived at Leconfield and a vast series of in-depth meetings and follow-up activities took place. His crew had arrived on site a little earlier so we managed to established relationships and working patterns prior to the arrival of 'The Master.' Try as I might I and despite not wanting to, shock, horror, I found myself beginning to like him, as did everyone else. The more time I spent with him, the more I came to admire him, this to my shame as I was, initially, rather dismissive of him. He wasn't in any way 'precious.' It was an object lesson for me of how not to judge a book by its cover. I found him to be a compassionate, intelligent, humorous, professional and patient individual, relentlessly determined to do his utmost to ensure that our documentary was the very best that it could be and that DST would be shown in a good light, despite filming a truthful 'warts and all' documentary.

Jeremy is an outrageously honest and forthright person who doesn't hesitate to raise his head above the parapet. He kept us in the loop at all stages, none of the 'luvvie' stuff that you get in the theatre. He was very accommodating with matters that we considered to be sensitive. He had the knack of easing heavy situations with the odd light-hearted comment. I remember when he first arrived and everyone was on their best behaviour, Jeremy said that he would never have imagined that he'd be in the back of a Mastiff. It was reassuring to see that he had a sense of humour. He was going to need it.

Ultimately when the show was aired it was ragingly successful and attracted a great deal of favourable comment for DST, the Army and the Ministry of Defence. The viewing figures were excellent. It undoubtedly benefitted DST by showing viewers that we weren't just there to annoy the local populace by filling up their roads with trucks and also that our prime concern was to turn out nothing but the best students who were to face more horrors and drama's than we could ever imagine. We could never have reached that size of audience under normal circumstances. As a Media Team we were absolutely thrilled with the results. A Media triumph – and there was great back-slapping throughout the land. It could so easily have gone the other way. We'd placed a a great deal of trust in Jeremy and the ITV Team, they were very professional and didn't let us down.

At the conclusion of filming, Jeremy took me to one side and much to my surprise said that he now considered me to be his friend – not only that but his friend for life! Again, I was cautiously judgemental and thought that once he disappeared through the camp gates that would be the last I would see of him. He has such an extremely busy life so why would he fit me into that sort of schedule – but he did. Both me and my wife Maggie have been to Dinner with him several times and had the pleasure of being invited to both the now defunct Granada TV Studios at Manchester and to his new studio set-up at Salford Quays to see him weave his magic. I had the great pleasure, as an old Thespian, of being ligged out on the couch in the Number One dressing room at Granada and wondering just who else had been in there such as Coronation Street stars Ena Sharples (Violet Carson), Elsie Tanner (Pat Phoenix), Annie Walker (Doris Speed) and my personal favourite – Albert Tatlock (Jack Howarth)? You have to be bordering on ancient to remember some of these names. Their photo's were still on the wall in the Granada Canteen and their ghosts walked. As an old 'Thespian' I love that sort of thing.

We had lunch in the Granada Canteen and it seemed quite surreal being sat there tucking into meat and two veg as various members of the august Coronation Street cast wandered in for their lunch. I recall seeing one extremely well known 'name' attempting to eat his lunch and saw him cut a pea in half! Supposes that they have to watch their figures, but cutting a pea in half seemed a little drastic to me. I have always gone for the full pea myself. One day there was a group of visiting students there chatting to Ken Barlow (William Roach). He was being very kind, posing for photo's and signing autographs when the canteen door opened and Jeremy swept in. The group surrounding William Roache just left him standing there and went straight across to Jeremy, clamouring for his attention. Ah the immediacy of popular television. Jeremy also introduced us to Graham Stanier, the Director of Aftercare for ITV and the Jeremy Kyle Show, who is also a tip-top geezer. We've been over to Salford to see the JK Show being recorded and watch as Jeremy goes from strength to strength. He's a good bloke and it's a pleasure to be numbered amongst his friends. When we've been sat in the studio watching the taping of his shows he often introduces us to his audiences (as his 'Honorary Uncle and Aunt')!

'SOME OF THE PLAYS AND FILMS'

I've always been involved in something to do with the stage, films and television in various capacities. It might only have been at a relatively low level on occasions, but I did it and loved it (still do). Here's some 'bits and pieces' that I've been involved with over my life-time. Obviously I can't include everything I've done in this book or it would be as long as the New English Bible. Just a few things, to give you something of a flavour.

'THE RING KING'

The comedy play 'The Ring King' about a failed Magician was for me an absolute joy and I had mountains of fun writing it then touring it around the local area. We took the play out on the road more than once, using a variety of talented local actors. The one and only Bryn Ellis, supported by my old mate Roger Peace and Angela Burkitt (nee Daysley) as 'Mother' were at the top of their game and we had some great fun, as I hope did the audiences, who were paying for the privilege. Because I took the play out on several different occasions it was necessary to use a variety of different actors and actresses. It's the old availability thing that often makes casting so difficult. We didn't make a fortune because we worked on the basis of 'profit share,' but it wasn't all about money.

As you do, you have to come up with all sorts of wheezes in order to get publicity for your play, fighting for some valuable space in the media with larger and well funded companies. There weren't as many local radio stations pumping information out as there are now. One particular wheeze we had was to get a generous hearted Rannoch Daly, Governor of Hull Prison, to join in a photo-stunt at the front of the prison where the Ring King (an inefficient

Magician) had him locked in a pair of handcuffs (surely a first for a Prison Governor)? It did the trick and we managed to get some juice out of the already hard squeezed publicity orange. Bums on seats was the reward.

We decided to take 'The Ring King' on a grand tour of Yorkshire and Lancashire. I'd been for a wander around Robin Hoods Bay with the Memsahib on a previous occasion and discovered, much to my surprise, that there was an old Chapel there that had been converted into a theatre, cunningly called 'The Old Chapel Theatre.' The area is absolutely delightful, albeit it a bit out in the sticks, but nevertheless we thought that there would be an audience to watch our comedy show. I managed to scrounge a decent truck from an old Army mate of mine (not a military truck I hasten to add – before howls of outrage emanate from furious tax-payer of Wetwang) with which to transport our props and scenery, plus lighting and heavy sound equipment. We booked the venue and drove down to Robin Hood's Bay in a fleet of cars, following the truck carefully down the exceedingly steep hill leading to the bottom of Robin Hood's Bay so that we could reach the venue to unload our scenery, costumes and props etc.

The village was full of merry holidaymakers, who applauded the efforts of our heavily perspiring truck driver (Bryn Ellis) who had to reverse up a steep hill leading to the theatre whilst trying not to demolish any of the ancient and picturesque property. The truck's engine was severely tested and I could smell a familiar 'burning' that I recognised as coming from the clutch. We stopped the truck fairly near to the venue to let it cool down, and decided to continue unloading the scenery, costumes and equipment from it 'by hand.' It was rather exciting moving large 'flats' from the truck up to the theatre, tottering along the cliff edges, particularly as there was a gusty wind blowing at the time – and on several occasions we nearly joined the ranks of the Kamikaze hang-gliders. We eventually got everything into the theatre, with much relief, and started to get things organised. Everything went swimmingly well, so we repaired to a local hostelry for a rest and spot of pre-show refreshment.

Then it was back to the 'theatre,' everything readied and tested, actors slathered in make-up and costumed, ready for the off. The audience that night can only be described as being 'thin.' Unfortunately, there were more people on stage than we had in the audience. Undaunted, we decided to continue with the performance. Incidentally, what we hadn't been told was that there was also an amateur production of 'Oklahoma' on that night 'just up t'road' and the majority of locals had gone, understandably, to see that show. You pay to learn. Technically, our show was a bit of a disaster in that the electrics of the venue couldn't handle our lighting and sound equipment requirements, although we'd been informed that it wouldn't be a problem on our initial recce. Looking back I suppose that it was quite amusing, for us anyway, because it seemed that every time we reached a particularly dramatic moment in the play – of which there were several – the bloody lights blew, pitching the entire venue into darkness. We could then hear the hurried footsteps of our 'Techie' thrashing across the theatre, by torchlight, to seek out the fuse-box and throw a switch so that we could continue.

In the true spirit of theatre (we didn't want to return any ticket money), we completed the show, took a bow or two and left to a smattering of applause from the Spartan audience. We 'struck the set,' loading all of our scenery, cossies and equipment onto the truck, ready to departed from the venue the following day. We were, lathered, with heavy hearts and very little loot to show for our efforts. Having said that, luckily we'd made enough to cover our costs, we were doing something that we loved - so it wasn't too bad. We lived to perform another day.

The cast and crew of the Cast Iron Theatre Company repaired to a local hostelry for further refreshments then at closing time tottered off to a local boarding house where we would be able to enjoy a decent night's kip before proceeding to our next venue in Lancashire the following morning. One of our red blooded younger male actors (no names no pack-drill) had consumed rather too much of the grape and spent a lot of the evening pursuing the Landlady's svelte and now fearful daughter around the house demanding that she come and share a late night beverage with him etc. The poor girl was mortified, feared for her virginity and was having none of it.

Our senior actor and company manager, Bryn Ellis, took the lad to one side and gave him a ferocious talking to about letting the side down with his over-amorous behaviour and ordered him to bed - without the lady of his desires accompanying him. Funnily enough I was watching TV only the other night and saw the now not so young stallion appearing in an insurance advert! A good bloke though, and a hardworking, much liked member of the Cast Iron Theatre Company.

Money was tight, so the company male's had to share bedrooms. In our particular room, one male actor, Ashley K Howard, had the single bed, whilst both me and Roger Peace shared a double bed for the night (let the men talk)! The next morning I woke up thoroughly refreshed after a cracking night's sleep, but with no sign of my kipping companions. What I'd failed to tell them was that I was a ferocious snorer. Because of the horrendous noise I had been making they'd been unable to get to sleep and had 'abandoned ship' at about four in the morning, going for a pre-dawn wander along the cold, deserted Robin Hood's Bay beach, killing time until the sun came up and a much longed for breakfast would be served.

The lads eventually sat at the breakfast table, cream-crackered whilst my face lit up with pure delight when the lovely Landlady came and said "Right lads, just so I know – do you want two fried eggs or three with your breakfasts?" She then delivered us all a very hearty 'full English' breakfast with great crispy chunks of black pudding and mountains of vein clogging fried bread. Health food be damned, we wanted something that would cling to our ribs! Just the job. After breakfast I jumped into my car and thrashed off over to Keighley in West Yorkshire to visit my dear old Ma (it was Mother's Day) leaving the others to crack on with preparing for the move of the company to our next venue at Clitheroe in faraway Lancashire.

Original Cast and Crew of 'The Ring King'
(Left to Right):
Ashley Howard, Ona Kvedaravicius, Graham Elwell, Roger Peace, T C, Bryn Ellis,
the divine Angela Burkitt (nee Daysley)

All was not well in Robin Hood's Bay. Apparently our truck started off nicely but gave up the ghost halfway up the very steep hill leading out of Robin Hood's Bay – t'was indeed the clutch that had burnt out! My very kind transport contact provided us with another truck, but we were trying his patience. It's only through the generosity of people such as sponsors and providers of various 'things' that little theatre companies like 'Cast Iron' survive and in doing so manage to keep live theatre going.

One final little 'happening' with 'The Ring King' was when we took the play to North Ferriby, on the outskirts of Hull. We did all of the usual, building the set, lights, sound etc and were ready for curtain up. Just as the house lights dimmed and the curtain rose for the opening scene of the play to begin, Angela Burkitt (nee Daysley), who was playing the part of Mother, was sat in her chair, front centre stage, ostensibly having a cup of tea and about to deliver her opening line, when someone backstage let out the most tremendous and ripest of farts. The sound of this anal explosion echoed around the North Ferriby auditorium and was quickly followed by an odious and undisguisable 'eggy' stench drifting throughout the theatre.

Angie was, alas, overcome by a fit of the giggles and struggled to continue performing. In the front row of the theatre were sat two elderly ladies (Angie could hear all of this going on). One old lady turned to the other and said "Ooooh, in't it clever what they can do nowadays, Ethnie, you can even smell it!" Whomsoever committed the farting offence never 'coughed' to doing it, but I'm determined that I'll get to the bottom of it one day! Until then, the miscreant is referred to by all of us as 'The Phantom Farter of Ferriby.'

Angela Burkitt (nee Daysley) as 'Mother' in the opening scene of 'The Ring King'

The play received some excellent notices and we were able to add various comments to our show publicity, such as:

> *'Hilarious'* – *'Stage and Television Today.*
> *'A very rewarding evening'* – *'East Yorkshire Viewpoint.'*
> *'Cast Iron Magic'* – *Hull Daily Mail.*
> *'Gets the Laughs'* – *Holderness Gazette.*

So we were doing something right and it's one of life's joys as a writer being able to make people laugh out loud, enjoy a good night at the theatre and perhaps forget some of their troubles. Live theatre, when it's done properly, you can't beat it.

'WATERHOUSE LANE'

I decided to write a play about prostitution in Hull, having once been driven past Waterhouse Lane in Hull and had it pointed out that that was where 'Ladies of the Night' plied there trade, just around the corner from the infamous Earl de Gray Pub. A true 'red light' area. The story popped into my head and I hit the keyboard to try and make some sense of it all. I eventually finished up with a play about three fictional prostitutes from different eras and what had happened that caused them tread down the prostitution path.

The three stories took place during the end of the 1890's, the World War 2 era and here and now. The play showed how these three women fell on hard times, having had no other option but to turn to prostitution as a means of surviving. I thought that it was a good script, containing, drama, humour and pathos, so – 'Tally Ho!'

To help publicise the play, now named 'Waterhouse Lane,' I got the three actresses playing the main roles to turn up at the actual location of Waterhouse Lane, shortly to be demolished, in Hull one sunny afternoon, wearing their tarty costumes, for a publicity shoot with the Hull Daily Mail newspaper. The photographer did his thing, made a few notes and then left. I went to get my car to take the actresses (still in costume) back home. As I parked up and got out of the car, a group of rough looking drunkards staggered around the corner from the Earl de Gray, obviously seeking female company, and spotted me with the three girls. One of the lads shouted at me "Are you going to shag 'em all then, you fat greedy bastard?" My face, puce with embarrassment, I ushered the tittering girls into my car and we legged it out of the area at speed. The drunkards shook their fists, blew raspberries and made rude gestures at us as we drove past them.

The Shady Ladies!
Claire McDougall (as Stacey Parker), Angela Burkitt (nee Daysley) (as Polly Stansfield) and Rena Kearns (as Renate Lappe)

The play went very well and was received with great enthusiasm at the various venues where it was performed. We even took the play to Askham Grange near York which, for those that don't know it, is an open prison for women. That was an interesting experience. After all of the usual security procedures at the prison, we started to erect our stage set and place the lighting and sound equipment in their gymnasium. Askham Grange is a lovely old building and I suppose if you're going to spend some time at one of Her Majesty's residences then that one didn't appear to be too bad. When I was a young Sergeant, one of my Army bosses had left the Army and been appointed a Deputy Governor in Her Majesty's Prison Service. One of his postings was at Dartmoor Prison and he'd invited both me and Maggie down to Dartmoor to have a look around. Askham Grange was a palace by comparison. The great temptation for the inmates at Askham Grange was, I suppose, that as the front gates are always open wide, not doing a runner was the key issue. Anyway, on a mafting hot summer's day we put up the set, donned costumes/makeup etc and did all of the usual pre-show preparations. I particularly enjoyed setting up the scenery and placing the props etc. It was a joy changing what was just some empty and soul-less spot into something special.

The only slight difficulty at Askham Grange was that we were performing the play in their Gymnasium where there was only a makeshift stage, which necessitated some of the actors entering from the rear of the 'auditorium.' Those actors who were doing so hid at the back of the auditorium, out of sight. The captive (sorry) audience arrived and we started the play off. What we didn't know was that the actors waiting at the rear of the auditorium, in a confined space, didn't have access to a lavatory and that one of the shall we say more mature actresses took desperately short. Not willing to nip through the audience in full costume and make-up or hold up the start of the show, she decided to nip behind a fire door and 'weigh anchor' in a convenient Tesco's plastic carrier bag. 'The show must go on!' Unfortunately as one thing led to another for the poor girl, her Number 1 morphed into a ferocious smelling Number 2. The other actors waiting to go on were blanching and gagging but nevertheless realised that when you've got to go – you've just got to go. It was lucky that there was Tesco plastic bag available for the purpose. Can you imagine if there hadn't been one. I'll leave that with you.

The show went particularly well, although it was rather unusual to see several members of the entirely female audience breast feeding their babies throughout the performance. Something of a first for me. As usual, straight after the show we 'struck the set' loaded it onto our vehicles, made our farewells and everyone headed off for home. I was told afterwards that the offending Tesco bag used as a temporary loo facility was placed delicately in the very rear of Roger Peace's car until it could be properly disposed of, but that the actors sharing the vehicle had to sit there in the heat of a fine summer's day suffering from the effects of the whiffy contents on the journey home, apparently made in silence. Ah, the glamour of show-business.

I eventually arranged for 'Waterhouse Lane' to be filmed in and around Hull and also for us to use the magnificent court house at Beverley for the sentencing scenes. Beverley based Dave Pearson was the brains behind the filming technicalities and we couldn't have managed the project without him and his expertise. As usual, we had a great deal of fun doing it and it's nice to have been able to capture a permanent record of both the play and those who took part.

A very fierce looking Stacy Parker (Ruth Dalton) in the dock at Beverley Court

Another unusual venue where we staged the play was on board the Beverley based barge 'The Syntan' as a fund-raiser for the 'The Beverley Barge Preservation Society.' They are a charity who must continually fun-raise in order to keep their heads and their barges above water. We had a great time performing the play and much fun was had. Although it was a maftingly hot day, the cast and crew just got on with it in the hot, confined space, such was their dedication. We managed to put up the 'Boat Full' signs and got a few quid in for 'The Syntan.' Makes everything worthwhile when that happens. The Syntan Barge is parked up on Beverley Beck not far from the town centre and is well worth a visit.

Performing on board the Beverley based barge 'The Syntan'
Rear Row – Left to Right: Roger Peace, T C, Ashley K Howard, Nick Beardshaw
Front Row – Left to Right: Ruth Pearson and Claire Winn

'BERNADETTE – THE VISIONS'

For some reason, can't remember why, I decided that my next offering would be a drama about Bernadette Soubirous (Saint Bernadette). For those that don't know it, Bernadette was a little peasant girl who had been playing out near a cave in Lourdes where she'd had a vision of the Virgin Mary. She then claimed that the Virgin Mary had spoken to her. These visitations happened to her more than once and when she spoke about them caused uproar locally and within the Catholic Church. Those sort of mysteries intrigue me. I'm not a conspiracy theorist but I do believe that there are some things beyond our comprehension.

The day after I'd decided to write the play, I was 'channel surfing' on the TV and 'cor blimey guv' the film that day was about Saint Bernadette, (the Franz Werfels 1943 version), starring Jennifer Jones as Bernadette Soubirous. Spooky coincidence. It's a lovely, charmingly innocent film. As usual I did a great deal of research before writing the play and initially was more than a little cynical about the whole 'Little Shepherdess has a vision of the Virgin Mary' thing. By the time I'd finished writing the play my cynicism had vanished and I'd changed my mind completely. I believe that something very spiritual had indeed occurred at Lourdes.

I have a couple of friends who have since visited Lourdes and they say that although the area itself is very commercially orientated, the grotto itself feels rather special. Inexplicably the body of Saint Bernadette lies at in the Chapel at the Church of St Goldard, Convent of Neves, where her remains are displayed in a crystal coffin, having been there since the 3rd of August 1925 and remain 'uncorrupted.' No-one can explain why that is.

The opening night of the play, staged in the most beautiful St Mary's Church in the centre of Hull, didn't go too well. Angela Burkitt (nee Daysley), who played the part of a young Nun, was just a little nervous and fluffed some of her opening lines, requiring some supportive whispering from the Prompt. The beads of sweat were pouring from her Nun's wimple as she battled valiantly on. You have to tread carefully, audiences can smell terror and it makes them uncomfortable. An unforgiving member of the audience stormed out of the church complaining that he was "not stopping to watch a play where the bloody prompt has more lines than the actress!" Still, it could have been worse, at least he hadn't asked for his money back, every penny counted. Needless to say, Angie soon got into her stride and eventually reduced the audience to sympathetic tears with her clever and riveting performance. Mr Nasty's loss, he missed out on a great night. Claire McDougal, as Bernadette Soubirous was excellent, her performance was both believable, innocent and very touching.

'OFF WITH HIS HEAD'

A while ago and before it became reality I was thinking one day, don't know why, that in the unlikely event that Prince Charles was to marry Camilla Parker-Bowles it could make for an interesting story, particularly as he was our future Monarch. So I fired up the kettle, made a brew and started to write a play called 'Off With His Head!'

In the play, a farce, Prince Charles had, by that time, been crowned King and, naturally, Camilla became his Queen. The Royal couple were attempting to visit Kingston-upon-Hull by Royal Train. There was disquiet on the streets and the good citizens of Hull had refused them entry into Hull Paragon Station, much to the King's outrage. King Charles was spitting tin tacks and was forced to wait at Arram Railway Station near Beverley before being whisked away to the nearby Army base at Leconfield for a spot of lunch whilst negotiations were carried out with Hull City Council to allow the King to proceed into Paragon Railway Station. Something along those lines. The play had a good, solid and reliable cast:

Bryn Ellis - as Sir Peregrine Pelham, ADC to the King.
David Sandford - as King Charles the 3rd.
Angela Burkitt (nee Daysley) - as a fiesty VIP Waitress, working in the Officers' Mess at Leconfield.
Barry Cowles - as scheming Colonel Lancelot Roper, the career Minded Commandant of the Central Defensive Driving School (CDDS), Leconfield

Gerald Fox - as a dashing young Captain at CDDS, Leconfield
Nick Beardshaw - as Acting Sergeant Arthur Clapsaddle, PA to the Commandant CDDS, Leconfield.

The 'World Premier' of the play took place in the Central Library, Hull, where the very supportive management team had very kindly given us access to a complete floor of the Library to stage the play. It meant getting in there each evening after the Library had closed 'for business' to build a relatively simple set and then striking the set after each show. It was very tiring as we didn't have a special team to do it, it was as usual all 'self-help.' Bit of an ache but worthwhile in order to give the play an airing. The play went extremely well and was enthusuastically supported throughout its relatively short run.

Much to my delight the audiences really enjoyed it and there was much hearty laughter throughout. It is a particular joy to a writer when he can take an audiences mind off the days's drudgery and make them laugh. If nothing else it helps them to forget any troubles they may have for a brief moment in time. It's also very fulfilling listening to people laugh and smiling at something that has emanated from your own bonce. Each audience, though, is different and will laugh in different parts of the play, sometimes where you expect it, sometimes where no-one has laughed before. I wish I could always put my (typing) finger on the magic of it all.

There was one particularly funny moment in the play when right at the very start the lights come up and there are clouds of 'steam' (good old disco smoke) and the sound effect of the 'Royal Steam Train' rolling into at Arram railway station, whistle blowing, carriage doors slamming etc. Running onto the platform getting ready to greet the Royal party is the Aide de Camp (played by Bryn Ellis). Bryn came on stage, rolled out a small piece of red carpet and did a bit of business with a tin of spray Pledge and a Yellow duster, hurriedly polishing and tidying up the Arram station sign and a bench prior to their Majesties stepping out of their railway carriage. Bryn extracted a casette player from the briefcase he was carrying and placed it reverentially on the platform before pressing a button to play some music and then standing to attention, saluting. The casette was supposed to play the National Anthem. Well, that was the plan.

On the opening night, despite everything being well prepared and checked, when Bryn entered, dusted the Station sign (first laugh) etc and pressed the relevant button on the casette player – nothing happened. There was a deathly silence, followed by a few more desperate pressings of the button. You could hear Bryns brain whirling and he glanced offstage, top lip stuck to his teeth, seeking inspiration. Suddenly a light came on in his head and he burst into song, warbling a very passable rendition of 'God Save Our Gracious Queen – er - King' and then carried on as if nothing untoward had occurred. It got a good laugh from the audience – so we kept it in.

Gifted raconteur and actor Barry Cowles played the scheming Commandant of Leconfield absolutely brilliantly. His unexpected death a few years later was an absolute tragedy and he is, of course, irreplacable. A loving husband, a genuinely nice man and an extremely talented actor who left us far too soon. David Sandford (Entrepeneur and Manager of Hull New Theatre for many years) played the King to perfection and Gerald Fox as the dashing and heroic Sandhurst type young Captain was spot on. Gerald is an actor par excellence and we were very fortunate to have him in the play. Nick Beardshaw was his usual excellent self as a snooty military PA and last but not least, the diminutive Angela Burkitt (nee Daysley) can only be described as being a comedic scream as the Officers' Mess Waitress. The sight of Angie being flung around the stage by Barry when a fight broke out at the Officers' Mess will stay with me forever. She grabbed the 'Commandant' around the neck and was swung around several times, just like you used to see in one of those old variety acts (it's called 'Apache Dancing'). Carefull choreographed and very brave. There were legs and fists flying everywhere.

They were an excellent and very supportive cast who gave their all throughout the run. There are so many truly talented people in the Hull and East Yorkshire areas, who – with apparent consumate ease – have the ability to breathe life into the written word. They do it for love, not money (although money helps)! Who knows, I might resurrect 'Off With His Head' at some stage in the future. Might have to change the lead characters to King William and Queen Catherine though.

'THE FILM - 'ROUNDAGAIN'

I was approached by an ex-Mayor of Beverley, Councillor Nev Holgate, to see if I would like to become involved in a film project about a well know local character/tramp who had lived on Beverley Beckside. The film could then be sold, the proceeds of which would be used to assist with the costs of restoring the 'Syntan' barge.

The restored Beverley based Barge – 'Syntan'

The tramp in the story was known by all as 'Roundagain' who had lived around the Beverley Beck area when it was a busy worksite. The film script was based on an excellent and very comprehensive tale penned by local author and historian, Bill Cooper. I adapted Bill's tale into a film script and shooting began. As Producer/Director I had my hands full, but with a talented cast it was enjoyable and not too taxing. It never is when working with talented and enthusiastic people.

I think that the only real problem we experienced throughout the whole production was in the Undertakers Parlour scene where the actress concerned was supposed to be a dead bod, laid in repose in an open coffin, but who was spooked at the last minute and refused point blank to climb into the coffin. I think she thought that she was tempting fate. The ornate coffin had been loaned to us by the nearby Defence School of Transport who used it when practicing funeral drill. I stepped in at short notice and volunteered my services to act as a corpse, donning a blond wig and looking rather fetching in a white nightgown. I leapt gingerly into the coffin which was set up on wooden trestles and waited for the filming to begin.

I remember that it was very uncomfortable in the coffin, but thinking to myself – with a touch of graveside humour, that it wouldn't really matter in real terms as the final occupant wouldn't be feeling anything anyway. The scene was filmed inside the cunningly disguised interior of the Syntan Barge. As Director I called out 'Action' from inside the coffin and the scene got underway in the darkened room, lit only by flickering candle-light and with recorded Salvation Army Brass Band music playing in the background to add a little gravitas to the situation.

Enter friends of the corpse who had come to view the stiff and pay their respects. The little tramp, Roundagain, was played by Nev Holgate and the Undertaker played with comedic genius by Roger Peace. The two were supposed to enter the funeral parlour and glance sorrowfully at the corpse in the laid out in the coffin before delivering their lines. It was supposed to be a sombre and touching event.

Things didn't go too well initially. Corpsing would be an appropriate term to use in this instance because when Nev and Roger walked over to the coffin and looked down at me, bewigged and prostrate in the coffin, they started to giggle. I could feel my face turning puce as I held my breath so that my chest wouldn't move and tried to keep my eyelids still whilst the filming was going on. The scene had to be shot many times before the giggling stopped and normality was restored. Eventually we got the scene 'in the can.' If you manage to get a copy of the film, one of the 'corpsing' scenes was left in, 'Blooper' style, at the end. Overall though, filming went well, mainly due to the technical genius and infinite patience of our local film expert, the ever enthusiastic Dave Pearce.

Once completed and packaged as a boxed DVD, the film was eventually marketed to raise funds for the Beverley Barge Preservation Society. The story itself was relatively straightforward and I like to think that it was both comedic and entertaining. I've never been one of those "I am a tea-pot" arty-farty style of writers. I like to tell a good story that can be understood and has a beginning middle and an end, and principally that entertains. Bill Cooper's story was excellent and made for easy adaption. I think it was Billy Connolly who once said:

"My definition of an intellectual is someone who can listen to the William Tell Overture without thinking of the Lone Ranger."

Coincidentally, we had a couple of ex-Beverley Town Mayors performing in the film, one being Councillor Nev Holgate and the other his colleague Councillor Matt Snowden. Distinguished or what!

Nev Holgate (in Wellies) filming 'Roundagain'

'Roundagain' was shot on a shoe-string, everything was scrounged, but we did our best and I like to think that it was an excellent effort which had the added bonus of recording some of the areas and activities in Beverley that now, sadly, no longer exist, having been demolished to make way for the new College, so segments of the film make an interesting historical record. The cast and crew, all unpaid volunteers, entered into the project with great gusto and we had a lot of fun doing it. It's well worth a look, if you can get your hands on a copy. The first batch sold like hot cakes! Just after filming had been completed, I was sat on a bench situated at the end of Beverley Beck, chatting to a rather elderly lady. I told her about the film – and she said that she remembered the little tramp 'Roundagain' from when she'd lived in the area as a little girl. It's a small world that we inhabit.

'SUP IT UP'

We, the 'Cast Iron Theatre Company' were planning to 'tour' a comedy I'd written called 'Sup it Up.' Money was a bit tight (as usual) and we couldn't really afford to be paying out humongous amounts of cash to the Performing Rights Society (PRS) for using someone else's music. My colleague Bryn Ellis and I decided that we'd write and perform our own song to introduce and end the play. That way it wouldn't cost us an arm and a leg every time we used it. So we sat down and cobbled something together.

We called our song 'Sup It Up' (not daft eh?) and then, rather imaginatively, named ourselves 'Klench and Trapp – The Yorkshire Rappers'. We recorded the song at a lovely little Studio, 'Wall 2 Wall,' in George Street, Hull run by a charming and charismatic bloke, the ex-drummer of Roy Wood's 'Wizzard' the talented Garry Burroughs, sadly no longer with us. Gary was very patient with the two of us and ultimately we finished up with a not too bad 'product' at the end of the session, man. The recording was certainly good enough to use to open and close the play.

Somehow, and to this day we honestly didn't know how, the rap duo 'Klench and Trapp' reached the semi-finals of a huge local talent competition that was taking place at the Tower Ballroom in Hull. As we hadn't performed it 'live' as it were, we could never quite work out how we had progressed to the semi-finals. Someone must have sent a copy of the song to the Judging Team. We hurriedly made the excuse that we would be on tour performing the play at the time the semi's were taking place and thereby avoided appearing on stage as the 'Yorkshire Rappers' – which would have been quite traumatic, not only for two middle-aged geezers, but for a paying audience. We did manage to get the song played on the BBC a couple of times but then, like the Titanic, 'Klench & Trapp,' sank without trace. The play did well and having our own song saved us quite a bit of money, money that would normally have been paid to the Performing Rights Society.

THE FILM - 'ALL OUT AT SEA (AUF HOHER SEE)'

I went over to Leeds, auditioned for and was fortunate enough to be selected to appear in a leading role (not difficult as there were only two of us in the film) in the comedy 'All Out at Sea', produced and directed by the eminent German Director, Imogen Kimmel. The leading actress playing opposite me was a perfectly delightful and very pretty young lady called Madeleine Wood. The film was all about a seedy railway booking office clerk who picked up a 'lady of the night,' took her home to his seedy flat and – well, you'll have to make the effort to see what happened then (nothing untoward, I assure you, it was a comedy). Suffice to say that such was the excellence of Imogen Kimmel's direction, the quality of the script and the superb acting (!) that the film eventually won an award at the Berlin Film Festival.

'All Out at Sea' was filmed in a seedy little house in Chapeltown, Leeds. The place was a pig hole and when I mentioned it to one of the blokes on the film, he replied rather huffily, "Well it's my pad actually and it isn't normally like this. It's dressed for the film." Duly chastened and removing my foot from my mouth I repaired to the back room to run through my lines. Filming progressed, we were in full make-up and I was wearing my best Marks and Spencer suit as it fitted me nicely. The last scene in the film culminated in having buckets of cold water thrown over me whilst at the same time the young actress was flicking the room's lights on and off to make the lights flash. The whole fantasy was supposed to be taking place on board ship in a stormy sea (in my character's seedy little mind).

I recall that at one stage the camera crew ran out of film, causing a bit of an eruption from Imogen – who was not to be tampered with. The crew received a fierce Germanic verbal lashing for their gross inefficiency and we, the poor actors – me pissed wet through and getting a bit hacked off – had to wait for resupplies of film to be rushed in. Filming eventually concluded at a about three o'clock in the morning with an 'It's a wrap my darlings!" from Imogen. I had been wearing contact lenses and had great difficulty seeing every time one of the crew threw a bucket of water over me (rather too enthusiastically I thought). It wasn't particularly glamorous, laid in a soaking bed, cold and unable to see properly whilst trying to deliver lines on cue. Don't know how Daniel Craig manages it.

Eventually changing out of my wet clothes I put on a, thankfully, dry green shell suit, which was in vogue at that time. I left my make-up on because it was very late and I had to drive back to home to Beverley. I could remove the makeup once I reached home. Farewells were said, kisses exchanged etc and off I drove into the night. On the outskirts of Leeds, heading for the M62, I saw lots of blue flashing lights and a police cordon blocking the road ahead. I was waved into side of the road by an armed Policeman. At the time I was driving a rather posh Mercedes Benz which was on loan to me from my Brother-in-law Richard, who was off skiving in South Africa or somewhere mysterious for a couple of months. The butch looking Policeman, wearing all the protective gear and carrying a weapon, instructed me to switch my engine off and get out of the car. His face was a picture when he saw a middle-aged, portly man getting out of a Merc, wearing a bright green shell-suit and streaky orange make-up. What I didn't know at the time was that my eye make-up had smeared, what with all of the water being thrown in my face, and I must have looked to all intents and purposes like a very tearful and sad old Queen.

The Officer invited me to explain where I'd been and what I was doing out at that time of the morning (it was by then about 2 o'clock). He'd also noted that laid across the back seat of the car was a soaking wet three piece suit. I explained that I'd been down in the Chapeltown area of Leeds (a not particularly salubrious place) filming and showed him a copy of the film script, which fortunately had my details printed on it. He visibly relaxed once he realised that I wasn't a member of some sort of pervy 'Golden Rain' group and we had a nice little chat. He asked me how long I'd been in films and I explained that it was a first and that in reality I was a Major in the Army (which I still was at that stage). He asked where my unit was and when I explained that it was at Leconfield, he told me that he'd done a driving course there. He became my new friend. The car was, by this time, surrounded by armed policemen who were, apparently, waiting for an illegal arms shipment to appear on the horizon at any moment and wanting to arrest the perps. I suppose my arrival broke the monotony. Anyway I left the lads to get on with their unenviable job and thrashed off into the night, seeking the M62 and the route home.

Talking of glamour, I made a film in Hull once which was shot using a technical method called 'Pixiliation' where one posed for each single shot – 'click' and then moved on. This process continued throughout the day until the storyboard was completed. As I recall, I was cast as a middle-aged fat bloke (don't know why) sat in his front room watching TV with his family, me wearing a seedy string vest, gray hair slicked back and with a huge bowl of cold spaghetti in front of me. All I had to do throughout day was sit there expressionless, (not difficult for me), and suck strands of spaghetti from the plate whilst watching TV, splattering the tomato juice from the spaghetti over my chest/string vest. All quite disgusting. Sat next me was a full sized skeleton which was posed to copy my actions and which also sucked up the spaghetti. Quite what it was all about I never found out – and I never got to see it. The usual copy was promised but never received. A consequence of that particular film was that I had and still have an intense dislike of Heinz spaghetti. We used to got through a shedfull of tins of the stuff at home, but no longer. I just thought - I've been in a spaghetti movie!

'LEAPS'
(Local Entertainers and Performers Society)

After my time with the BBC's Councils had finished I found myself at something of a loose end and looking for something else to do. Whilst at a BBC meeting in Hull I'd bumped into a bloke from Hull called Mally King. Mally was in the process of establishing and launching a charity that was to be called LEAPS. I was interested in what he was doing, so decided to offer my services to help him. Mally was ex-RAF, but that wasn't his fault.

LEAPS, as a concept, was mooted in 2007, leading to it being formally established on the 1st of January 2008. It was established primarily to raise the profile of training and education for entertainers, both young and those more experienced, within Hull and the East Riding of Yorkshire. Principally this was achieved by performers being involved in shows that were staged at Hull New Theatre, Hull City Hall and Bridlington Spa Theatre, all major venues at which they would not normally have the opportunity to appear. A positive spin-off from LEAPS activities was that because of show income, support could, and was, made available for deserving local charities/causes throughout Hull and the East Riding of Yorkshire, using the talents and expertise of our Artistes, Members and Friends. Later on a series of shows called 'Voices of Angels' was introduced by LEAPS where groups of performers staged shows in local churches in order to help them raise funds. They proved to be popular and continue to be so.

LEAPS wholeheartedly encourages the participation of younger entertainers in their shows, particularly those who have not been involved in the larger more professional style of show. That way they gain the vital experience and stage-craft needed for their future careers in the highly competitive entertainment field.

Since its inception LEAPS has gone from strength to strength. They select at least two local charities each year on whom to focus their support. It's great being involved with LEAPS and heartening to see just how performers develop, how positive they become and what they can achieve.

Chairman of LEAPS – Mally King with Comedian (and LEAPS Patron) Billy Pearce
Presenting a cheque to the RNLI at Bridlington

With West Hull Community Presenter Mike Woodhouse – July 2014
Drumming up support for our shows

we're supported by some very enthusiastic Patrons and 'Friends':

'PATRONS OF LEAPS'
Jeremy Kyle, Mick Miller, Billy Pearce, Steve Womack, Edwina Hayes, Elkie Brooks, Carlo Paul Santanna, Jimmy Cricket, Rufus Stone, Robin Colvill (Grumbleweeds), Phil Hunt, Lee Clark (President at Associated Board of Dance, Fellow of Associated Board of Dance, FAAD.FBTDA, AIDTA, Dance & Music), and BBC Radio Humberside's Simon Pattern

'FRIENDS OF LEAPS'
Rory Bremner, Victoria Wood, Brotherhood of Man, James Toseland,

If you're interested in what we at LEAPS get up to, why not have a look at our website:
leaps.org.uk

'GRAHAM 'GRUMBLEWEED' WALKER'

Tragically, we lost one of our greatest supporters, our Patron, Graham 'Grumbleweed' Walker. A lovely man and a comedic genius.

I first met Graham Walker of the comedy group 'The Grumbleweeds' when they came to Hamm in West Germany as part of a Combined Services Entertainment (CSE) Show package that I'd been tasked to organize. It all went swimmingly well and we had a great night, the troops being regally entertained by the brilliantly funny Grumbleweeds. After the show I'd organised some supper for the lads and that's how I got chatting to Graham.

A number of years later I was on a cruise in the Western Mediterranean with the Memsahib when who should I bump into but Graham Walker, who was performing that night in the on-board show alongside his equally brilliantly funny colleague Robin Colvill. We had a good chat and a laugh and when I mentioned that I was employed, at the Defence School of Transport, Leconfield, Graham – who had a life-long interest in big trucks, said that he'd like to visit the unit and have a good look around. He would be working locally in the pantomime at Hull New Theatre that year, so I got it organized and eventually he came over to Leconfield and had a brilliant 'Trucks 'R' Us' day out with us. It was a delight to be in his company that day (or any other day).

The late Graham 'Grumbleweed' Walker

I was, (and still am), involved with the local charity group LEAPS, staging variety/musical shows in and around Hull and the East Riding of Yorkshire using voluntary local talent. Graham liked what he heard about LEAPS and showed an interest, so we invited him to become a Patron, an invitation that he kindly accepted, supporting us with his special kind of unbounded enthusiasm from the word go.

I received a 'phone call from Graham one day telling me that, sadly, he had been diagnosed with throat cancer, but that the prognosis wasn't quite as bad as he thought it would be, and he'd been told that the medics could do something about it. I won't waffle on, suffice to say that Graham fought a long, heroic battle with the disease but in the end he succumbed. His death was such a tragic loss to his family and his many friends, particularly his performing partner Robin Colvill (an equally talented and hilarious man), to the world of entertainment and to all those that knew and loved him. A truly generous, supportive, spirited, clever and funny man who is sorely missed.

It's not all – 'Work and no play' with LEAPS. Whilst involved with the staging of a charity show at Hull's premier venue the delightful City Hall, I was wandering around the main stairwell at the entrance to the Hall, when I spotted my old mate from 'Cast Iron' the actor Bryn Ellis. Bryn was recovering from the effects of a nasty back operation as a result of which he had to use a wheelchair. I should explain, Bryn and I are both great fans of the TV comedy 'Black Adder.' Bryn occasionally referred to me as 'Baldrick' whilst I referred to him as 'Slack Bladder.' Silly, but there we are, chaps.

Anyway, Bryn had come to see our show and was sat in his wheel-chair waiting for the lift to arrive to take him up to the Auditorium. I shouted at him in a loud military fashion, "Slack Bladder, sit up straight in that damned wheelchair!!" then went across to speak to him. To my abject horror as I drew near I saw that the occupant, now sitting rigid in the said wheelchair wasn't Bryn Ellis at all, but some poor innocent theatre-goer who looked just like him.

The occupant of the wheel-chair was sitting ramrod straight whilst waiting for the disabled lift to arrive. I, in courageous fashion, walked straight past the poor man and pretended that I was talking to someone else in the distance. The lift fortuitously appeared and the 'victim' thankfully scuttled into it, disappearing out of my life. I have never felt quite so embarrassed, well – perhaps I have, but no more 'Slack Bladder' moments for me.

'AN EQUITY MOMENT'

As a member of Actors Equity I attended the monthly meetings that were held in the Seamen's Mission near Hull docks (since moved). On this particular hot summer's evening I had arrived early so went to the bar to order a nice cool pint of something or other. For some reason, I know not why, I said to the Barman, using an effete voice and affecting a lisp, "Whooooo, in't it th'ticky' I'll have a pint, pleathe!" I don't know why I chose to speak like that, but I did. The Barman was totally nonplussed, nodded and poured me a pint. He then winked and surreptitiously nodded his head towards a very large woman stood next to me at the bar. That was when things started to go vaguely awry. The woman, a Gorgon, stood next to me at the bar was what can only be described as a muscle-bound she-man mountain, with pendulous breasts crammed into a sweaty 'T-Shirt' and a complexion like a tin of condemned veal. We were the only ones in there so it was written in the stars that we were destined to converse at some stage of the proceedings.

She looked at me and smiled, revealing the odd yellowed and tobacco stained tooth, then lisped – to my horror – "Yeth, you're right mate, it ith – th'ticky!" Aaaaaagh! This left me in an immediate and dangerous quandary i.e. was she just joining in the general 'lisping' banter or did she herself have a lisp? Discretion being the better part of valour, (it would have been easy for her to knock seven bells out of me), I decided to keep up the pretence of having a lisp just to be on the thafe thide. The Les Dawson look-alike did in fact sport a ferocious lisp. We continued to have an excruciatingly long conversation, full of the letter 's' - both lisping merrily for some thirty very long, nerve-wracking minutes until I heard someone say, much to my relief, that the Equity meeting was about to begin.

I quickly finished my drink, nodded at the lady mountain and said, "Well, nice th'peaking to you – th'ee you then!" and legged it into the meeting. Thankfully I haven't th'een her since. You'll recognise her if you ever bump into her. She's six foot tall, huge bee-hive hairstyle and has two names tattooed on the knuckles of her hands – 'Lidl' on the left – 'Aldi' on the right. Take my advice and think twice before you lithp.

'THE HIGH SHERIFF ACCIDENTALLY POLISHES HIS JEWELS'

After many, many hours of intensive studying and burning the midnight oil, my beloved wife Maggie had qualified for the award of an MSc. A brilliant achievement in its own right, but even more so when considering that she had also worked full time throughout her studies in a complex, busy and demanding job. It made me very proud of her. Anyway, come the day of the formal Presentation Ceremony at the rather grand Hull City Hall, I sat up in the gallery to watch the presentations taking place. This is always preceded by the grand entrance of the great and good, wearing their finery, indicating which Doctorates they themselves had achieved. All very colourful and oozing tradition. It was such a thrill seeing all those youngsters, not only from Great Britain, but from all around the world being presented with their formal degrees and various other awards for their hard earned academic achievements. They were so proud of themselves and it restored one's faith in humanity.

One member of the said 'great and good' in attendance was the High Sheriff. Here's a bit of information culled from notes provided by 'The High Sheriffs Association of England and Wales,' just to help me paint a picture for you:

'The ceremonial uniform that is worn by male High Sheriffs today is called Court Dress. It has remained essentially unchanged since the late seventeenth century and consists of a black or dark blue velvet coat with steel-cut buttons, breeches, shoes with cut-steel buckles, a sword and a cocked hat. A lace jabot is worn around the neck. Some High Sheriffs wear their military uniform instead of Court Dress. Ceremonial uniform is worn at a wide variety of functions but when not wearing Court

Dress, a High Sheriff will wear a badge of Office on a ribbon.'

Members of the 'great and good', wearing their various formal rigs, proceeded grandly towards the stage of the City Hall to take their allocated seats. On this occasion, the City Macebearer and the City Swordbearer, preceded the High Sheriff (who shall remain nameless to preserve the dignity of his high office), who was wearing the traditional 'Court Dress' as described above. The High Sheriff progressed regally down the auditorium, nodding graciously at the lesser beings, heading towards the stage. Hanging dangerously at his side was a relatively small, glittering ceremonial sword. Treading carefully up the stage stairs he swept towards his plush seat, centre stage, to thunderous applause, and then attempted to sit down. That is when things went a little awry for him.

As he sat down, the sword slipped between his legs and walloped him fairly and squarely, how can I put this delicately, right in the 'Crawfords' to much sympathetic 'Ooooing' from the assembled masses. I have never seen a man stand up so quickly in my life. His face was puce, eyes and jabot bulging. It was quite obvious to all of us that the short, sharp slap that had been administered to his reproductive department by the blade of the sword had completely taken the wind out of his sails. There was a definite sharp intake of breath from the males witnessing the incident. The High Sheriff quickly eased the sword from in between his legs, pretending that he cared not a jot, and sat down once again – this time a little more gingerly. His dignity had been affronted by circumstance.

For the remainder of the ceremony he looked as if he was in a certain amount of discomfort and kept crossing and uncrossing his legs. What made it even funnier that he had to keep standing up and sitting down throughout the ceremony and the assembled masses were was waiting with bated breath for the sword to slap him on his privates again. Alas, I was overcome with the titters and sat in the cheap seats sniggering like a naughty schoolboy. I'd actually met the High Sheriff on a previous occasion at a social function and found him to be just this side of Lord Snooty, not only that, he'd been rather rude and overbearing to the lady with whom I shared an office at the time, (the exotically named Scheherazade Williams), when he rang one day about a visit – so I thought that in essence he had received his come-uppance and received not an ounce of sympathy from me. He deserved a slap in the 'nads.' Anyway, Maggie was eventually called up on stage for her formal presentation, shortly after which we swept off into Hull to celebrate her achievement at a local hostelry. The look of pride and sense of achievement on her face as she received her 'Masters' will stay with me forever, (as will the look of horror on the puce and florid fizzog of the High Sheriff who, when he eventually left the stage, was walking with a definite semi-mincing delicate gait, as a result of his mishap with the sword).

'NEARLY FULL CIRCLE'

That's about it really. Things, for me, have come full circle. I've retired from the Ministry of Defence, leaving the Realm to look after itself. I've very recently returned from a tour of the Far East with my beloved Wife, Maggie and our two dear friends, Major Peter Todd and Lady Linda Todd. We had a really brilliant time whilst out there, the girls hitting the shops big style on Singapore's Orchard Road, whilst Peter and I did a bit of "When I" by re-visiting places there from our military youth. We hired a taxi and went to have a look at what was Peter's old army base at Nee Soon. I'd also done a couple of courses there and was looking forward to having a nose around. Some of you may be familiar with the place which appears in the movie 'Virgin Soldier's' which, like Peter's wallet, still gets an occasional airing on TV.

Despite us both having heroically helped the Singaporeans to hurtle back the communist hordes, a scaringly smart, efficient Singapore Army Duty Sergeant wouldn't let us have a look inside the camp for security reasons, despite our pathetic protestations and wheedlings that we were two old soldiers who'd travelled thousands of miles just to see the place. Our pleas went unanswered and we were only allowed to stand at the main gate looking forlornly in at the barracks, where some of the things still looked familiair, even after all these years. Bit of a disappointment really, but who knows, might get back there again some day.

Emotional return to Nee Soon, Singapore

All was not lost. Peter, who had served in Singapore with the REME at the same time as I'd been there, (athough I don't think that we ever crossed paths), decided that we should have a look around nearby Nee Soon village, where although there had been many changes, there were several places that he remembered. We then stopped off at a roadside hostelry for a chilled flagon of 'Tiger Beer' at 'The Famous Kitchen', Sembawang Road, where we were made to feel extremely welcome. The owner, Jenny Foo, had spotted us both recuperating at an outside table from the heat and came out to have a chat with us. Jenny was herself a 'Child of the Sixties' and recalled much of the period we were talking about. We then spent a pleasant hour sat in the sizzling Singapore sun talking our way down memory lane whilst fettling a few pints of Tiger Beer. We had our photo taken, which will by now be adorning the wall of 'The Famous Kitchen.' See if you can spot us if ever you have the opportunity to pop in there – and say hello to Jenny for us!

Jenny Foo, stood directly behind Peter Todd

One of the places we wanted to visit was the troop's main watering hole in Singapore, The NAAFI's 'Britannia Club' which is now a police station – (quite appropriate when I remember some of the shenanigans that went on in that fine establishment).

Although we could have a good look around the outside of the 'Brit' Club, once again we couldn't get inside. Back in the day, copius amounts of Tiger and Anchor beer were consumed there at the side of the swimming pool, whilst many of the military patrons, pissed out of their skulls, leapt from the upper balcony of the club, dropping down a couple of floors into the said swimming pool – just to cool down or simply to let off a bit of steam. Many a squaddie was led off to the British Military Hospital (BMH), whimpering, to have a broken limb repaired, to unsympathetic cheering from various others in advanced states of disrepair. The 'balconeers' who survived the experience usually then basked in the dying rays of the sun, drying off and continuing the drinking motion before heading off to the flesh pots. It was the done thing to top up with beer at the NAAFI run 'Brit Club' which was sold at at very affordable prices, before hitting the more salubrious establishments in Singapore City.

Luckily we managed to have a look around at what was RAF Seletar where I'd served with the 15 (Air Despatch) Regiment RCT. The village where I'd spent so many hours boozing and carousing, not too far from the main gates of RAF Seletar – Jalan Kayu – was no longer sited there but was now a mile further down the road. Another memory bubble burst; no more 'Pop's Canteen' for a ferocious curry, or 'Doris's Fish & Chip Emporium' for a touch of the non-exotic, but it was still nice to see the old 'plaice.' 'Pops Canteen' had been a joy to behold. It was a little cafe inside which were small booths that each held four patrons or so. The curries served there were truly ferocious and much in demand by the troops. One of 'Pop's' infamous curries, washed down with a nicely chilled Tiger beer just couldn't be bettered. One's mouth felt as if it had been blow-torched and a cold beer was de rigeur.

At the front counter of Pop's Canteen was a huge, wood fired black metal cauldron which bubbled along merrily as pieces of meat were continually added into the evil brew to keep it topped up. It was rumoured that the cauldron hadn't been emptied since the end of World War 2, just continually added to. We cared not a jot –'Pops' curries were always cheap and delicious, if somewhat fiery. One always paid the price the following morning as nature took its inevitable course. It was once pointed out by some wag that you never saw a dog or a cat in Jalan Kayu village, which when we thought about it was quite true.It didn't bear thinking too much about what had gone into that cauldron to 'beef up' the curries......

The weekends activities inevitably began with a curry and a beer or two at Pops, then we'd hail a 'Pirate' taxi to take us downtown Singapore, usually the Union Jack Club, or the Brit Club, for the usual fun and games. We were encouraged to use taxis as the public transport was, at that time, rather basic. We had reasonable wages and pirate taxis were cheap, so why not? Anyway, like a lot of places, Pop's Canteen and Dot's Chippy were no more. It's quite sad to go and see where these places used to be, makes you sad. Shouldn't do it.

Entrance to RAF Seletar (as was)

If you really want to get a flavour of what Singapore was like in the good old days, right underneath the equivalent of their 'London Eye' in the centre of Singapore is the 'Singapore Flyer' where they've recreated a facsimile of what Singapore used to look like in the good old days. It's brilliant.

It even smells the same, that very special 'Eau de Monsoon Drain.' It's a veritable time capsule with lots of small stalls producing wonderful and much remembered local food. Whilst there we consumed a couple of 'Anchor and Tiger Beers' those delightfully chilled local brews that both Peter and I thoroughly enjoy. We sat there savouring the memorable food, the smells and soaking up the ambience and atmosphere, for that brief moment in time, as we were transported back to being young, bold warriors, making it a point of honour to refresh both our memories and gullets. If you're ever in 'Singers' it's well worth paying a visit there. It's exactly what the place used to be like.

Ah, such golden, irreplaceable memories. Singapore has completely changed but is still such a joy to visit. So clean and so safe. Not once did we see any bad behaviour or were we treated with discourtesy. Unlike here in Great Britain, the Singaporeans have great respect for their elders and their manners are beyond criticism. Yes, the Singaporeans were as lovely as we remembered them. We did all of the usual touristy things, including visiting a much changed Bugis Street, now a street market, that replaced a very colourful area where many and varied delights were available for the Patrons (another book in itself) and of course the visit wouldn't have been the same without having a Singapore Sling or two at the much vaunted Rafffles Hotel, (where both Peter and I had been when we were to young lads). The haunt of the idle rich. On the day we visited we couldn't gain access to the 'Writers Bar,' which was a great disappointment to me.

Who knows, if we could put up with the jet leg then a return visit might be on the books. Unfortunately we didn't have the time to have a proper, lengthy look around Singapore, which is just oozing with things to see. We'd visited quite a few areas on that holiday, Malaysia, Thailand, been chased around the jungle by Kimodo Dragons, that sort of thing. All very educational – and if nothing else we now knew how to pronounce 'Phuket,' realising that we'd mispronounced it for a number of years. We were, however, fortunate enough to have sufficient time on our hands on the last day of our holiday to pay a visit to the market in China Town in Singers – which is absolutely brilliant and recommended. There's even an equivalent there of our Poundshops there, called 'The Two Dollar Shop.' It's full of unusual items and a great place for small gifts. Loved the visit, even though at times it was a bit sad as we were surrounded by the ghosts of my military colleagues and memories of how things 'used to be.'

Very shortly after our return to the UK, I was walking around Beverley with my wife Maggie when we were passed by a group of Neanderthals, farting, belching, smoking and eating chips out of styrofoam packaging, 'effing and jeffing' and caring not a jot for those around them. There was litter blowing around the streets, chewing gum and fag ends everywhere and not a policeman to be seen. Home Sweet Home. Nice to be back! What must foreign visitors think of us?

So there you have it. That's just a small portion of my life laid bare for you to have a look at. I hope that you've enjoyed reading this as much as I enjoyed writing it –(if you've got this far). It's not been a bad old life and as I receive my Corps Magazine and read other bits of e-mails, Facebook etc and note that many of my old mates are dropping off the perch with monotonous regularity, I'm glad I decided to put some of my memories on paper. If nothing else this will be a bit of a keepsake for our beloved daughter Sara, who, fortunately, doesn't know the half of what her little old Dad got up to in a previous life. I would get the back of my legs smacked and sent to bed if she did.

Thank you for giving up some of your valuable time (and presumably money) to read this. You've made an old man very happy. Not willing to rest on my laurels, I recently completed another book with Beverley author, Harry (Brian) Clacy, which caused us much hilarity whilst being written. It's called 'Tell it like it wasn't.' Work now begins on my next book, so that will keep these little arthritic pinkies of mine busy flitting across the keyboard. I'm still very much involved with the local registered charity Local Entertainers and Performers Society (LEAPS) helping young, inexperienced entertainers and raising money for local charities. It's a joy to be involved with and very rewarding to be able to do something positive. I'll keep at it is long as they'll put up with me and as long as I'm able to totter around.

The research for my next book entailed me travelling down to London and spending some time in Highgate Cemetery, amongst others. My wife, Maggie, being eminently sensible, declined my offer to accompany me to Highgate and spent the day hitting the shops in Regent Street. I was trying to find the grave in Highgatew of the comedian Max Wall so that I could take a photograph of his gravestone for inclusion in the next book.

The weather that day was atrocious, it was cold and tippling down as I travelled to Highgate Cemetery by bus, from the centre of London. If you ever do the journey I recommend that you travel by bus as you get to see a lot of things that you normally wouldn't when sat upstairs on a double-decker. On reaching Highgate Cemetery, I spent a lot of time trying to find Max Wall's final resting place, to no avail. I thought to myself, "Well Max, if I don't find you in the next couple of minutes mate, you can go and whistle, I'm off!" It was tippling down and I was getting a bit fed up.

At that precise moment I slipped on some wet grass, went base over apex, (or arse over tit if you prefer), and landed flat on my rump, floundering around in the wet, clinging mud. I was covered in it and looked like a grave-digger. Defeated and depressed, I glanced up and I kid you not, right in front of me was the very gravestone I had been seeking.

Max Wall

Max Wall had had the last laugh. I picked myself up, wrung my trousers out, took the required photo and hobbled off out of Highgate Cemetery, thoroughly depressed, pissed wet through and covered in mud, attracting wary glances from other visitors who probably thought that I'd spent the night there. Phase Two of the research operation. I moved on to the next venue on my list, Golders Green Crematorium, to take some more photo's. Golders Green Crematorium – what an exotic and exciting life I lead. At least it had stopped raining and I eventually arrived at Golders Green, semi dried out. I continued to get some suspicious glances from other people visiting the crematorium, i.e. a damp old person, covered in mud, limping around the place (I was suffering from a bout of Bursitis at the time which did nothing for my hobbling).

Anyway, I tottered around the grounds, took several photo's that I needed and then, to my delight, discovered that not only were there toilets (water tablets kicking in) but that there's a small cafe within the grounds of the Crematorium dispensing welcome refreshments, so I went for a cup of tea. Totally lacking in discipline, despite having had a 'full English' that morning, I ordered a morale boosting toasted cheese sandwich and a most reviving mug of Rosy Lee. The cheese on the toast was unexpectedly hot and I burned my lips – would there be no end to the misery? I cared not a jot, I was clemmed.

So there I sat, bad leg aching, still wet through, covered in mud, decidedly crumpled and sporting a trout pout that an aged jazz trumpeter would have been proud of. I finished my cup of tea and left before the young lady behind the counter called the Police. She kept glancing at me covertly and I'm sure that she thought I was some old Jakey that had wandered in off the streets of Golders Green. Finishing my repast, I hobblerd back to the Bus Station and returned to central London to meet my wife Maggie in Regent Street, where I was promptly ordered to return to our hotel and get smartened up. Oh, we do see life, or on that occasion, death. So, as you, hopefully, read this book I'm cracking on with the next one. If you happen to come across some old codger totterng around a cemetery, taking photo's and scribbling furiously, fear not - the odds are that it'll be me. If you're not scared by the apparition, please say hello!

'A LITTLE BREAK IN HAWORTH'

To celebrate the end of writing this book, my beloved wife Maggie and I decided to have a weekend break and pay a visit to Haworth in West Yorkshire. We'd visited the Bronte Parsonage quite a few years previously when we'd been courting and thought that it would be nice to return there to have a look around. All went swimmingly well, (it was, as usual, tippling down), so we decided to grab a spot of lunch in a locally hostelry and wait for the weather to clear. Whilst having a look at the menu on an outside wall of a pub, my beloved lost her footing on a wet flagstone, fell and broke her arm. For the record, drink had not been taken at that stage. Off we thrashed to Airedale General Hospital at nearby Skipton for medical treatment. Say what you like about our National Health Service, but Maggie received excellent treatment (fairly) quickly there and was given some welcome pain relief whilst I pottered back and forth putting money into the ever open maw of the bloody parking meter. What a country, you pay to be ill! The Accident and Emergency Department was being refurbished, which meant that we had to join a rather long queue of fellow sufferers, sat in a long gloomy corridor. Our daughter Sara rang me whilst we were sitting there. My answer phone had the Beatle's 'Help' as the call notification – which boomed out and around the hospital passageway. It made everyone laugh and we all started chatting, breaking the ice and lifting the atmosphere. I wanted to include the opening words of the song 'Help' here, just to give you an idea of their appropriate content for the occasion and see why people laughed. I wrote to ex-Beatle, Sir Paul McCartney for permission to do so, but never got a reply, so I won't be buying his CD's anymore. That'll teach him. He must have been busy in Abbey Road that day.

'END PIECE'

So there it is – or was. My formative years spent happily in a smog filled Northern mill town, followed by thirty years in the Army, followed by two years of ducking and diving, then back to a relatively routine life as a Civil Servant in the Ministry of Defence, which lasted a mind blowing further eighteen years. Forty eight years of my life for Queen and Country, a year with the Cast Iron Theatre Company in Hull and a year as Chief Officer with the Anlaby Community Care Association. Where does time go?

I now move forward into the final phase of my life, with a great deal to look forward to. Baldness, poor eyesight, hearing deteriorating (sometimes selective), teeth not so good – the prospect of incontinence and the inevitable onset of a bad memory. I can't remember what else I was going to list - see, it's started already! Ah that was it, the prospect of incontinence and the onset of bad memory, hang on – didn't I just say that. My old friend, the actor Roger Peace, made me laugh out loud the other week. We were chatting on the 'phone and he said that his memory was starting to fail. He found himself in an upstairs bedroom (his, I hasten to add) holding a plate of steaming hot food and didn't quite know why he'd taken it up there. He had originally been on his way to the dining room. Watch Out! - they're coming for us!

Right, must go. Time to take my Blood Pressure/Gout/Warfarin/Water tablets etc. Even a visit to the local Doctor's surgery can't be taken for granted any more as the insidious and despicable Conservative government continues to try and privatise everything where they spot some sort of opportunity to make money. Perhaps we're heading right back to where for me it all began when just before 1947 my Mother had to save up enough money to pay for Doctor's visits prior to me being born. Similarly, the Conservatives have been hard at worked depleting our beloved Armed Forces to levels not seen since we were having the odd spat with Napoleon Bonaparte whilst we continue to send billions of pounds to all sorts of criminals so that they can continue to maintain their Mercedes Benz fleets and palaces abroad. We never seem to learn, do we?

Things change with such rapidity that sometimes I can't keep up with it all. I mean, for instance - we have several different coloured dust-bins, emptied on dates that one has to list on a complex chart and each bin has to contain different types of rubbish - oh, see what's happened, I've gone off on one now! I've turned into 'furious of Beverley.' Thanks for reading this and I hope that you enjoyed at least some of it. It's semi-autobiographical but doesn't cover everything that I've done and been involved in, although I've tried to give you a general flavour of how 'A boy from nowhere' went somewhere and did all sorts of things. All manner of people have tottered through these pages – from Royalty to Reprobates. Now, though, I'll have a bit of a rest, get my breath back and then crack on with my next book. No peace for the wicked, eh!

So, my best wishes to you and to all those with whom I've served and those I've crossed paths with as I've meandered through life. Whilst you've been reading this, if I've made you smile, or pause for thought – then that's brill. If I've upset anyone along the way, it probably wasn't intended (well, perhaps some of it was). Like you, I've just been trying to survive and get through each day. But, eeeh by gum, it's all had its moments. TTFN and always remember:

**'Don't wait for your ship to come in –
Row out and meet it!'**

Printed in Great Britain
by Amazon